Poetry for Pleasure
THE HALLMARK BOOK OF POETRY

Poetry for Pleasure

THE HALLMARK BOOK OF POETRY

SELECTED AND ARRANGED
BY THE EDITORS OF
HALLMARK CARDS, INC

DOUBLEDAY & COMPANY, INC.
GARDEN CITY, NEW YORK
1960

LIBRARY OF CONGRESS CATALOG CARD NUMBER 60–15176
COPYRIGHT © 1960 BY HALLMARK CARDS, INC.
ALL RIGHTS RESERVED
PRINTED IN THE UNITED STATES OF AMERICA
FIRST EDITION

The compilers and the publisher have made every effort to trace the ownership of all copyrighted poems. While expressing regret for any error unintentionally made, the publisher will be pleased to make the necessary correction in future editions of this book.

AMERICAN SCANDINAVIAN FOUNDATION for "Synnove's Song" by Björnstjerne Björnson, "O, Let Me Kiss" and "A Pair" by Karl Gjellerup, "Tora's Song" by Knut Hamsun, "A Bathing Girl" by Johannes Jensen, "A Vagrant" and "Imagined Happiness" by Erik Axel Karlfeldt, "The Child of Peace" by Selma Lagerlof, "Home," "Fellow-Citizens" and "How Easily Men's Cheeks Are Hot" by Verner von Heidenstam; all translated by Charles Wharton Stork; "The Boy and the Flute" by Björnstjerne Björnson, translated by Sir Edmund Gosse; all reprinted by permission of the American Scandinavian Foundation.

GEORGE ALLEN & UNWIN for "The Morning Hours" from THE MEANING OF THE GLORIOUS KORAN by Mohammed Marmaduke Pickthall, reprinted by permission of George Allen & Unwin, Ltd.

APPLETON-CENTURY-CROFTS, INC. for "The Jazz of This Hotel" from GOING TO THE STARS by Vachel Lindsay. Copyright, 1926, D. Appleton & Co. Reprinted by permission of the publishers, Appleton-Century-Crofts, Inc.

AUGUSTANA BOOK CONCERN for "Beauty Is Most at Twilight's Close" by Pär Lagerkvist, translated by Kenneth Laycock, from MODERN SWEDISH POEMS, copyright Augustana Book Concern. Used by permission.

5

6

mings; from "IS 5" copyright, 1926, by Horace Liveright; renewed, 1954, by E. E. Cummings. Reprinted from POEMS 1923–1954 by *E. E. Cummings;* "The Tides of Love" from SELECTED POEMS OF T. A. DALY, copyright, 1936, by Harcourt, Brace and Company, Inc.; "The Hippopotamus," "The Hollow Men," "Lines for Cuscuscaraway and Mirza Murad Ali Beg," and "Preludes" from COLLECTED POEMS 1909–1935 by *T. S. Eliot,* copyright, 1936, by Harcourt, Brace and Company, Inc. and Faber & Faber, Ltd.; "Children of Light" from LORD WEARY'S CASTLE, copyright, 1944, 1946, by Robert Lowell; "Childhood" copyright, 1956, by Ned O'Gorman. Reprinted from THE NIGHT OF THE HAMMER by *Ned O'Gorman;* "Song: Under the Bronze Leaves" from ANABASIS by *Saint-John Perse,* translated by *T. S. Eliot,* copyright, 1938, 1949, by Harcourt, Brace and Company, Inc.; "Lessons of the War; Naming of Parts" from A MAP OF VERONA AND OTHER POEMS, copyright, 1947, by Henry Reed; "Primer Lesson" from SLABS OF THE SUNBURNT WEST by *Carl Sandburg,* copyright, 1922, by Harcourt, Brace and Company, Inc., renewed, 1950, by Carl Sandburg; "In an Iridescent Time" by *Ruth Stone.* First published in *The New Yorker* (under the title "Laundry"), © 1958 by Ruth Stone. Reprinted from IN AN IRIDESCENT TIME by *Ruth Stone;* "Edgar A. Guest Considers 'The Good Old Woman Who Lived in a Shoe' and the Good Old Truths Simultaneously" from SELECTED POEMS AND PARODIES OF LOUIS UNTERMEYER, copyright, 1935, by Harcourt, Brace and Company, Inc. "Caliban in the Coal Mines" from CHALLENGE by *Louis Untermeyer,* copyright, 1914, by Harcourt, Brace and Company, Inc., renewed, 1942, by Louis Untermeyer; "Spendthrift" copyright, 1958, by I. A. Richards. Reprinted from GOODBYE EARTH AND OTHER POEMS by *I. A. Richards;* "Sonnet" from THINGS OF THIS WORLD, © 1956, by Richard Wilbur. All reprinted by permission of Harcourt, Brace and Company, Inc.

HARPER & BROS. for "The Jaguar" from THE HAWK IN THE RAIN by *Ted Hughes.* Copyright © 1957 by Ted Hughes; "God's World," "Lament" and "The Return" by *Edna St. Vincent Millay* from COLLECTED POEMS, *Edna St. Vincent Millay,* Harper & Brothers. Copyright 1913, 1921, 1934, 1940, 1948 by Edna St. Vincent Millay, by permission of Norma Millay Ellis. Reprinted by permission of Harper & Brothers.

HOLT, RINEHART & WINSTON, INC. for "For City Spring" by *Stephen Vincent Benét* from SELECTED WORKS OF STEPHEN VINCENT BENÉT. Rinehart & Co., Inc. Copyright 1935 by Stephen Vincent Benét; "Nancy Hanks" by *Rosemary Carr Benét* and three Rhymes by *Stephen Vincent Benét from* A BOOK OF AMERICANS, Rinehart & Co., Inc. Copyright, 1933, by Rosemary and Stephen Vincent Benét;

11

13

15

17

"A Memory" from SELECTED POEMS, by L. A. G. *Strong;* "On His Books" from SONNETS AND VERSE by *Hilaire Belloc* and "Grandmamma's Birthday" from LETTERS FROM HILAIRE BELLOC. Reprinted by permission of A. D. Peters, Ltd.

ACKNOWLEDGMENTS

This book is the product of much work by many persons. Thanks are due, first of all, to the hundreds of Hallmark dealers and employees who suggested poems for inclusion. The Kansas City Public Library and the University of Kansas City Library provided considerable assistance in locating books and poems. Mr. Richard B. Sealock and Miss Della Cortner of the Kansas City Public Library were particularly helpful. The manuscript was prepared under the general editorial direction of Webster Schott, Maurice Nugent, Carl Goeller, and Katherine Davis. Portions of the manuscript were typed by Louise Van Vooren, Ronalee Redford, Laura Deal, Orleen Eckhoff, Sandra Jensen, Aileene Neighbors, Judy Sears, Mary Margaret Gentry, and Jane Turner. All or part of the manuscript was read by Peter Seymour, Elliott Valentine, Arnold Shapiro, and Ray Watson. Valuable suggestions about the manuscript were made by Paul Engle of the State University of Iowa, Karl Shapiro of the University of Nebraska, and Thorpe Menn and Dwight Pennington of the Kansas City Star. Jeannette Lee supervised the designing of the jacket, endpapers, and illustrations. The jacket and endpapers were designed by Norman Engler. The jacket photograph is by William B. Bryer, M.D. The illustrations are the work of Walter Swartz, Jim Hamil, and Frank Szasz. The book was designed by Joseph P. Ascherl. Joe Kipp offered continuously good advice about the whole project. Robert V. Breen of Carl Byoir & Associates was particularly helpful in the planning of the book. And the counsel and enthusiasm of Sam Vaughan of Doubleday & Co. were essential to the successful completion of the book.

Contents

Taste and Times

Several months ago Doubleday and Company asked us whether we would like to gather a group of poems together in a book. Their reasons were that Hallmark had worked a long time in a field which demands attention to both good taste and clear communication, and that our efforts with television and fine art suggested we might be able to come up with a book which would be both popular and worthwhile. We liked this idea.

When I was a young man in a small bookstore back in Nebraska in the early 1900s, it would have been unheard of for a business organization to be involved in assembling an anthology of poetry. But we live in different times now, and I take this book to be a healthy sign of the new interest in everything in the arts in the United States today. We've grown up in our ability to appreciate the things that make life worth living. There are many reasons why. Today you can hear great symphonies, great statesmen and great poets on long-playing records. In just a few hours from New York or Kansas City you can fly to the Mayan ruins in Guatemala or the beautiful old countryside in Britain. You can see splendid reproductions of the world's great paintings in any number of magazines. Through television you can acquaint yourself with ways of life altogether different from your own. All these and many others have had a tremendous, uplifting effect on public taste.

Taste is becoming more refined. Our ability to appreciate the finer things in life has increased in every respect. Personally, I have seen these gradual changes in taste during a half century of watching the American public improve its taste from year to year in the selection of greeting cards. I am amazed when I look back ten years at the cards people preferred then; and when I look back twenty years, I am shocked. At Hallmark we see new evidence of the improvement in taste every year. It is accelerating, improving faster all the time. I just don't agree with the talk I sometimes hear about the American public having the mind of a twelve-year-old. Our people have greater capabilities than that. They will live up to what you expect of them.

Furthermore, the twelve-year-old mind today is quite a mind. The twelve-year-old of today would have been a match for some of the twenty-year-olds when I was a young man.

We know there is widespread public appreciation for fine writing and fine acting in television—our own broadcasts have proved this. We've found that just about everyone likes Shakespeare's plays when they are well done—not just the highbrows and college professors, but the man in the street and the family in the living room. Public interest in serious poetry seems to be growing, too. We've published several great poets of the past on Hallmark Cards (Wordsworth, Shakespeare, Tennyson, FitzGerald) as well as a number of fine contemporary poets (Pasternak, MacLeish, Engle, and Williams). They sell.

This collection of poems is designed to be a pleasure to read over a long period of time. True, it expects something from you in return. It expects your attention. But it will reward you for your effort and time. When the job of selecting and organizing the poems in this book was finished, I took the manuscript home and read it. I found a lot of pleasure, some thrills, and even inspiration in these poems. I hope and believe you will too.

Joyce C. Hall, President
Hallmark Cards, Inc.

Kansas City, Missouri
June 1960

Poetry, Yes

On a brilliant May morning a four-year-old girl with fresh blue eyes and corn-silk hair ran up to our breakfast table, talking to herself and to any listening thing nearby:

> Jack and Jill
> Went up the hill,
> To fetch a pail of water;
> Jack fell down,
> And broke his crown,
> And Jill came tumbling after!

The child laughed, climbed up on the bench, and ordered her bowl of shredded wheat. And I was left to think of what her recitation had meant. Nothing? No, everything, for she had said how to begin with poetry.

Surely her play with words belonged somewhere in the history of poetry. For through its several thousand years poetry has always been said or sung, beginning with ancient chants and incantations, then taking the form of primitive songs, becoming Oriental odes, changing into the early elegiac Greek couplets and heady Roman lyrics, growing into Dark Age ballads, and finally evolving into the charged language we call poetry in comparatively modern times. Change has had its way with poetry, but the elementary condition of poetry has never changed. Poetry may be read silently, but it cannot be felt that way. For this it must be said aloud, as it was from its start.

The other side of my May reverie was that the whole episode occurred spontaneously, for the sheer joy of the words bursting forth from a little girl whose spirit matched the morning. She was in love with the sound of the words: the way they marched and danced together, the silly delight of the rhymes, the bounce of the rhythm. She may or may not have known what "fetch" and "crown" meant; I will have to ask her some time. Nor did she care about why these words were put in this particular order, or whether it was tragedy or comedy she described (both, of course, are in the poem) as she galloped into the kitchen.

The reason for recalling this is not to say that we should be child-like in approaching poetry, but to insist that poetry's first pleasure is the same pleasure the child finds—the picture-magic of sound discovered in music, an art which is closer kin to poetry than prose is. Listen to the ring of these lines, light in meaning but full of music, from Poe's "The Bells":

> Hear the sledges with the bells,
> Silver bells!
> What a world of merriment their melody foretells!
> How they tinkle, tinkle, tinkle,
> In the icy air of night!
> While the stars that oversprinkle
> All the heavens seem to twinkle
> With a crystalline delight;
> Keeping time, time, time,
> In a sort of Runic rhyme, . . .

Or read aloud the first stanza from D. H. Lawrence's "The Sea." Certainly this poem is something more than an array of words. But Lawrence's root idea is an ordinary one: the sea is cruel and lonely. The rolling, swelling patterns of sound move the poem away from the cliché behind it. Meaning is less relevant than sonorous beauty:

> You, you are all unloving, loveless, you;
> Restless and lonely, shaken by your own moods,
> You are celibate and single, scorning a comrade even,
> Threshing your own passions with no woman for the
> threshing-floor,
> Finishing your dreams for your own sake only,
> Playing your great game around the world, alone,
> Without playmate, or helpmate, having no one to
> cherish,
> No one to comfort, and refusing any comforter.

This is the sea in sound, and when you examine the poem more closely, also the sea in impersonal reality.

It may be interesting to search the first lines of Gerard Manley Hopkins's poem, "Spring and Fall"

1

> Márgarét, are you gríeving
> Over Goldengrove unleaving?
> Leaves, like the things of man, you
> With your fresh thoughts care for, can you?

and practice amateur psychoanalysis on a child who weeps over the facts of botany. Or to settle for yourself whether Paul Engle's daughter was crying, white with anger and filled with cold-blooded hatred, in his poem "You Can't Be Wise":

> Denied, she screamed in rage and ran away.
> I yelled. She halted, rigid in her going.
> Water frozen in the act of flowing.

Hopkins's little girl honors life while mourning the inevitability of death, displaying a highly precocious and disturbing emotionalism. In Engle's poem the figure of speech using "water" implies tears; the words "frozen" and "rigid," cold hatred.

But if all of these inferences are valid and you make them, they have little effect on your first pleasure of hearing Hopkins's melodious lament or the suffering, stabbing quickness of Engle's lines. The first delight of poetry comes spontaneously with the words. For the poem's meaning is forever wedded to its utterance; the form itself expresses the truth of the poem. This is what Archibald MacLeish was talking about when he wrote: *A poem should not mean/But be*. The early meaning of a poem is in the form, its pattern of sound and our emotional response to these sounds.

MUSIC AND MEANING

The parallel between poetry and music is obvious. But we don't demand that the harmonies or rhythms of music mean anything beyond themselves, although such matters do carry significance for specialists in the field. We don't ask what Enesco's "Rumanian Rhapsodies" are about; they may be occult or even subversive for all we know or care. How we respond to Bach's precisely iridescent "Brandenburg Concertos" has nothing to do with what we think the music and the composer may be trying to say to us. We don't ask what music *means* because music isn't the way we communicate with one another day after day. We know that music is harmonic poetry, that it speaks to us in an extraordinary way, that it will not withstand the bloodless analysis of science. It is, we say, art.

But with language we are in another habit. Words stand for things. We expect words to mean something and always the same some-things. This is where we get into trouble with poetry. The poet doesn't use words the way the rest of us do. He chooses his words and phrases for their sounds and rhythms, and poets' notebooks and revised drafts reveal how often they collect verbal images or alter their lines for these effects alone. The poet takes old words and ar-ranges them together in new ways. They still possess all of their old meanings, but they acquire new meanings because of their nearness to one another or because the poet discovers new meanings for them in life. New emotions are wrung from old language. The poet invents new figures of speech. His expressions and impressions are superim-posed. His subconscious and conscious sensibilities are dredged and disciplined until through an act of language he has defied all the limits of language and has created joy or anguish or emptiness which is greater than reality.

This is what happens in poetry: the poet attempts to give voice to the inexpressible. His command to language has always been that it struggle to exceed itself. When Edgar Allan Poe writes that

> Once upon a midnight dreary, while I pondered,
>> weak and weary,
> Over many a quaint and curious volume of forgotten lore,—
> While I nodded, nearly napping, suddenly there came
>> a tapping,
> As of some one gently rapping, rapping at my chamber door

it is not only a bird that Poe's narrator hears summoning him. It is the inevitable course of man, the end of life, total darkness:

> And the Raven, never flitting, still is sitting, still is sitting
> On the pallid bust of Pallas just above my chamber door;
> And his eyes have all the seeming of a demon's that is dreaming,
> And the lamp-light o'er him streaming throws his shadow on
>> the floor;
> And my soul from out that shadow that lies floating on the floor
> Shall be lifted—nevermore!

Death waits. Death takes all. The raven is both a bird and more-than-a-bird. It is the end of hope, the unknowable, blackness. "The Raven" is not a poem one clips and carries in his billfold, but we respond to it because we go with Poe as his mind reaches beyond his words.

If you can suppress your imagination when you read "Thirteen Ways of Looking at a Blackbird" by Wallace Stevens, you draw only a blank. The poem seems abstract to the point of mystery, although blackbirds turn up in every stanza. But give Stevens your head and you will discover that every time he used the word "blackbird" he had something else in mind—the persistence of life, the search of conscience, man standing on the needle point of nature. And very likely he continuously enjoyed the whimsy of placing "blackbird" and its implications in such extraordinary surroundings. Here are the first eight stanzas of this remarkable poem which flies away with the imagination. They speak of a reality beyond the borders of language:

I

Among twenty snowy mountains,
The only moving thing
Was the eye of the blackbird.

II

I was of three minds,
Like a tree
In which there are three blackbirds.

III

The blackbird whirled in the autumn winds.
It was a small part of the pantomime.

IV

A man and a woman
Are one.
A man and a woman and a blackbird
Are one.

V

I do not know which to prefer,
The beauty of inflections
Or the beauty of innuendoes,
The blackbird whistling
Or just after.

VI

Icicles filled the long window
With barbaric glass.

The shadow of the blackbird
Crossed it, to and fro.
The mood
Traced in the shadow
An indecipherable cause.

VII

O thin men of Haddam,
Why do you imagine golden birds?
Do you not see how the blackbird
Walks around the feet
Of the women about you?

VIII

I know noble accents
And lucid, inescapable rhythms;
But I know, too,
That the blackbird is involved
In what I know.

POETRY AND ICEBERGS

The way to read a poem is with an open mind, not an open dictionary. A good poem doesn't need a dictionary. The poem itself provides the meanings for the words the poet puts to work. It seems too simple to be true. Yet there is no other way. You discover meaning by reading the poem, but more than once, and aloud. And if that won't do the trick, read another poem. Art is undemocratic. Not all poems are written for all readers. Reading poetry must be a pleasure, not a social responsibility. Poetry is supposed to be beautiful, not an intellectual obligation. The first beauty lies in language, where poetry and everyone who reads it must begin. But language is only the means by which poetry fulfills its promise. A poem is like an iceberg. We see the peak and project the depth. The union between the poem and the reader as he follows the lines down below the surface into the poem's profusion of possible meanings is the great, recurrent pleasure of reading poetry. The poet fuses all of his experience with all of our experience, and each time we read a poem we find something new about the poem, ourselves, and the rest of life. What we discover in the poem is as much read into as written into the poem. But the greatest poets—Shakespeare, Whitman, Yeats, and whomever one turns to again and again—fill their poems with possibilities for meaning and emotional response. Their poetry, as all lasting poetry, operates on several levels of experience at once. Whitman's "Cavalry Crossing a Ford" steals the ear with its rhythms: *A line in long array* or *Scarlet and blue and snowy white/The guidon flags flutter gaily in the wind.* The language is alive and spoken. No poetic sweet talk, no mythology. Simultaneously in the mind's eye flashes the picture of the column crossing the stream and stopping to drink. Read with greater care the poem becomes like an impressionistic painting, a study in swift movement and subtle shading. From first line to last the poem moves with the cavalry troop; the action of the poem is wedded to the subject of the poem. With more thought "Cavalry Crossing a Ford" begins to seem peculiarly American in its unconscious contrast of the exhausted men and the brazen pennants of the Civil War. It is a gentle song to the bond Whitman felt with everything American, including contradictions. And read in the 1960s "Cavalry Crossing a Ford" is also a hymn to the last romantic war in history. Such is hindsight. But everything we know goes into our reading of the poem.

The best poem seizes your mind the first time you read it. There is an immediate impact. You feel the poem even though you cannot describe the feeling precisely or quickly. By the second or third reading the poem becomes part of you. You own it. You possess it in ways that only you can, for you have set the poem's limits. This is what H. M. Tomlinson must have meant when he said that "the reader who is illuminated is in a real sense, the poem." Poetry says what the same words (or different words) arranged in any other order cannot say. This is why analyzing or paraphrasing a poem can never substitute for the experience of personally discovering the poem. You can say what a little girl's smile is like. Or you can describe the scatter of stars on a black night. But will you settle for words when you can have the smile? And can an astronomer's lecture take the place of your wandering wonder when you are lost in the stars? The poem itself is the miracle of feeling and intelligence, and it is possible to make a good argument that any poem which can survive being taken apart and laid out like a gear box is no poem at all. The successful poem puts us into a new relationship with life, a relationship which never existed before. Poetry is a way of seeing things, and as a result feeling these relationships which never existed before. It is not rhythm, rhyme or figures of speech; these are only the means to poetry's ends. Poetry is the quality of awareness: emotion captured and surrendered.

TIME'S TEMPER

A few pages earlier I said change has had its way with poetry. I should have said change has had its way with men. For like the other arts, poetry does not grow in a laboratory dish, thriving in airy isolation. Poetry is intimately related to everything happening to people and their world. It is contemporaneous, expressing the special sensibilities of its age. The greatest poets, often unconsciously, record the psychological stresses and tensions of their era and make us participants in them. Poetry reflects the new realities of man's condition, and as often as not it has brought these new visions out of darkness and made them public. The process of catching up—the closing of the gap between what the poet perceives and what the mass of his readers may have yet to discover—has produced both poetry's great successes and great losses.

Boris Pasternak once called poetry "the expression of the birth pangs of the new in the world." Through history these pangs have been accompanied by cries of misunderstanding. In the early 1600s when John Donne and the "new" metaphysical poets following Shakespeare began writing, Ben Jonson complained that "now nothing is good that is natural . . . (the) writhed and tortured is considered the more exquisite . . . Nothing is fashionable til it be deform'd." Another critic said the metaphysical imagery and sophisticated language of Donne, James Cowley, and Thomas Carew were "ingenious nothings . . . mere embroideries upon cobwebs." Two hundred years later a major critical journal of the day said Wordsworth's "Ode on the Intimations of Immortality" was "illegible and unintelligible" and could give "no analysis or explanation of it." When it first appeared, Coleridge's "Christabel" was called a "rhapsody of delirium." Shelley's "Prometheus Unbound" was a "tissue of insufferable buffoonery" and his "Adonais" was a "mere collection of bloated words heaped on each other without order, harmony, or meaning." But we know now that Donne was the first poet to give voice to the new vision of the universe as seen by Kepler and Galileo. We know now that Wordsworth's contemporaries were hearing backwards, were deaf to poetry whose majesty lay in simplified diction. Now we know that Shelley had found a new lyrical relationship between man and his world.

Like life, poetry continually renews and reorganizes itself. It is forever discovering, as Shelley said, the previously "unapprehended relations of things and perpetuates their apprehension." Greek and Roman poetry trembled with such adjustments. Medieval lyrics rearranged Christian ideals and earthly urges to such an extent that a man could carry on his love affairs in church. Writers of the ancient, rigorous Chinese odes so successfully invested their poetry with the peculiar symbolism of their times that we still cannot say what the peach trees are for in their poems about wedding ceremonies.

In our own time the readjustment of poetry has been nothing less than a literary upheaval, with all the manifestoes, rivalries, labels, slogans and war cries of a revolution. It has been as misunderstood as any poetry in history and its conceptions have been so far in advance (or behind, depending on your vantage point) of public sensibilities that our poetry has almost, but not quite, lost its audience.

THE SPIRIT OF THE NEW

The poetry we call "modern" is already old; it began in the late nineteenth and early twentieth century, born of radical changes in the way men lived and thought of themselves. It came as a reaction against growing materialism in Europe and America; it came as an expression of the poet's estrangement from public life; it came as a symptom of the great social and ideological complexities of industrialization. Under the new conditions of life in the early twentieth century, the traditional rhetoric of poetry seemed dead and false, the traditional emotions seemed phony. The poetry of the past did not conform to the experience of the present. Science was replacing the arts as the chief interpreter of human behavior, and to place himself in the new era the poet was compelled to find new ways of knowing about man. Aesthetic values were being displaced by commercial values, and the poet's reaction was to create art for its own sake. Against the disorderliness of the age, as Arthur Rimbaud said, the poet went about an intentional "disordering of the senses." In the other arts—painting, music and to a lesser degree, sculpture—much of the same was happening. Old forms were fractured.

Surprisingly, the first outlines of what is modern in poetry were drawn in the United States, where Edgar Allan Poe was practicing what he called "a suggestive indefiniteness." In Poe a group of young literary insurgents in France found their model, and French Symbolism became the first full-scale modernist movement in poetry. Led by Charles Baudelaire the Symbolists created a new kind of poetry in which one poetic symbol or image implied a second, and in which one sensual impression was used to suggest still another. They dealt almost exclusively in these symbols, and the meaning (but not the music) of their poetry required lengthy symbolic analysis. The example of the Symbolists spread almost immediately through the rest of the civilized world. From Symbolism came Russian and Italian Futurism and lines designed to bring the modern style of speed and dynamism to poetry. From French Symbolism came English and American Imagism and free-verse filled with cadence, foreign language and the imagined excitements of the poet. And from the Symbolists came T. S. Eliot and scholarship-as-poetry, erudition-as-craftsmanship, and the ideal of a poetry so transparent that we cannot see the poetry in it: "Poetry with nothing poetic about it, poetry standing naked in its bare bones . . . We should not see the poetry, but . . . what the poem *points* at." A hard and stark age begot a hard and stark poetry.

The social antagonism of the earliest modern poetry has run its course by now. But all poetry of the twentieth century has fallen heir to the stylistic legacy of the Symbolist revolution. Contemporary poetry is irregular in rhyme and rhythm. It operates without reference to a recognizable body of poetic technique. It follows no Baedeker's guide of approved mythology or poetic allusion. The stilted expressions, the great heroes, the passionate loves, the gingerbread rhetoric of the old poetry are gone. Modern poetry's language is common even though its metaphors are not. The modern poet lays down no linguistic underbrush for the mind to cut through. Lines like T. S. Eliot's

> When the evening is spread out against the sky
> Like a patient etherized upon a table

or Boris Pasternak's

> The Caucasus lay spread before our gaze,
> An unmade bed, it seemed, with tousled sheets

seize the imagination because they assault us directly. Here is life vivid and filled with surprise. In their later years, W. H. Auden, Eliot, Pasternak, and others turned to theology for comfort, but these are the endings of these poets, not their beginnings; and religion in contemporary poetry is primarily an English-language phenomenon. One finds little of it in modern Italian, German or French poetry. The poet of our time most often finds his inspiration in conscience, the common man, the social interplay, the new cosmos of the new scientific era. When he deals with nature, the contemporary poet writes from nature, not about nature. Suggestiveness, the association of one idea with another, is inherent in art. But the contemporary poet magnifies the power of suggestion by leaping at random from one impression to the next. The relationships in contemporary poetry are arbitrary. They are decreed by the poet, not by the laws of logic or the reasonableness of cause and effect.

ATTENTION, PLEASE

Most twentieth-century poetry does demand greater attention than much of the poetry preceding it, particularly the highly formalized lyrics of the romantic periods of English literature. But the age we live in requires all of our wits. And effort is relative anyway. You must expend it whether you lift a brick or move a mountain. The question is always one of purpose.

Poetry has never been easy reading. It has always demanded the best the mind can muster. Shakespeare's sonnets are not simple-minded jingles waiting to be set to soap. They are exceedingly complex poems rich in the glories of language. Read his "Sonnet XV" with the same degree of attention you give a subscription renewal letter and see what happens:

> When I consider every thing that grows
> Holds in perfection but a little moment,
> That this huge stage presenteth naught but shows
> Whereon the stars in secret influence comment:
> When I perceive that men as plants increase,
> Cheered and checked even by the self-same sky,
> Vaunt in their youthful sap, at height decrease,
> And wear their brave state out of memory;
> Then the conceit of this inconstant stay
> Sets you most rich in youth, before my sight,
> Where wasteful Time debateth with Decay,

To change your day of youth to sullied night;
And, all in war with Time for love of you,
As he takes from you, I engraft you new.

It's beautiful to the ear. But it must be read two or three times to find the intelligence it transmits. Then you discover that Shakespeare was saying to a mistress or a patron: as time wears you down I build you up; you may be getting older, as all we must, but I renew your beauty by writing to you.

One can go on and on doing this. Follow Browning, if you can, quickly around the rose bush in "Women and Roses":

I will make an Eve by the artist that began her,
Shaped her to his mind!—Alas! in like manner
They circle their rose on my rose tree

Or try to paraphrase what goes on in John Donne's magnificent first stanza of "Song," written some 250 years ago:

Goe and catche a falling starre,
Get with child a mandrake roote,
Tell me where all past yeares are,
Or who cleft the Divel's foot;

Lines like Pope's *Swift on his sooty pinions flits the Gnome,/ And in a vapor reached the dismal dome* may have had significance centuries ago, but one can't be sure what they mean now. Vapors are no longer a physical malady, but what you get from Vick's to cure one. If Pound's wanderings through Oriental history and Eliot's troubling fascination with culture seem unfriendly, one only needs turn to John Milton and consider V*exed Scylla, bathing in the sea that parts/Calabria from the hoarse Trinacrian shore* or accept a visitation of Shelley's relentless "azure heavens," "unpavilioned vistas," and "fast influencings holding an unremitting interchange with the clear universe."

The charged quality is as peculiar and necessary to poetry as walking on two legs is to man. No poet who has made easiness his attribute has ever contributed to the permanent body of words and ideas we call literature. "I never meant my poetry," said Robert Browning, "to be a substitute for an after-dinner cigar." When the sidewalk critics of modern poetry cite the good, old (and often embarrassingly mawkish) poetry of a few centuries ago as models of clarity and communication, one can only conclude that they have either faulty memories, or less charitably, that they have never read poetry at all. One is entitled to ask whether the detractors of modern poetry are rushing home of an evening to take in the glories of Byron's "Childe Harold's Pilgrimage" or Tennyson's "Idylls of the King," or whether, instead, the time isn't being spent with the idol of electronics.

IS ANYONE LISTENING?

Let's admit that the most influential poets of the past fifty years have cared little about speaking into the Public Ear. But let's also admit that we cared not to listen. Our system of values, our media of communications, our lack of traditions in the arts, the emphasis our society places on the practical as opposed to the impractical— all have worked against the contemplative attractions of poetry. We have never read much poetry and therefore we can't understand that poetry is not designed to replace the newspaper, but is intended to enhance our awareness of life. Poetry is unessential for Man's survival; you cannot eat it. But poetry is essential for civilization's survival, for it represents all that is humanizing in mankind. Because everything, except thinking, is easy in the twentieth century, we expect poetry to be as simple as opening baked beans with an electric can opener. We operate on the misassumption that poetry doesn't require our highest intelligence and our best attention. But it does. Poetry is a way of feeling, thinking, and then knowing. And modern poetry has absorbed more ideas from more sources—Freud, Marx, Lincoln, Einstein, Whitehead—than any poetry in history. It was bound to; we have learned more about ourselves in the past one hundred years than in civilization's previous several thousand years.

Reading poetry has not been our style; we've been too busy with the gross practical matters which poetry escapes. But in Japan poetry is part of the way of life. Businessmen are almost as likely as poets to write Haiku. In France statesmen and politicians write poetry as professionals, but in the United States the businessman who reads poetry can generally stop conversation simply by saying so. The press marvels at the fact that William Carlos Williams has been a successful physician as well as a distinguished poet. And our journalists still haven't recovered from the discovery that the late Wallace Stevens, while writing some of the most refined poetry of his era,

35

was also a vice president of a Hartford insurance company and an expert in claims on surety bonds.

Karl Shapiro insists with vigor and appealing candor that one of the things wrong with modern poetry is that it is so scholarly it has to be taught in college. But would modern poetry have to be taught if it had been as blessed as the other arts by the advances of modern technology? FM radio and the long-playing record have brought great music, free or at small cost, to all of us. High-speed, high-precision lithography and silk-screen printing have made inexpensive reproductions of great paintings the symbol of popular culture. But how many of the multi-million-circulation weekly magazines or Sunday supplements regularly publish poetry in their pages? Perhaps if our poetry were clear enough it would find the big audiences. On the other hand, our most straightforward poets—Robert Frost, Carl Sandburg, Winfield Townley Scott, Mark Van Doren, Engle, Shapiro—can count on their fingers the times their poetry has appeared in the popular magazines. How can we acquire an understanding of modern poetry if we never see it where we do most of our reading?

Obscurity cannot be the sole reason for the public's estrangement from poetry. Dylan Thomas was never an easy poet, yet his public readings were great successes. During the 1950s Robert Frost's lectures and recitations drew audiences of thousands of persons even though his poems demanded all the reverence he himself brought to them. In April 1956, some 13,700 persons came to hear T. S. Eliot speak in Minneapolis.

IN DAYS AHEAD

Is it only wishfulness to think better days may be ahead? Long-playing records by poets reading from their works may establish a public tradition for poetry, spoken, as it must be. Prose writings by poets like John Ciardi and Paul Engle are turning up everwhere—in all sorts of magazines and books. Poet-critics like Ciardi and Shapiro are making poetry interesting to read about, and the poet, not without risk, is becoming a public figure again. He must, in order to be heard amidst the shouts of the age. The paperback phenomenon is working to poetry's benefit; publishers at last are bringing out collections of new modern verse at prices which put poetry within almost everyone's economic reach. More and more poets are lecturing, worrying about their isolation, and writing with a clarity absent in the poetry which began the modern-poetry revolution. Our poets want to be read. I know of no poet who believes with Stanley Kunitz that American poetry is in its Silver Age because poetry is going unread and the poet can write to please himself. If the Silver Age is poetry without readers, then the Golden Age would have to be poetry without poets.

Poetry needs readers the way the stars need the sky. For we give poetry its meaning. This above all is what the little girl on the May morning was saying. Poetry will be whatever we make of it: the music of our moods, the emotions we cannot locate in other language, the special sensibilities of our age. Because poetry comes from our depths it is the way we say yes to life at the height of our humanity.

This collection of poems is for readers rather than poets. It is for pleasure rather than scholarship. It covers as much of 2000 years of poetry as possible within some 500 pages and without forgetting that in the nature of things we are most strongly drawn to English-language poetry and the poetry of our own times.

Many of these poems are old. You will remember reading them often, perhaps with pleasure, and probably with chalk on your hands. But there is also plenty here to grow on. A good many of these poems have never appeared in an anthology before, and most of them never together before. Of course, not every poem in this collection is for every reader; such is impossible. But everyone who picks this book up should be able to find in it somewhere (and more than once) a voice that speaks to him as if it were his own and as if it had never been heard in the world before.

—WEBSTER SCHOTT

Kansas City, Missouri
May–June, 1960

Poetry for Pleasure
THE HALLMARK BOOK OF POETRY

New Voices

POETS FOR OUR TIMES

A voice is new until it has been heard. Some of the poets in this section are older than others in years lived, but are not older in attention paid to their poetic speech.

The art of poetry is never constant. Where it remains most the same it is the most untraditional, for tradition is that the rhythmical, heightened and imaginative language which is poetry always alters as the young poets walk out of the dark of time into astonishing daylight.

As the Nineteen-Sixties begin, it is obvious that the new voices are speaking in their own solid way. They are more concerned with the open expression of human feeling, not hiding it under a stone of objective image, the reader left to guess from his own shrewdness that it is there. William Merwin speaks of "love's delicacy or its quiet assurance," in a line which the poets of the Twenties and Thirties might well have been incapable of writing.

Poet after poet in this decade is concerned with the theme which John Frederick Nims states in his poem "Midwest," where he finds "Conspicuous on our fields the shadow of man." This is a direct statement which many recent poets would have found distasteful.

Along with this acceptance of emotion, there has come a greater concern with solid form. These new poets are writing in carefully calculated stanzas. The push toward security in our lives at mid-century has apparently given these voices the impetus to find comfort in fixed form, sharp stanza, exact rime. Control of language is everywhere tightening, as poets rely on the security of firm line and rhythm.

Above all, these new voices are speaking with warmth and delight, with the refusal to let the immediate unknown destroy them. As the times offer their destructive threat, poetry seems to become more important, as the expression of that area of man which is most himself, most worth saving, most the uniqueness of his mortal life.

It is important to note that this is not simply the attitude of poets in the United States, but of the recent poet wherever he has raised his eloquent voice, from Missouri to Japan.

—PAUL ENGLE

MIDWEST

John Frederick Nims

Indiana: no blustering summit or coarse gorge;
No flora lurid as disaster-flares;
No great vacuities where tourists gape
Nor mountains hoarding their height like millionaires.
More delicate: the ten-foot knolls
Give flavor of hill to Indiana souls.

Topography is perfect, curio-size;
Deft as landscape in museum cases.
What is beautiful is friendly and underfoot,
Not flaunted like theater curtains in our faces.
No peak or jungle obscures the blue sky;
Our land rides smoothly in the softest eye.

Man is the prominent fauna of our state.
Elsewhere circus creatures stomp and leer
With heads like crags or clumps. But delirious nature
Once in a lucid interval sobering here
Left (repenting her extravagant plan)
Conspicuous on our fields the shadow of man.

SO LONG FOLKS, OFF TO THE WAR

Anthony Ostroff

When I was little, oh a very small boy,
With a Ford, fish, and go fly your kite,
I lived in a house in a cookie jar joy,
With a bed, game, and I'm it tonight.

I wore short pants and had dimples in my knees,
With a Whitney-Pratt, call me that again.
I had a girl friend more pretty than you please,
With a top, bee, and so's your old man.

I played in the street, oh I never saw school,
With a Campbell can, and knock *that* off,
I hid and I sought and I broke THE rule,
With a me, who, and why don't you cough?

When I was happy, oh a very small boy,
With a sink, stove, and jump in the lake,
I made mud huts I would never destroy,
With a strap, please, be good for my sake.

I didn't grow much, and then I grew fast,
With a book, bat, and why don't you try?
I never was first, but I was never last,
With a good, bad, and who knows why?

I grew like grass, Oh! we said, Like corn!
With an ache, break, and which way to go?
I dreamed some nights that I'd never been born,
With a glad, sad—I still don't know.

THE AIRMAN WHO FLEW OVER
SHAKESPEARE'S ENGLAND

Hyam Plutznik

A nation of hayricks spotting the green solace
    Of grass,
And thrones of thatch ruling a yellow kingdom
    Of barley.

In the green lands, the white nation of sheep.
    And the woodlands,
Red, the delicate tribes of roebuck, doe
    And fawn.

A senate of steeples guarding the slaty and gabled
    Shires,
While aloof the elder houses hold a secret
    Sceptre.

To the north, a wall touching two stone-grey reaches
  Of water;
A circle of stones; then to the south a chalk-white
  Stallion.

To the north, the wireless towers upon the cliff.
  Southward
The powerhouse, and monstrous constellations
  Of cities.

To the north, the pilgrims along the holy roads
  To Walsingham,
And southward, the road to Shottery, shining
  With daisies.

Over the castle of Warwick frightened birds
  Are fleeing,
And on the bridge, faces upturned to a roaring
  Falcon.

BEYOND THE HUNTING WOODS

Donald Justice

I speak of that great house
Beyond the hunting woods,
Turreted and towered
In nineteenth-century style,
Where fireflies by the hundreds
Leap in the long grass,
Odor of jessamine
And roses, canker-bit,
Recalling famous times
When dame and maiden sipped
Sassafras or wild
Elderberry wine,
While far in the hunting woods
Men after their red hounds
Pursued the mythic beast.

I ask it of a stranger,
In all that great house finding
Not any living thing,
Or of the wind and the weather,
What charm was in that vine
That they should vanish so,
Ladies in their stiff
Bone and clean of limb,
And over the hunting woods
What mist had maddened them
That gentlemen should lose
Not only the beast in view
But Belle and Ginger too,
Nor home from the hunting woods
Ever, ever come?

ELEGY

Robert Layzer

I

Whenever we touched, I thought of the Lying-in Hospital.
Those women were big as the houses they hoped to fill,
Not slender like you: too bulky to be desired
But swollen and snug as after a Thanksgiving dinner.
They were digesting some really important secret
And I remembered, when you moved out of my arms,
That we had our own secrets to fill the room.

II

We slept. I dreamed or simply remembered a room
Where the laughter of nursing mothers lay like the hum
Of telephones on the air. A woman sat
On the edge of her bed and combed her hair and laughed,
Bare to the waist, the gentle curve of her back
Partly in shadows of the late afternoon
And partly illumined by my clear desire.

Your hand had slipped from mine and I was afraid
To wake you, if I took you in my arms,
From that ambiguous dream that smoothed your face
Into the semblance of complete content.
The moonlight picked out objects in the room.
What did I lack? The bed and books were there,
Your breathing, and the secrets of the room.

APRIL INVENTORY

W. D. Snodgrass

The green catalpa tree has turned
All white; the cherry blooms once more.
In one whole year I haven't learned
A blessed thing they pay you for.
The blossoms snow down in my hair;
The trees and I will soon be bare.

The trees have more than I to spare.
The sleek, expensive girls I teach,
Younger and pinker every year,
Bloom gradually out of reach.
The pear tree lets its petals drop
Like dandruff on a table top.

The girls have grown so young by now
I have to nudge myself to stare.
This year they smile and mind me how
My teeth are falling with my hair.
In thirty years I may not get
Younger, shrewder, or out of debt.

The tenth time, just a year ago,
I made myself a little list
Of all the things I'd ought to know;
Then told my parents, analyst,
And everyone who's trusted me
I'd be substantial, presently.

I haven't read one book about
A book or memorized one plot.
Or found a mind I didn't doubt.
I learned one date. And then forgot.
And one by one the solid scholars
Get the degrees, the jobs, the dollars.

And smile above their starchy collars.
I taught my classes Whitehead's notions;
One lovely girl, a song of Mahler's.
Lacking a source-book or promotions,
I showed one child the colors of
A luna moth and how to love.

I taught myself to name my name,
To bark back, loosen love and crying;
To ease my woman so she came,
To ease an old man who was dying.
I have not learned how often I
Can win, can love, but choose to die.

I have not learned there is a lie
Love shall be blonder, slimmer, younger;
That my equivocating eye
Loves only by my body's hunger;
That I have poems, true to feel,
Or that the lovely world is real.

While scholars speak authority
And wear their ulcers on their sleeves,
My eyes in spectacles shall see
These trees procure and spend their leaves.
There is a value underneath
The gold and silver in my teeth.

Though trees turn bare and girls turn wives,
We shall afford our costly seasons;
There is a gentleness survives
That will outspeak and has its reasons.
There is a loveliness exists,
Preserves us. Not for specialists.

IN AN IRIDESCENT TIME

Ruth Stone

My mother, when young, scrubbed laundry in a tub,
She and her sisters on an old brick walk
Under the apple trees, sweet rub-a-dub.
The bees came round their heads, and wrens made talk.
Four young ladies each with a rainbow board
Honed their knuckles, wrung their wrists to red,
Tossed back their braids and wiped their aprons wet.
The Jersey calf beyond the back fence roared;
And all the soft day, swarms about their pet
Buzzed at his big brown eyes and bullish head.
Four times they rinsed, they said. Some things they starched,
Then shook them from the baskets two by two,
And pinned the fluttering intimacies of life
Between the lilac bushes and the yew:
Brown gingham, pink, and skirts of Alice blue.

JAPAN THAT SANK UNDER THE SEA

Satoru Sato

When night falls,
Japan that sank under the sea
    (Possibly it may have sunk, for next morning
    I found myself between the blind clouds
    And the old inhuman water.)
Comes up afloat in the heavens,
Like a lantern hanging.
Yes, that is an antique paper-lantern,
A candle-light muffled with an amber-colored Japanese paper.
There, the surrounding darkness is deep,
Especially deep because of the vague candle-light.
But, where are the crowds of people so familiar to me?
What swells up the darkness
Is the thick glossy foliage.

What fortune is told by this sight?
I don't see Tokyo anywhere; don't see anything modern.
Only the lantern remains,
Only the antique silence
Keeps in form the melancholy of the long history.

From far down below some noise is heard,
A noise like that of waves . . . or is that . . . ?
It is too early to reveal itself.

A RENEWAL

James Merrill

Having used every subterfuge
To shake you, lies, fatigue, or even that of passion,
Now I see no way but a clean break.
I add that I am willing to bear the guilt.

You nod assent. Autumn turns windy, huge,
A clear vase of dry leaves vibrating on and on.
We sit, watching. When I next speak
Love buries itself in me, up to the hilt.

THE GARDEN AT ST. JOHN'S

May Swenson

Behind the wall of St. John's in the city
 in the shade of the garden the Rector's wife
 walks with her baby a girl and the first
 its mouth at her neck seeking and sucking
 in one hand holding its buttocks its skull
 cupped by the other her arms like a basket
 of tenderest fruit and thinks as she fondles
 the nape of the infant its sweat is like dew
 like dew and its hair is as soft as soft
 as down as the down in the wingpits of angels

The little white dog with the harlequin eye
 his tail like a thumb feet nimble as casters
  scoots in the paths of the garden's meander
   behind the wall of St. John's in the city
    a toy deposed from his place in her arms
     by this doll of the porcelain bone
      this pale living fruit without stone

She walks where the wrinkling tinkling fountain
 laps at the granite head of a monk
  where dip the slippery noses of goldfish
   and tadpoles flip from his cuspid mouth
    a miracle surely the young wife thinks
     from such a hard husband a tender child
      and thinks of his black sleeves on the hymnbook
       inside the wall of St. John's in the city
        the Ah of his stiff mouth intoning Amen
         while the organ prolongs its harmonious snore

Two trees like swans' necks twine in the garden
 beside the wall of St. John's in the city
  Brooding and cool in the shade of the garden
   the scrolled beds of ivy glitter like vipers
    a miracle surely this child and this garden
     of succulent green in the broil of the city.

  She thinks as setting the bird-cries apart
   she hears from beneath the dark spirals of ivy
    under the wall of St. John's in the city
     the rectal rush and belch of the subway
      roiling the corrugate bowels of the city
       and sees in the sky the surgical gleam
        of an airplane stitching its way to the West
         above the wall of St. John's in the city
          ripping its way through the denim air

ECCLESIASTES
Joseph Langland

Out of the icy storms the white hare came
Shivering into a haven of human arms;
It was not love but fear that made him tame.

He lay in the arms of love, having no name
But comfort to address. Shaking alarms
Out of the icy storms, the white hare came

Across the haunted meadows crackling with game.
What evil eye pinpointed his soft charms?
It was not love but fear. That made him tame

Among the chilling hail and scattering aim.
Helpless against the sport of ancient farms,
Out of the icy storms the white hare came

Thinking, perhaps, it leaped through icy flame,
Thinking, with instinct, hate or trust disarms.
It was not love. But fear that made him tame

Leaped again in his heart; his flesh became
Translated into havens. From sudden harms
Out of the icy storms the white hare came;
It was not love but fear that made him tame.

THE JAGUAR
Ted Hughes

The apes yawn and adore their fleas in the sun.
The parrots shriek as if they were on fire, or strut
Like cheap tarts to attract the stroller with the nut.
Fatigued with indolence, tiger and lion

Lie still as the sun. The boa-constrictor's coil
Is a fossil. Cage after cage seems empty, or
Stinks of sleepers from the breathing straw.
It might be painted on a nursery wall.

But who runs like the rest past these arrives
At a cage where the crowd stands, stares, mesmerized,
As a child at a dream, at a jaguar hurrying enraged
Through prison darkness after the drills of his eyes

On a short fierce fuse. Not in boredom—
The eye satisfied to be blind in fire,
By the bang of blood in the brain deaf the ear—
He spins from the bars, but there's no cage to him

More than to the visionary his cell:
His stride is wildernesses of freedom:
The world rolls under the long thrust of his heel.
Over the cage floor the horizons come.

NORTH

Philip Booth

North is weather, Winter, and change:
a wind-shift, snow, and how ice ages
shape the moraine of a mountain range.

At tree line the chiseled ledges
are ragged to climb; wind-twist trees
give way to the trust of granite ridges,

peaks reach through abrasive centuries
of rain. The worn grain, the sleet-cut,
is magnified on blue Northwest days

where rock slides, like rip-tide, break out
through these geologic seas. Time
in a country of hills is seasonal light:

alpenglow, Northern lights, and tame
in October: Orion, cold hunter of stars.
Between what will be and was, rime

whites the foothill night and flowers
the rushes stilled in black millpond ice.
The dark, the nightfall temperatures

are North, and the honk of flyway geese
high over valley sleep. The woodland
is evergreen, ground pine, spruce,

and deadwood hills at the riverbend.
Black bear and mink fish beaver streams
where moose and caribou drink: beyond

the forests there are elk. Snowstorms
breed North like arctic birds that swirl
downhill, and in a blind wind small farms

are lost. At night the close cold is still,
the tilt world returns from sun to ice.
Glazed lichen is North, and snowfall

at five below. North is where rockface
and hoarfrost are formed with double grace:
love is twice warm in a cold place.

THE MADMAN

Constance Urdang

At first, he wondered why he should be spared;
Observed, of all the windows, none was barred,
And every door swung open at a word.

The garden welcomed him; the angel's sword
Flowered before his eyes like Aaron's rod;
At first he wondered that he should be spared.

The beasts had grown so tame they hardly stirred;
The wall uncoiled its length without a guard
Where every door swung open at a word,

And trees bowed low to offer all they had.
The woman swore he was her only lord
Although, of all the windows, none was barred.

He called it Eden (but it was the world),
And so, until it was too late, ignored
The lucid glass that sealed the windows hard;

No longer troubled to pronounce the word.
But at the end, when towering clouds hurled
Boomerangs at him, and the thunder roared

At him one terrible and final chord,
He knew at last that he had not been spared,
Ran screaming from the mirror, and was mad.

CHILDHOOD

Ned O'Gorman

Childhood is when the mouth tastes earth.
When the body is the body's sign;
When there is no studied end to time;
When hands join and make a cradle.

The child races through the snow in circles
and hears on the swing the sound of air;
the world's grave mummery is everywhere
and the sun like a falcon swerves toward his wrist.

There are drummers drumming and red sails
making April conquests in the bay;
the flesh is still a flurried sound of clay;
kites go as high as God and there are birds.

Though children are not passionate
they feel the thigh against the sheet;
When there is thunder they will weep;
Stairs go down to halls and rooms are darknesses.

The child is verb and hieroglyphic of his day
and sits and broods like a thinking flame;
That is called the playing of the game;
A child tends to glory like a pirate in a church.

And suffering fills him up with light
that holds its lumen for another time;
And one day as he plays he'll see a sign
and lift his arms and cry aloud like Man.

HOUSE AND SHUTTER

Lewis Turco

Like a fleet thief, this sparrow has
stolen stillness. He keeps it in a
purse of bones. The aperture in which he
quit quickening is thin: an airy dimness
between our house and its fake shutter.

Here's a sparrow that couldn't fall.
I cannot even pry him loose. The
shutter has been stunned with bolts; the wall won't
drop its trophy. For certain, bird, you did not
fly diving into quiet. It is

your tail that caught you up and will
not let you down. How in heaven did
you back to your demise? This December
sky seems somewhat grimmer for your defection.
The overcast will not be cast off.

* * *

So this small absence is noted and
duly recorded. His mate impatiently
waits near the crack into which he crept for
warmth. It will be a cold day elsewhere,
my lady, before this midwest

wind hovers about his flight again.
One feather works loose. It falls. The overcast
is cued: a flake has launched an avalanche.
My sympathy is for both you birds,
but less for the live, for at least

(For all or any hurt a sparrow
feels) when winter learns to thaw there's always spring.
Death will shrink to due proportion: a bird's
eye view of a worm, perhaps. But right
now, be vigilant with your grief,

wife. Snow is vital too. It sucks what
warmth was left today when wings hung fire.

PALERMO, MOTHER'S DAY, 1943
William Belvin

Among those who promised us our honors,
Someone said we'd killed a hundred each;
And since our knowledge of events was vague,
We used the digits in our dim additions:
Sometimes I deck zeroes out in lashes
To make crude, comic eyes that will not cry.

Hell's a harbor for the guilty; but
Were we not innocent of the spectacle
In our high and ornamental boxes?
There is no need to say we bluntly murdered;
I memorized the scene in my crossed glasses:
I swear there were not even marionettes.

I could fear the image of a planting;
Yet we knew no sense of sowing (though our seeds
Were miracles that rooted, boled, and bloomed,
Fertilized and fruited in a flash)
For we were timorously tending other ground,
Where rude berries brambled gratuitously.

But at length the sound of women's voices
Will fracture all the sealed rooms of the air,
And all the little rooms that time has bricked
Against my knowledge of that soiled city
Will suddenly sympathize with the vibrations
Of distant propellers meaning no malice but death.

FOR THE GRAVE OF DANIEL BOONE
William Stafford

The farther he went the farther home grew.
Kentucky became another room;
the mansion arched over the Mississippi;
flowers were spread all over the floor.
He traced ahead a deepening home,
and better, with goldenrod:

Leaving the snakeskin of place after place,
going on—after the trees
the grass, a bird flying after a song.
Rifle so level, sighting so well
his picture freezes down to now,
a story-picture for children.

They go over the velvet falls
into the tapestry of his time,
heirs to the landscape, feeling no jar;
it is like evening; they are the quail
surrounding his fire, coming in for the kill;
their little feet move sacred sand.

Children, we live in a barb-wire time
but can follow the old hands back—
the ring in the light, the knuckle, the palm,
all the way to Daniel Boone,
hunting our own kind of deepening home.
From the land that was his I heft this rock.

Here on his grave I put it down.

SAMUEL SEWALL

Anthony Hecht

Samuel Sewall, in a world of wigs,
Flouted opinion in his personal hair;
For foppery he gave not any figs,
But in his right and honor took the air.

Thus in his naked style, though well attired,
He went forth in the city, or paid court
To Madam Winthrop, whom he much admired,
Most godly, but yet liberal with the port.

And all the town admired for two full years
His excellent address, his gifts of fruit,
Her gracious ways and delicate white ears,
And held the course of nature absolute.

But yet she bade him suffer a peruke,
"That One be not distinguished from the All";
Delivered of herself this stern rebuke
Framed in the resonant language of St. Paul.

"Madam," he answered her, "I have a Friend
Furnishes me with hair out of His strength,
And He requires only I attend
Unto His charity and to its length."

And all the town was witness to his trust:
On Monday he walked out with the Widow Gibbs,
A pious lady of charm and notable bust,
Whose heart beat tolerably beneath her ribs.

On Saturday he wrote proposing marriage,
And closed, imploring that she be not cruel,
"Your favorable answer will oblige,
Madam, your humble servant, Samuel Sewall."

CINDERELLA

Cynthia Pickard

It was too dark in the chimney corner to see
Whether the floors I scrubbed ever had any shine;
When the food she made me fix turned out not fine
The witch wore out her broom beating me.

She purred for the mirror and gurgled at her beauty
And that of her daughters, but never never mine.
Once I gazed in a bucket of water and thought in
It I saw sparkles. She watched and went Tee Hee.

Then the wonder was. A godmother to the scene!
She was the one, she was the really dear
Who carried a wand whenever she came near
And said: Rest. Be beautiful. Be a queen.
She led me out on a footlog and said *Look*
And lo! a shining brightness was the brook.

ABRAHAM'S KNIFE

George Garrett

Where hills are hard and bare,
rocks like thrown dice, heat
and glare that's clean and pitiless,
a shadow dogs my heels, limp
as a drowned man washed ashore.
True sacrifice is secret, none
to applaud the ceremony, nor
witness to be moved to tears.
No one to see. God alone
knows, whose great eye winks not,
from whom no secrets are hid.

My father, I have loved you,
love you now, dead ten years.
Your ghost shadows me home.
Your laughter and your anger still
trouble my scarecrow head like wings.
My own children, my sons, study
my stranger's face. Their flesh,
bones frail as a small bird's,
is strange, too, in my hands.
What will become of us?
I read my murder in their eyes.

EARTH AND I GAVE YOU TURQUOISE

N. Scott Momaday

Earth and I gave you turquoise
    when you walked singing
We lived laughing in my house
    and told old stories
You grew ill when the owl cried
We will meet on Black Mountain

I will bring corn for planting
  and we will make fire
Children will come to your breast
  You will heal my heart
I speak your name many times
The wild cane remembers you

My young brother's house is filled
  I go there to sing
We have not spoken of you
  but our songs are sad
When Moon Woman goes to you
I will follow her white way

Tonight they dance near Chinle
  by the seven elms
There your loom whispered beauty
  They will eat mutton
and drink coffee till morning
You and I will not be there

I saw a crow by Red Rock
  standing on one leg
It was the black of your hair
  The years are heavy
I will ride the swiftest horse
You will hear the drumming hooves

FOR HER SAKE

Alastair Reid

Her world is all aware. She reads
omens in small happenings, the fall of a teaspoon,
flurries of birds, a cat's back arching,
words unspoken, wine spilt.
She will notice moods in handwriting,
be tuned to feelings in a room,
sense ill-luck in a house, take heed of ghosts,
hear children cry before the sound has reached her,

stay unperturbed in storms, keep silence
where speech would spoil. Days are her changes,
weather her time.

Whether it be becalmed in cool mornings
of air and water, or thunderstruck through nights
where flesh craves and is answered, in her, love
knows no division, is an incarnation
of all her wonder, as she makes
madness subside, and all thought-splintered things
grow whole again.

Look below. She walks in the garden,
preoccupied with paths, head bent,
beautiful, not at rest, as objects are,
but moving, in the fleck of light and shade.
Her ways are hers, not mine. Pointless to make
my sense of her, or claim her faithfulness.
She is as women are, aware
of her own mystery, in her way faithful
to flowers and days; and from the window's distance,
I watch her, haunted by her otherness.

Well to love true women, whose whims are wise,
whose world is warm, whose home is time,
and well to pleasure them, since, last of all,
they are the truth which men must tell,
and in their pleasure, houses lighten,
gardens grow fruitful, and true tales are told.
Well to move from mind's distance
into their aura, where the air
is shifting, intimate, particular.

And of true women, she, whose eyes illumine
this day I wake in—well to mark
her weather, how her look is candid,
her voice clear-toned, her heart private,
her love both wild and reticent.
Well to praise and please her, well to make
this for her sake.

AMERICAN PRIMITIVE
William Jay Smith

Look at him there in his stovepipe hat,
His high-top shoes, and his handsome collar;
Only my Daddy could look like that,
And I love my Daddy like he loves his Dollar.

The screen door bangs, and it sounds so funny,
There he is in a shower of gold;
His pockets are stuffed with folding money,
His lips are blue, and his hands feel cold.

He hangs in the hall by his black cravat,
The ladies faint, and the children holler:
Only my Daddy could look like that,
And I love my Daddy like he loves his Dollar.

NOTES ON A CHILD'S COLORING BOOK
Robert Patrick Dana

These lines are a discipline he would avoid,
For they impose a limit upon his will
And demand of him dimension, plane, and angle,
Shape of birthday cake and shapeless hill.

But he persists. His swift ungoverned stroke
Uncoils, snakelike, or like live garden hose,
And flaring in a mess of early jonquils,
Charges with terror a pale-eyed cat's repose.

Nor is color, for him, what merely meets the eye.
It is, rather, a maneuver of the mind
Which penetrates the surface of his page
To reveal what lies below, or just behind.

Take, for example, this simple lakeside scene.
A boy, his dog cavorting at his back,
Wades in the shallows. The boy is blue and orange,
The cocker green. The sky and the lake are black.

These are childhood's commonplace events
In which the forms of things stand not quite pure
But touched with light—for the artless will is hard,
And the vision trembling at the eye is sure.

We come to know the author through his book.
Here, through the daily violence of their lives,
Snake, cat, boy, and cocker move,
And line with line, color with color strives.

THE GREAT WAVE: *Hokusai*

Donald Finkel

> But we will take the problem in its most obscure
> manifestation, and suppose that our spectator is
> an average Englishman. A trained observer, care-
> fully hidden behind a screen, might notice a dila-
> tion in his eyes, even an intake of his breath,
> perhaps a grunt.
>
> From *The Meaning of Art* by HERBERT READ

It is because the sea is blue,
Because Fuji is blue, because the bent blue
Men have white faces, like the snow
On Fuji, like the crest of the wave in the sky the color of
Boats. It is because the air
Is full of writing, because the wave is still: that nothing
Will harm these frail strangers,
That high over Fuji in an earthcolored sky the fingers
Will not fall; and the blue men
Lean on the sea like snow, and the wave like a mountain leans
Against the sky.

                              In the painter's sea
All fishermen are safe. All anger bends under his unity.
But the innocent bystander, he merely
'Walks round a corner, thinking of nothing': hidden

Behind a screen we hear his cry.
He stands half in and half out of the world; he is the men
But he cannot see below Fuji
The shore the color of sky; he is the wave, he stretches
His claws against strangers. He is
Not safe, not even from himself. His world is flat.
He fishes a sea full of serpents, he rides his boat
Blindly from wave to wave toward Ararat.

MASTERS

Kingsley Amis

That horse whose rider fears to jump will fall,
Riflemen miss if orders sound unsure;
They only are secure who seem secure;
    Who lose their voice, lose all.

Those whom heredity or guns have made
Masters, must show it by a common speech;
Expected words in the same tone from each
    Will always be obeyed.

Likewise with stance, with gestures, and with face;
No more than mouth need move when words are said,
No more than hand to strike, or point ahead;
    Like slaves, limbs learn their place.

In triumph as in mutiny unmoved,
These make their public act their private good,
Their words in lounge or courtroom understood,
    But themselves never loved.

The eyes that will not look, the twitching cheek,
The hands that sketch what mouth would fear to own,
These only make us known, and we are known
    Only as we are weak:

By yielding mastery the will is freed,
For it is by surrender that we live,
And we are taken if we wish to give,
    Are needed if we need.

EARLY SUPPER

Barbara Howes

Laughter of the children brings
  The kitchen down with laughter.
While the old kettle sings
Laughter of children brings
To a boil all savory things.
  Higher than beam or rafter,
Laughter of children brings
  The kitchen down with laughter.

So ends an autumn day,
  Light ripples on the ceiling,
Dishes are stacked away;
So ends an autumn day,
The children jog and sway
  In comic dances wheeling.
So ends an autumn day,
  Light ripples on the ceiling.

They trail upstairs to bed,
  And night is a dark tower.
The kettle calls; instead
They trail upstairs to bed,
Leaving warmth, the coppery-red
  Mood of their carnival hour.
They trail upstairs to bed,
  And night is a dark tower.

From I AM WAITING

Lawrence Ferlinghetti

I am waiting for my case to come up
and I am waiting
for a rebirth of wonder
and I am waiting for someone
to really discover America

66

and wail
and I am waiting
for the discovery
of a new symbolic western frontier
and I am waiting
for the American Eagle
to really spread its wings
and straighten up and fly right
and I am waiting
for the Age of Anxiety
to drop dead
and I am waiting
for the war to be fought
which will make the world safe
for anarchy
and I am waiting
for the final withering away
of all governments
and I am perpetually awaiting
a rebirth of wonder.

THE ATTIC

Henri Coulette

We have ascended to this paradise,
Make-believe angels hurrying to our choirs.
Imagination is our Sunday vice;
We are alone, alone with our desires.

We are enchanted by the sound of rain;
Darkness, half-light, and light combine and blur.
This is the national treasury of Cockaigne,
Of which we are the keepers, as it were.

Time is our Midas. We are of his line;
His touch descends to us on either side—
That golden touch. One gesture will refine
This dust into such realms as dust would hide.

These beads are pearls disguised as imitations.
This broken chair, my dear? It is a throne
From which you may survey the lesser nations,
Those lands that cannot claim you as their own.

This box contains the music of the spheres;
Its Swiss machinery records the stars.
Ever the listener given to fancy hears
The strings of Venus and the drum of Mars.

Time and Imagination—what are they?
They are, my dear, the pseudonyms of Change,
The smooth, indifferent author of our play,
Master of both the common and the strange.

My sister, it is autumn in Cockaigne,
And we are weary, for we've come so far
—Too far to be enchanted by the rain.
We are alone, alone with what we are.

POEM

Donald D. Olsen

We used to float the paper boats in spring,
And had to run to keep their slipping pace
Along the curb. My sister Bett would race
Wide-hipped ahead and clear the snow and things.

At night in summer, naked through the park
She ran; and jumping off the diving tower
Her cobalt splash evinced unhuman power.
She ran in summer, white against the dark.

An empty bedroom still remains. It brings
To mind her giant hips and pumpkin hair.
She won the giggling contest at the fair.
What else a quiet, empty room can bring
I do not know. She raced against the dark.
Carved on a tree, her name is in the park.

RETURN TO LANE'S ISLAND
William H. Matchett

The grass is short and newly yellow-green
That feathered then fawn-tawny in the moonlight.
The sun is precise though a mist drifts in from the sea.
Calm on the furthermost rock the seagulls preen,
While a soft-swirling-silver solitary finger
Of driftwood clutches at the sudden shore.
My thoughts, like the ceaseless rote of the rolling waves,
Rise and return, lose their momentum, then linger
And slowly withdraw, to rise and return once more.

Here, single-file, in near silence, we three
Followed the footpath that night, unable to reach
Out to each other, caught in our separate selves,
I yearning to share in the deeper awareness that saves
Other men from the sickening sorrow of self-separation.
Frail in the moonlight, the soft wind fondling your hair,
You climbed to the point while he waited below on the beach,
And I followed, halfway, until, held by an old hesitation,
Unable to speak, I found myself motionless there
Where I could not escape the rote of the rolling waves.

AT THE NADIR
Gerta Kennedy

February brings despair:
in every house a harried pair.

Common and uncommon cold
keep most lambs within the fold.

This is the month when suicide
stealthy creeps on human pride.

All sophisticated wives
lock up axes, carving knives.

New England scarecrow, dressed in sleet,
you can be short, but never sweet.

Moderns

POETS AT MID-CENTURY

Modern poetry has been accused so often of obscurantism that the charge has become a literary cliche. The fashion is to condemn contemporary poetry without a reading or even a hearing.

But the stereotype will not work. Some modern poetry is abstract to the point of incomprehensibility. Some of it is as classic in form as the models in the Greek Anthology. Some of it is profound in its simplicity. Some of it is exquisitely beautiful.

The poems which follow were selected for two reasons. First, they are broadly representative of the work of some of the best contemporary poets in the United States and the rest of the world. Second, they are eminently readable. There are poems here, to appropriate John Ciardi's remark about his own work, that will "make you hear a voice you will welcome into your head."

THE ROAD NOT TAKEN

Robert Frost

Two roads diverged in a yellow wood,
And sorry I could not travel both
And be one traveler, long I stood
And looked down one as far as I could
To where it bent in the undergrowth;

Then took the other, as just as fair,
And having perhaps the better claim,
Because it was grassy and wanted wear;
Though as for that the passing there
Had worn them really about the same,

And both that morning equally lay
In leaves no step had trodden black.
Oh, I kept the first for another day!
Yet knowing how way leads on to way,
I doubted if I should ever come back.

I shall be telling this with a sigh
Somewhere ages and ages hence:
Two roads diverged in a wood, and I—
I took the one less traveled by,
And that has made all the difference.

A REFUSAL TO MOURN THE DEATH,
BY FIRE, OF A CHILD IN LONDON

Dylan Thomas

Never until the mankind making
Bird beast and flower
Fathering and all humbling darkness
Tells with silence the last light breaking
And the still hour
Is come of the sea tumbling in harness.

And I must enter again the round
Zion of the water bead
And the synagogue of the ear of corn
Shall I let pray the shadow of a sound
Or sow my salt seed
In the least valley of sackcloth to mourn

The majesty and burning of the child's death.
I shall not murder
The mankind of her going with a grave truth
Nor blaspheme down the stations of the breath
With any further

Elegy of innocence and youth.
Deep with the first dead lies London's daughter,
Robed in the long friends,
The grains beyond age, the dark veins of her mother,
Secret by the unmourning water
Of the riding Thames.
After the first death, there is no other.

THE WAKING

Theodore Roethke

I wake to sleep, and take my waking slow.
I feel my fate in what I cannot fear.
I learn by going where I have to go.

We think by feeling. What is there to know?
I hear my being dance from ear to ear.
I wake to sleep, and take my waking slow.

Of those so close beside me, which are you?
God bless the Ground! I shall walk softly there,
And learn by going where I have to go.

Light takes the Tree; but who can tell us how?
The lowly worm climbs up a winding stair;
I wake to sleep, and take my waking slow.

Great Nature has another thing to do
To you and me; so take the lively air,
And, lovely, learn by going where to go.

This shaking keeps me steady. I should know.
What falls away is always. And is near.
I wake to sleep, and take my waking slow.
I learn by going where I have to go.

TRUE NIGHT

René Char

Translated by Jackson Mathews

With a stronger wind,
A lamp less dim,
We must find the stopping place
Where night will say "Come in";
And we shall know it's true
When the glass goes black.

THE FLOWER

Robert Penn Warren

Above the beach, the vineyard
Terrace breaks to the seaward
Drop, where the cliffs fail
To a clutter of manganese shale.
Some is purple, some powdery-pale.
But the black lava-chunks stand off
The sea's grind, or indolent chuff.
The lava will withstand
The sea's beat, or insinuant hand,
And protect our patch of sand.

It is late. The path from the beach
Crawls up. I take you. We reach
The vineyard, and at that path angle
The hedge obtrudes a tangle
Of leaf and green bulge and a wrangle
Bee-drowsy and blowsy with white bloom,
Scarcely giving the passer-by room.
We know that the blossomy mass
Will brush our heads as we pass,
And at knee there's gold gorse and blue clover,
And at ankle, blue malva all over
—Plus plants I don't recognize
With my non-botanical eyes.
We approach, but before we get there,
If no breeze stirs that green lair,
The scent and sun-honey of air
Is too sweet comfortably to hear.

I carry you up the hill.
In my arms you are sweet and still.
We approach your special place,
And I am watching your face
To see the sweet puzzlement grow,
And then recognition glow.
Recognition explodes in delight.
You leap like spray, or like light.
Despite my arm's tightness,
You leap in gold-flitter and brightness.
You leap like a fish-flash in bright air,
And reach out. Yes, I'm well aware
That this is the spot, and hour,
For you to demand your flower.

When first we came this way
Up from the beach, that day
That seems now so long ago,
We moved bemused and slow
In the season's pulse and flow.
Bemused with sea, and slow
With June heat and perfume,
We paused here, and plucked you a bloom.

So here you always demand
Your flower to hold in your hand,
And the flower must be white,
For you have your own ways to compel
Observance of this ritual.
You hold it and sing with delight.
And your mother, for our own delight,
Picks one of the blue flowers there,
To put in your yellow hair.
That done, we go on our way
Up the hill, toward the end of the day.

But the season has thinned out.
From the bay edge below, the shout
Of a late bather reaches our ear,
Coming to the vineyard here
By more distance thinned.
The bay is in shadow, the wind
Nags the shore to white.
The mountain prepared the night.
By the vineyard we have found
No bloom worthily white,
And the few we have found
Not disintegrated to the ground
Are by season and sea-salt browned.
We give the best one to you.
It is ruined, but will have to do.

Somewhat better the blue blossoms fare.
We find one for your hair,
And you sing as though human need
Were not for perfection. We proceed
Past floss-borne or sloughed-off seed,
Past curled leaf and dry pod,
And the blue blossom will nod
With your head's drowsy gold nod.
Let all seasons pace their power,
As this has paced to this hour.
Let season and season devise
Their possibilities.
Let the future reassess

All past joy, and past distress,
Till we know Time's deep intent,
And the last integument
Of the past shall be rent
To show how all things bent
Their energies to that hour
When you first demanded your flower.

And in that image let
Both past and future forget,
In clasped communal ease,
Their brute identities.

The path lifts up ahead
To the rocca, supper, bed.
We move in the mountain's shade.
But the mountain is at our back.
Ahead, climbs the coast-cliff track.
The valley between is dim.
Ahead, on the cliff rim,
The rocca clasps its height.
It accepts the incipient night.
Just once we look back.
On sunset, a white gull is black.
It hangs over the mountain crest.
It hangs on that saffron west.
It makes its outcry.
It slides down the sky.
East now, it catches the light
Its black has gone again white,
And over the rocca's height
It gleams in the last light.
It has sunk from our sight.
Beyond the cliff is night.

It sank on unruffled wing.
We hear the sea rustling.

It will rustle all night, darling.

THE PULSE

Mark Van Doren

One thing is sure
When most are not:
That there is cold,
That there is hot,

That winter stars
Are swollen blue
And that bright summer
Bulges too—

Getting the same
Black sky with child;
And both are big,
And both are wild.

There is no error
In the frost;
With warmth away
No warmth is lost;

Waves are coming
Of a time
That has been written
In slow rhyme:

Hot and cold,
And cold and hot—
All things may fail,
But this one not.

Though hate and love
And mercy cease,
Under the rippling
Vapor-fleece

Of earth goes warmth
Pursuing cold
And neither is young,
And neither is old.

CARTOGRAPHY

Louise Bogan

As you lay in sleep
I saw the chart
Of artery and vein
Running from your heart,

Plain as the strength
Marked upon the leaf
Along the length,
Mortal and brief,

Of your gaunt hand.
I saw it clear:
The wiry brand
Of the life we bear

Mapped like the great
Rivers that rise
Beyond our fate
And distant from our eyes.

DIALOGUE

Howard Nemerov

O father, answer me,
Why, why must money be?
The stones along the shore,
The leaves upon the tree

Are worth as much and more.
Why must we labor for
Our greasy greenery
When such fine things are free?

* * *

The leaf, alas, will die,
And crumble in your hand,
And the stone's color dry
To dullness on the sand.

And only money, son,
Retains its character
When withered in the sun
Or dried in the salt air.

POPLAR

Gottfried Benn
Translated by Christopher Middleton

Restrained,
with branch and young shoot undisclosed
to cry the louder out into the blue of sky—:
trunk only, all enclosure,
tall and shivering,
a curve.

Medlar is fugitive,
killer of seed,
and when have blessing clefts of lightning
roared round my shaft,
disuniting,
casting far and wide
the thing once tree?
Who ever saw a wood of poplars?

Individual,
restless at night and through the day
over the gardens' mignonetted
sweet deliquescence gaping wide
that sucks its roots and gnaws its bark
insignia of cries on its crowned brow it offers
dead space opposing,
to and fro.

IT MAY BE

Max Jacob

Translated by Wallace Fowlie

It may be that a strange dream
Seized you tonight,
You thought you saw an angel
And it was your mirror

In her flight Eleonore
Undid her long hair
To rob the dawn
Of the sweet object of my desire.

You should think no longer
Of some faithful husband.
I am the lover, I have wings
I will teach you to fly.

May the muse of falseness
Bring to the end of your fingers
That scorn which is but a dream
Of the shepherd prouder than a king.

MOST LIKE AN ARCH THIS MARRIAGE

John Ciardi

Most like an arch—an entrance which upholds
and shores the stone-crush up the air like lace.
Mass made idea, and idea held in place.
A lock in time. Inside half-heaven unfolds.

Most like an arch—two weaknesses that lean
into a strength. Two fallings become firm.
Two joined abeyances become a term
naming the fact that teaches fact to mean.

Not quite that? Not much less. World as it is,
what's strong and separate falters. All I do
at piling stone on stone apart from you
is roofless around nothing. Till we kiss

I am no more than upright and unset.
It is by falling in and in we make
the all-bearing point, for one another's sake,
in faultless failing, raised by our own weight.

229

José Garcia Villa

There was a perfect tree.
There was a perfect fruit.
Around it curled
Beautiful Lucifer!

There was a perfect man.
There was a perfect woman.
But beautiful Eve
Passioned for the fruit.

Beautiful Lucifer held it.
Beautiful Eve took it!
The perfect woman
Passed the fruit to Adam.

Beautiful Lucifer hid now!
Beautiful God wrathed now.
Adam and Eve
Birthed the world now.

CREDO

Robinson Jeffers

My friend from Asia has powers and magic, he plucks a blue leaf
    from the young blue-gum
And gazing upon it, gathering and quieting
The God in his mind, creates an ocean more real than the ocean, the
    salt, the actual Appalling presence, the power of the waters.
He believes that nothing is real except as we make it.

I humbler have found in my blood
Bred west of Caucasus a harder mysticism.
Multitude stands in my mind but I think that the ocean in the bone
vault is only
The bone vault's ocean: out there is the ocean's;
The water is the water, the cliff is the rock, come shocks and flashes of
reality.
The mind
Passes, the eye closes, the spirit is a passage;
The beauty of things was born before eyes and sufficient to itself; the
heartbreaking beauty
Will remain when there is no heart to break for it.

1934

Donald Hall

In nineteen-thirty-four I spent July
At a small farm, my mother's father's. I
Was five years old. Father got *White's News-Letter,*
Friday, which said that things were looking better.
Bright Model A's kept speeding past each day,
Fouled by the eagles of the N. R. A.,
And blew their brassy horns at us, the farm
Where nothing and no one ever came to harm.
Men walked along the ditch, alone or in twos,
Stopping to let the sand out of their shoes,
And saw the house stretch back, a decent wall
Of clapboard, like a house they could recall.
They always stopped. My father said they might
Burn us and all the cattle up at night,
If we refused them food. Grandmother spread
The butter that she churned upon the bread
The baker peddled, airy, corrupt and stale,
And dipped them milk, out of my grandfather's pail,
And answered that we had no work right here,
Leastwise right now, but maybe they could peer
Up north a ways, perhaps and possibly.

At any rate, she knew that she could see
Pine timber trucking south in a heavy load
Five or six times a day. They took the road
Up north, or hopped a freight at Danbury where
Freight stopped to give the mail a thoroughfare.
Who needed mail in nineteen-thirty-four?
Somebody did, who needed it before.

BIG CRASH OUT WEST

Peter Viereck

They call streets "boulevards" and build them huge
Where grandpa's oxcart could not budge;
Here's room for elbows, land of the brave fourth gears.
Speed is the bridge for spanning loneliness.
Until.

This is the western way to die.
And when the car stops burning, thar he'll lie,
Surrounded by the brothers of his lodge.
O Crash for whom their boredoms cry,
Is there—in your sensuous instant—time to guess
At what's unspent, unsensuous years
Never hot with doubt nor faith nor reverence for tears?

HANS CHRISTIAN ANDERSEN
IN CENTRAL PARK

Hy Sobiloff

O statue, stand still!
Your arms are filled with children
Whose lollipop fingers stick to you.

The artist's hand brought your soul back to stay
He gave your face a weathered brow
Made your limbs relax and set you down.

Your wisdom lives in a park where children play
Where boats float under lost balloons
Miniatures floating in children's ideas of safety.

Hans Andersen, they run to your homage
Full of warm noises
In a language of bubble and gum.

They fondle your face with noses running
See you through the transparent lake,
And though you are bronzed with age
They know you are theirs.

MUSEUM PIECE

Richard Wilbur

The good gray guardians of art
Patrol the halls on spongy shoes,
Impartially protective, though
Perhaps suspicious of Toulouse.

Here dozes one against the wall,
Disposed upon a funeral chair.
A Degas dancer pirouettes
Upon the parting of his hair.

See how she spins! The grace is there,
But strain as well is plain to see.
Degas loved the two together:
Beauty joined to energy.

Edgar Degas purchased once
A fine El Greco, which he kept
Against the wall beside his bed
To hang his pants on while he slept.

TWO LIVES AND OTHERS

Winfield Townley Scott

Beyond the field where crows cawed at a hawk
The road bent down between oaks, pines, and maples,
Maples skimming the air with terra cotta.
The oaks spat acorns over scurries of squirrels.
Moss crunched stiff underfoot, and overhead
The sky was freezing gradually, white across blue.
We hurried our walk through shadows, yet it was
A noticeable sort of afternoon:
We honored a faded robin and considered
The importance of the color gray on bluejays.
A woodchuck all an urgent clumsiness,
Made his tumbling run, then he saw us,
Plunged, hid, and screamed his whistle of fear.
Round the next bend to twilight we went past
A solitary house, one room lamplighted,
An old man at supper alone facing the wall.
If he was aware of us he gave no sign.
We circled home, that last day before snow.

I WAKENED TO A CALLING

Delmore Schwartz

I wakened to a calling,
A calling from somewhere down, from a great height,
Calling out of pleasure and happiness,
And out of darkness, like a new light,
A delicate ascending voice,
Which seems forever rising, never falling
Telling all of us to rejoice,
To delight in the darkness and the light,
Commanding all consciousness forever to rejoice!

BOY WITH HIS HAIR CUT SHORT
Muriel Rukeyser

Sunday shuts down on this twentieth-century evening.
The L passes. Twilight and bulb define
the brown room, the overstuffed plum sofa,
the boy, and the girl's thin hands above his head.
A neighbor's radio sings stocks, news, serenade.

He sits at the table, head down, the young clear neck exposed,
watching the drugstore sign from the tail of his eye;
tattoo, neon, until the eye blears, while his
solicitous tall sister, simple in blue, bending
behind him, cuts his hair with her cheap shears.

The arrow's electric red always reaches its mark,
successful neon! He coughs, impressed by that precision.
His child's forehead, forever protected by his cap,
is bleached against the lamplight as he turns head
and steadies to let the snippets drop.

Erasing the failure of weeks with level fingers,
she sleeks the fine hair, combing: "You'll look fine tomorrow!
You'll surely find something, they can't keep turning you down;
the finest gentleman's not so trim as you!" Smiling, he raises
the adolescent forehead wrinkling ironic now.
He sees his decent suit laid out, new-pressed,
his carfare on the shelf. He lets his head fall, meeting
her earnest hopeless look, seeing the sharp blades splitting,
the darkened room, the impersonal sign her motion,
the blue vein, bright on her temple, pitifully beating.

THE HORSE CHESTNUT TREE
Richard Eberhart

Boys in sporadic but tenacious droves
Come with sticks, as certainly as Autumn,
To assault the great horse chestnut tree.

There is a law governs their lawlessness.
Desire is in them for a shining amulet
And the best are those that are highest up.

They will not pick them easily from the ground.
With shrill arms they fling to the higher branches,
To hurry the work of nature for their pleasure.

I have seen them trooping down the street
Their pockets stuffed with chestnuts shucked, unshucked.
It is only evening keeps them from their wish.

Sometimes I run out in a kind of rage
To chase the boys away: I catch an arm,
Maybe, and laugh to think of being the lawgiver.

I was once such a young sprout myself
And fingered in my pocket the prize and trophy.
But still I moralize upon the day

And see that we, outlaws on God's property,
Fling out imagination beyond the skies,
Wishing a tangible good from the unknown.

And likewise death will drive us from the scene
With the great flowering world unbroken yet,
Which we held in idea, a little handful.

FOR MARY

Kenneth Rexroth

In the evening, just before
Sunset, while we were cooking
Supper, we heard dogs, high on
The west ridge, running a deer.
With unbelievable speed
They quartered down the hillside,
Crossed the gulch, climbed the east ridge
And circled back above us.
As they rushed down again, I
Ran to catch them. The barking

Stopped when they reached the creek bed.
As I came near I could hear
The last terrified bleating
Of a fawn. By the time I
Got there it was already dead.
When the dogs caught sight of me,
They scurried guiltily away.
The fawn was not torn. It had
Died of fear and exhaustion.

My dearest, although you are
Still too young to understand,
At this moment horrible
Black dogs with eyes of fire and
Long white teeth and slavering
Tongues are hunting you in the dark
Mountains to eat your tender heart.

NIGHT MUSIC

Chester Kallman

Night:
And the taut
Flight in the wing of the bat
Becomes the wing, and the river
Is led
From the river bed to hover
Through the resounding space.
Hang wolfsbane, wait
Alone, the night
Will bring you and your lover
Face to face;
And the river under
Our refuge, whispering thunder,
Far below
Will run, will run,
Will know, will know, will know.

THE BOARDER
Louis Simpson

The time is after dinner. Cigarettes
    Glow on the lawn;
Glasses begin to tinkle; TV sets
    Have been turned on.

The moon is brimming like a glass of beer
    Above the town,
And love keeps her appointments—"Harry's here!"
    "I'll be right down."

But the pale stranger in the furnished room
    Lies on his back
Looking at paper roses, how they bloom.
    And ceilings crack.

DREAM VARIATIONS
Langston Hughes

To fling my arms wide
In some place of the sun,
To whirl and to dance
Till the white day is done.
Then rest at cool evening
Beneath a tall tree
While night comes on gently,
    Dark like me,—
That is my dream!

To fling my arms wide
In the face of the sun,
Dance! whirl! whirl!
Till the quick day is done.
Rest at pale evening. . . .
A tall, slim tree. . . .
Night coming tenderly
    Black like me.

LATE AIR

Elizabeth Bishop

From a magician's midnight sleeve
    the radio-singers
distribute all their love-songs
over the dew-wet lawns.
    And like a fortune-teller's
their marrow-piercing guesses are whatever you believe.

But on the Navy-Yard aerial I find
    better witnesses
for love on summer nights.
Five remote red lights
    keep their nests there; Phoenixes
burning quietly, where the dew cannot climb.

SEA PIECES

Robert Fitzgerald

I. September six o'clock:
The young tinted faces
Pale in the harbor.

The sail falls shaking;
The water smiles from the prow.

Low sun, a cooler light
Exhaled; low evening stains
Waterblue under beeches.

The longlegged children
Are furling their sails
In the air like clear water,

The water like air, like mist.

II. Cool cheek to cheek
And long gaze of children:

Mark how the gull's intent
Wings half-golden
Tremble in sea-flaw.

Hand in hand, warm thought
To lie together, as light
Leaves the dark land of ocean:
Pallor above purple
Slow horizons fuming

Evening, star of the sea.

THE CONNECTICUT ELM

Emma Swan

The tall elm
stands in a field
as answer for
virgin forest

under its shadows
cows repose
on a summer day
and chew the cud

what air over them
stirs the leaves
they do not ask
nor what birds sing.

The river winds
continually nearer
swallowing the soil

and when it has eaten
the roots right out
from under the tree

the tree will fall
with all the leaves
swirling to the water

and what will be left
of magnificence in
Connecticut then?

CRADLE SONG

Louis MacNeice

Sleep, my darling, sleep;
    The pity of it all
Is all we compass if
    We watch disaster fall.
Put off your twenty-odd
    Encumbered years and creep
Into the only heaven,
    The robbers' cave of sleep.

The wild grass will whisper,
    Lights of passing cars
Will streak across your dreams
    And fumble at the stars;
Life will tap the window
    Only too soon again,
Life will have her answer—
    Do not ask her when.

When the winsome bubble
    Shivers, when the bough
Breaks, will be the moment
    But not here or now.
Sleep and, asleep, forget
    The watchers on the wall
Awake all night who know
    The pity of it all.

THE ZULU GIRL

Roy Campbell

(to F. C. Slater)

When in the sun the hot red acres smoulder,
Down where the sweating gang its labour plies,
A girl flings down her hoe, and from her shoulder
Unslings her child tormented by the flies.

She takes him to a ring of shadow pooled
By thorn-trees: purpled with the blood of ticks,
While her sharp nails, in slow caresses ruled,
Prowl through his hair with sharp electric clicks.

His sleepy mouth plugged by the heavy nipple,
Tugs like a puppy, grunting as he feeds:
Through his frail nerves her own deep languors ripple
Like a broad river sighing through its reeds.

Yet in that drowsy stream his flesh imbibes
An old unquenched unsmotherable heat,
The curbed ferocity of beaten tribes,
The sullen dignity of their defeat.

Her body looms above him like a hill
Within whose shade a village lies at rest,
Or the first cloud so terrible and still
That bears the coming harvest in its breast.

SUN AND CLOUD

Melville Cane

"Stand aside
And clear out of my path;
I will not be denied,"
The swaggering sun in his wrath
Cried out of the cloud.

"I refuse to be cowed;
You're an arrogant bully,"
Retorted the cloud,
"And my rights to the sky are as fully
Established as yours,
As long as heaven endures."

The empty blusterer
Recedes, withholds his torrid luster,
As, tranquilly, across the darkening lawn,
The gradual shade is drawn.

ADONIS

H.D.

I

Each of us like you
has died once,
each of us like you
has passed through drift of wood-leaves
cracked and bent
and tortured and unbent
in the winter frost—
then burnt into gold points,
lighted afresh,
crisp amber, scales of gold-leaf,
gold turned and re-welded
in the sun-heat.

Each of us like you
has died once,
each of us has crossed an old wood-path
and found the winter leaves
so golden in the sun-fire
that even the life wood-flowers
were dark.

II

Not the gold on the temple-front
where you stand

is as gold as this,
not the gold that fastens your sandal,
nor the gold reft
through your chiseled locks
is as gold as this last year's leaf,
not all the gold hammered and wrought
and beaten
on your lover's face,
brow and bare breast
is as golden as this.

Each of us like you
has died once,
each of us like you
stands apart, like you
fit to be worshiped.

YOU CAN'T BE WISE

Paul Engle

Denied, she screamed in rage, and ran away.
I yelled, She halted, rigid in her going,
Water frozen in the act of flowing.
Then suddenly her fearful face turned gay,
I'll come right back, she called, and laughed. Like wood
Amazed at turning into violin,
At having such a sweet, wild voice within,
She was amazed at turning into good.

Bright as a fragment of the first creation,
Her hand took mine and I could feel it glow,
For love was in her like a lamentation.
What does a mere man do with such surprise?
Don't punish, give your love, and simply know
Wisdom is knowing when you can't be wise.

dominic has a doll
E. E. Cummings

dominic has
a doll wired
to the radiator of his
ZOOM DOOM

icecoalwood truck a
wistful little
clown
whom somebody buried

upsidedown in an ashbarrel so
of course dominic
took him
home

& mrs dominic washed his sweet
dirty
face & mended
his bright torn trousers(quite

as if he were really her &
she
but)& so
that

's how dominic has a doll
& every now & then my
wonderful
friend dominic depaola

gives me a most tremendous hug
knowing
i feel
that

we & worlds
are
less alive
than dolls &

dream

TO A CHAMELEON

Marianne Moore

Hid by the august foliage and fruit
  of the grape-vine
  twine
    your anatomy
      round the pruned and polished stem,
      Chameleon.
      Fire laid upon
    an emerald as long as
    the Dark King's massy
  one,
could not snap the spectrum up for food
  as you have done.

O TO BE A DRAGON

Marianne Moore

    If I, like Solomon, . . .
    could have my wish—

my wish . . . O to be a dragon,
a symbol of the power of Heaven—of silkworm
size or immense; at times invisible.
Felicitous phenomenon!

SNAKE

Theodore Roethke

  I saw a young snake glide
  Out of the mottled shade
  And hang, limp on a stone:
  A thin mouth, and a tongue
  Stayed, in the still air.

It turned; it drew away;
Its shadow bent in half;
It quickened, and was gone.

I felt my slow blood warm.
I longed to be that thing,
The pure, sensuous form.

And I may be, some time.

AUTO WRECK

Karl Shapiro

Its quick soft silver bell beating, beating,
And down the dark one ruby flare
Pulsing out red light like an artery,
The ambulance at top speed floating down
Past beacons and illuminated clocks
Wings in a heavy curve, dips down,
And brakes speed, entering the crowd.
The doors leap open, emptying light;
Stretchers are laid out, the mangled lifted
And stowed into the little hospital.
Then the bell, breaking the hush, tolls once,
And the ambulance with its terrible cargo
Rocking, slightly rocking, moves away,
As the doors, an afterthought, are closed.

We are deranged, walking among the cops
Who sweep glass and are large and composed.
One is still making notes under the light.
One with a bucket douches ponds of blood
Into the street and gutter.
One hangs lanterns on the wrecks that cling,
Empty husks of locusts, to iron poles.

Our throats were tight as tourniquets,
Our feet were bound with splints, but now,
Like convalescents intimate and gauche,

We speak through sickly smiles and warn
With the stubborn saw of common sense,
The grim joke and the banal resolution.
The traffic moves around with care,
But we remain, touching a wound
That opens to our richest horror
Already old, the question Who shall die?
Becomes unspoken Who is innocent?
For death in war is done by hands;
Suicide has cause and stillbirth, logic;
And cancer, simple as a flower, blooms.
But this invites the occult mind,
Cancels our physics with a sneer,
And spatters all we know of denouement
Across the expedient and wicked stones.

LITTLE STEAMBOAT

Oscar Williams

The harbor wears a look of space
But hides its foggy fists:
The little steamboat's sudden face
Comes dawning through the mists.

It stares at clouds whose charging bulls
Are roaming china skies:
On plates of blue, lie black sea gulls,
And steel pearls are their eyes.

The little steamboat, like a dream
Of distance through a spinet,
Sails up the tightrope of a gleam,
The skyline of a minute.

She comes from thirteen wicked coasts,
Five-cornered is her heaven,
And every man aboard her boasts
The sins that number seven.

And so she sports and snorts in rhyme
And spits at lolling lands
And beats the thin, tin sides of time
With hot and foggy hands.

BEFORE HARVEST

Robert Fitzgerald

Deep and soft and far off over country
A train whistle is explaining something strange
To the cool night, so long, sweet, far away.

In your dark rooms under the elm branches,
Stir, O sleepers in the country towns,
Auburn, Divernon, Chatham, Jacksonville . . .
This is the ebb and weary hour of night.

Only a child benumbed with dreaming
Wakes and listens to the visiting rain
Lick its tongues in the leaves and pass away.

ON MINDING
ONE'S OWN BUSINESS

James Wright

Ignorant two, we glide
On ripples near the shore.
The rainbows leap no more,
And men in boats alight
To see the day subside.

All evening fins have drowned
Back in the summer dark.
Above us, up the bank,
Obscure on lonely ground,
A shack receives the night.

I hold the lefthand oar
Out of the wash, and guide
The skiff away so wide
We wander out of sight
As soundless as before.

We will not land to bear
Our will upon that house,
Nor force on any place
Our dull offensive weight.

Somebody may be there,
Peering at us outside
Across the even lake,
Wondering why we take
Our time and stay so late.

Long may the lovers hide
In viny shacks from those
Who thrash among the trees,
Who curse, who have no peace,
Who pitch and moan all night
For fear of someone's joys,
Deploring the human face.

From prudes and muddying fools,
Kind Aphrodite, spare
All hunted criminals,
Hoboes, and whip-poor-wills,
And girls with rumpled hair,
All, all of whom might hide
Within that darkening shack.
Lovers may live, and abide.
Wherefore, I turn my back,
And trawl our boat away,
Lest someone fear to call
A girl's name till we go
Over the lake so slow
We hear the darkness fall.

THERE IS NOTHING
FALSE IN THEE

Kenneth Patchen

There is nothing false in thee.
In thy heat the youngest body
Has warmth and light.
In thee the quills of the sun
Find adornment.
What does not die
Is with thee.

Thou art clothed in robes of music.
Thy voice awakens wings.

And still more with thee
Are the flowers of earth made bright.

Upon thy deeps the fiery sails
Of heaven glide.

Thou art the radiance and the joy.
Thy heart shall only fail
When all else has fallen.

What does not perish
Lives in thee.

TWO EGRETS

John Ciardi

"Look!" you said. "Look!"

On Easter morning two egrets
flew up the Shrewsbury River
between Highlands and Sea Bright

like two white hands
washing one another
in the prime of light.

Oh lemons and bells of light,
rails, rays, waterfalls, ices—
as high as the eye dizzies

into the whirled confetti
and rhinestones of the breaking blue
grain of lit heaven,

the white stroke of the egrets
turned the air—a prayer
and the idea of prayer.

TO THE STONE-CUTTERS

Robinson Jeffers

Stone-cutters fighting time with marble, you foredefeated
Challengers of oblivion,
Eat cynical earnings, knowing rock splits, records fall down,
The square-limbed Roman letters
Scale in the thaws, wear in the rain. The poet as well
Builds his monument mockingly;
For man will be blotted out, the blithe earth die, the brave sun
Die blind, his heart blackening:
Yet stones have stood for a thousand years, and pained thoughts
found
The honey peace in old poems.

DAWN

William Carlos Williams

Ecstatic bird songs pound
the hollow vastness of the sky
with metallic clinkings—
beating color up into it
at a far edge,—beating it, beating it
with rising triumphant ardor,—

stirring it into warmth,
quickening in it a spreading change,—
bursting wildly against it as
dividing the horizon, a heavy sun
lifts himself—is lifted—
bit by bit above the edge
of things,—runs free at last
out into the open—! lumbering
glorified in full release upward—

songs cease.

PLOUGHING ON SUNDAY

Wallace Stevens

The white cock's tail
Tosses in the wind.
The turkey-cock's tail
Glitters in the sun.

Water in the fields
The wind pours down.
The feathers flare
And bluster in the wind.

Remus, blow your horn!
I'm ploughing on Sunday,
Ploughing North America.
Blow your horn!

Tum-ti-tum,
Ti-tum-tum-tum!
The turkey-cock's tail
Spreads to the sun.

The white cock's tail
Streams to the moon.
Water in the fields.
The wind pours down.

DOCTORS' ROW

Conrad Aiken

Snow falls on the cars in Doctors' Row and hoods and headlights;
snow piles on the brownstone steps, the basement deadlights;
fills up the letters and names and brass degrees
on the bright brass plates, and the bright brass holds for keys.

Snow hides, as if on purpose, the rows of bells
which open the doors to separate cells and hells:
to the waiting-rooms, where the famous prepare for headlines,
and humbler citizens for their humbler deadlines.

And in and out, and out and in, they go,
the lamentable devotees of Doctors' Row;
silent and circumspect—indeed, liturgical;
their cries and prayers prescribed, their penance surgical.

No one complains—no one presumes to shriek—
the walls are very thick, and the voices weak.
Or the cries are whisked away in noiseless cabs,
while nurse, in the alley, empties a pail of swabs.

Miserable street!—through which your sweetheart hurries,
lowers her chin, as the snow-cloud stings and flurries;
thinks of the flower-stall, by the church, where you
wait like a clock, for two, for half-past two;

thinks of the roses banked on the steps in snow,
of god in heaven, and the world above, below;
widens her vision beyond the storm, her sight
the infinite rings of an immense delight;

all to be lived and loved—O glorious All!
Eastward or westward, Plato's turning wall;
the sky's blue streets swept clean of silent birds
for an audience of gods, and superwords.

A PACT

Ezra Pound

I make a pact with you, Walt Whitman—
I have detested you long enough.
I come to you as a grown child
Who has had a pig-headed father;
I am old enough now to make friends.
It was you that broke the new wood,
Now is a time for carving.
We have one sap and one root—
Let there be commerce between us.

ARS POETICA

Archibald MacLeish

A poem should be palpable and mute
As a globed fruit

Dumb
As old medallions to the thumb

Silent as the sleeve-worn stone
Of casement ledges where the moss has grown—

A poem should be wordless
As the flight of birds

A poem should be motionless in time
As the moon climbs

Leaving, as the moon releases
Twig by twig the night-entangled trees,

Leaving, as the moon behind the winter
leaves,
Memory by memory the mind—

A poem should be equal to:
Not true

For all the history of grief
An empty doorway and a maple leaf

For love
The leaning grasses and two lights above the sea—

A poem should not mean
But be.

PRIMER LESSON

Carl Sandburg

Look out how you use proud words.
When you let proud words go, it is not
    easy to call them back.
They wear long boots, hard boots;
        they walk off proud; they can't
        hear you calling—
Look out how you use proud words.

A STORM FROM THE EAST

Reed Whittemore

Their house faces east, is protected by trees
From winds from the Gulf which (the weatherman says) prevail
In that section; but a correction
Is due (of the thesis, or maybe the house),
Since, for three days, from the east, a preeminent gale
Has frozen, through sweaters and sweaters, both husband and
    spouse.

They have an unspoken agreement that they will be surly
Unto each other, and any intruders
For the duration. And they have kept it,
One refusing to talk, cook or sweep the place,
The other composing briefs for his side of the case,
And watching gulls fight for dead fish, as the wind blows.

They have children, too, but are keeping them properly cowed
Until the storm drops (or the children), at which time the patter
Of tiny feet will again be allowed,
And the oldest may even stop asking what is the matter.

They have love, too—put away, put away, while they fret
About the injustices done them; life and no mail.
Oh, when will the wind die down, weatherman, and let
What is so be so, what prevails prevail?

From PLAIN SONG

Jean Cocteau
Translated by Wallace Fowlie

I

I have sung, to deceive the evil-sounding clock of time,
    In twenty ways.
And thus have I avoided the praise of habit
    And the noble coldness.

It is little if habit crowns a glory
    When its head is old;
A long love must often amaze the heart
    By being brief.

Then, always young, free of rewards
    And carrying some book,
You half see the games, the drills, the dances
    Which will form tomorrow.

That is why death terrifies me just as much,
    And makes eyes at me;
It's a great voice murmuring in my ear:
    Think of my rendez-vous;

Let the people go home, let the door close,
    Let the wine turn;
Let a dead body be placed in the tomb;
    I am your divine name.

BACKWATER POND: THE CANOEISTS

W. S. Merwin

Not for the fishermen's sake
Do they drop their voices as they glide in from the lake,
And take to moving stealthily on that still water,
Not to disturb its stillness, hour on hour.
So that when at last a turtle, scuttling
Surprised from a stump, dives with a sudden splashing,
It startles them like a door slamming;
And then there is a faint breeze and echo of laughter
Dying as quickly, and they float still as before
Like shadows sliding over a mirror
Or clouds across some forgotten sky,
All afternoon, they cannot say why.

HER EYES

John Crowe Ransom

To a woman that I knew
Were eyes of an extravagant hue:
Viz., china blue.

Those I wear upon my head
Are sometimes green and sometimes red,
I said.

My mother's eyes are wet and blear,
My little sister's are not clear,
Poor silly dear.

It must be given to but few,
A pair of eyes so utter blue
And new;

Where does she keep them from this glare
Of the monstrous sun and the wind's flare
Without any wear;

And were they never in the night
Poisoned by artificial light
Much too bright;

And had the splendid beast no heart
That boiled with tears and baked with smart
The ocular part?

I'll have no business with those eyes,
They are not kind, they are not wise,
They are two great lies.

A woman shooting such blue flame
I apprehend will get some blame
On her good name.

THE SUMMING-UP

Stanley Kunitz

When young I scribbled, boasting, on my wall,
No Love, No Property, No Wages.
In youth's good time I somehow bought them all,
And cheap, you'd think, for maybe a hundred pages.

Now in my prime, disburdened of my gear,
My trophies ransomed, broken, lost,
I carve again on the lintel of the year
My sign: Mobility—and damn the cost!

BELL TOWER

Léonie Adams

I have seen, O desolate one, the voice has its tower,
The voice also, builded at secret cost,
Its temple of precious tissue; not silent then,
Forever. Casting silence in your hour.

There marble boys are leant from the light throat,
Thick locks that hang with dew, and eyes dew-lashed,
Dazzled with morning,—angels of the wind,
With ear a-point for the enchanted note.

And these at length shall tip the hanging bell,
And first the sound must gather in deep bronze,
Till, rarer than ice, purer than a bubble of gold,
It fills the sky to beat on an airy shell.

THE DEATH OF THE
BALL TURRET GUNNER

Randall Jarrell

From my mother's sleep I fell into the State,
And I hunched in its belly till my wet fur froze.
Six miles from earth, loosed from its dream of life,
I woke to black flak and the nightmare fighters.
When I died they washed me out of the turret with
    a hose.

TO MY MOUNTAIN

Kathleen Raine

Since I must love your north
of darkness, cold, and pain,
the snow, the lonely glen,
let me love true worth,

the strength of the hard rock,
the deafening stream of wind
that carried sense away
swifter than flowing blood.

Heather is harsh to tears
and the rough moors
give the buried face no peace
but make me rise,

and oh, the sweet scent, and purple skies!

A PRAYER

Vernon Watkins

If I dare pray for one
Gift in the coming age
That might protect my son
On every shifting stage
Keeping his joy as true
As now he feels in play
Fetching the ball I threw
Or pitched from day to day
Safe in a cot where sleep
Finds him still clasping toys
Until I step and stoop
And loose them with no noise,
I pray that he may have
Recourse in argument
After the falling wave
To what remains unspent,
That he may stoop and dare
To gather for his own
In that loud, hostile air
One word's deliberate throne,
I mean the uncounted praise,
The bridegroom's calm return
For which all nights and days
In speculation burn.
There where the breakers fly
Scattering their bridal lace,
Where instantly joy's eye
Rejects the commonplace,
Let him find strength to throw
Compromise to the winds
Though constancy forego
All but his truest friends,
The drift of broken vows,
Creating from despair
His Christ-appointed house,
That in the testing hour

Of hostile circumstance
His soul may put on power,
The impotence of chance
Revealing in his hold
On envy's taunting mind
Like Samson, tranquil-souled,
Who remained strong, though blind.

SEASIDE GOLF

John Betjeman

How straight it flew, how long it flew,
    It clear'd the rutty track
And soaring, disappeared from view
    Beyond the bunker's back—
A glorious, sailing, bounding drive
That made me glad I was alive.

And down the fairway, far along
    It glowed a lonely white;
I played an iron sure and strong
    And clipp'd it out of sight,
And spite of grassy banks between
I knew I'd find it on the green.

And so I did. It lay content
    Two paces from the pin;
A steady putt and then it went
    Oh, most securely in.
The very turf rejoiced to see
That quite unprecedented three.

Ah! seaweed smells from sandy caves
    And thyme and mist in whiffs,
In-coming tide, Atlantic waves
    Slapping the sunny cliffs,
Lark song and sea sounds in the air
And splendour, splendour everywhere.

POEM FOR EPIPHANY

Norman Nicholson

Three Kings stepped out of my body,
Walked across the sand by the wild sea
From December into January.

A King stepped out of my head,
And before him the sand was red
And the sea gold,
And he beheld
The landscape like an empire and found in
Even a sycamore leaf the plan of his domain.
And he offered the gold of his sight
The regimen of his thought
To the Child born that night.

A King stepped out of my breast
Who had the bearing of a priest.
To him the moon's movement
Was a sacrament,
And the taste of water and of wine,
The touch of bread and the weight of a stone.
And he offered the frankincense of the heart,
Prayer swung in the censer on the charcoal alight,
To the Child born that night.

A King stepped out of my loins,
And black as grapes were his skin and his veins.
In him was the anger of sex
Where the blood like a sea on the shingle breaks,
The pride of living, the longing for further birth
Because of the presentiment of death.
And he offered the myrrh of tiredness, the untight'n-
    ing of the fingers from the nerve's root
To the Child born that night.

Three Kings stepped out of my body
But only my two eyes between the three—
Only my two eyes and the wild skies to see.

QUIET

Giuseppe Ungaretti
Translated by Allen Mandelbaum

The grape is ripened, tilled the field,
the mountain severs from the clouds.

On the dusty mirrors of summer
Fallen is the shadow.

Between uncertain fingers
Their glistening is bright,
And distant.

With the swallows flees
The final harrowing.

THE EXPRESS

Stephen Spender

After the first powerful plain manifesto
The black statement of pistons, without more fuss
But gliding like a queen, she leaves the station.
Without bowing and with restrained unconcern
She passes the houses which humbly crowd outside,
The gasworks and at last the heavy page
Of death, printed by gravestones in the cemetery.
Beyond the town there lies the open country
Where, gathering speed, she acquires mystery,
The luminous self-possession of ships on ocean.
It is now she begins to sing—at first quite low
Then loud, and at last with a jazzy madness—
The song of her whistle screaming at curves,
Of deafening tunnels, brakes, innumerable bolts.

And always light, aerial, underneath
Goes the elate meter of her wheels.
Steaming through metal landscape on her lines

She plunges new eras of wild happiness
Where speed throws up strange shapes, broad curves
And parallels clean like the steel of guns.
At last, further than Edinburgh or Rome,
Beyond the crest of the world, she reaches night
Where only a low streamline brightness
Of phosphorus on the tossing hills is white.
Ah, like a comet through flames she moves entranced
Wrapt in her music no bird song, no, nor bough
Breaking with honey buds, shall ever equal.

THE BURNING OF BOOKS

Bertolt Brecht

When the Regime ordered that books with dangerous teachings
Should be publicly burnt and everywhere
Oxen were forced to draw carts full of books
To the funeral pyre, an exiled poet,
One of the best, discovered with fury, when he studied the list
Of the burned, that his books
Had been forgotten. He rushed to his writing table
On wings of anger and wrote a letter to those in power.
Burn me, he wrote with hurrying pen, burn me!
Do not treat me in this fashion. Don't leave me out. Have I not
Always spoken the truth in my books? And now
You treat me like a liar! I order you:
Burn me!

THE UNWANTED

C. Day Lewis

On a day when the breath of roses
Plumpened a swooning breeze
And all the silken combes of summer
Opened wide their knees,

Between two sighs they planted one—
A willed one, a wanted one,
And he will be the sign, they said, of our felicities.

Eager the loins he sprang from,
Happy the sheltering heart:
Seldom had the seed of man
So charmed, so clear a start.
And he was born as frail a one,
As ailing, freakish, pale a one
As ever the wry planets knotted their beams to thwart.

Sun locked up for winter;
Earth an empty rind:
Two strangers harshly flung together
As by a flail of wind.
Oh was it not a furtive thing,
A loveless, damned, abortive thing—
This flurry of the groaning dust, and what is left behind!

Sure, from such warped beginnings
Nothing debonair
Can come? But neither shame nor panic,
Drugs nor sharp despair
Could uproot that untoward thing,
That all too fierce and froward thing:
Willy-nilly born it was, divinely formed and fair.

SONG: UNDER THE BRONZE LEAVES

Saint-John Perse
Translated by T. S. Eliot

Under the bronze leaves a colt was foaled. Came such an one who laid
bitter bay in our hands. Stranger. Who passed. Here comes news of
other provinces to my liking. —"Hail, daughter! under the most
considerable of the trees of the year."

For the Sun enters the sign of the Lion and the Stranger has laid his
finger on the mouth of the Dead. Stranger. Who laughed. And tells us

of an herb. O from the provinces blow many winds. What ease to our ways, and how the trumpet rejoices my heart and the feather adept of the scandal of the wing! "My Soul, great girl, you had your ways which are not ours."

Under the bronze leaves a colt had been foaled. Came such an one who laid this bitter bay in our hands. Stranger. Who passed. Out of the bronze tree comes a great bruit of voices. Roses and bitumen, gift of many gestes to the year, and by the roads of all the earth the Stranger to his ways. . . . "Hail, daughter! robed in the loveliest robe of the year."

WINTER NIGHT*

Boris Pasternak
Translated by Eugene M. Kayden

The snow was falling soft and slow
From land to land.
A candle flamed upon a table;
A candle flamed.

As midges of the summer swarm
Against a candle flame,
Outside the snowflakes swarmed against
The windowpane.

The blizzard modeled on the glass
White stars and arrows.
A candle flamed upon a table;
A candle flamed.

And soft along the ceiling lingered
Two flaring shadows:
Cross-folded arms, cross-folded legs,
And destiny.

Two little shoes fell to the floor,
Fell with a thud.
And soft the candle shed wax tears
Upon a dress.

The world lay soundless in the snow
Within the frosty night.
A candle flamed upon the table;
A candle flamed.

A draft then shuddered in the flame.
The fever of temptation,
It raised the cross of angel wings
Upon a wall.

Day after day through February
The snow came down.
A candle flamed upon a table;
A candle flamed.

From IN TIMES OF WAR

VIII

W. H. Auden

He turned his field into a meeting-place,
And grew the tolerant ironic eye,
And formed the mobile money-changer's face,
And found the notion of equality.

And strangers were as brothers to his clocks,
And with his spires he made a human sky;
Museums stored his learning like a box,
And paper watched his money like a spy.

It grew so fast his life was overgrown,
And he forgot what once it had been made for,
And gathered into crowds and was alone,

And lived expensively and did without,
And could not find the earth which he had paid for,
Nor feel the love that he knew all about.

SPENDTHRIFT

I. A. *Richards*

Home again?
How?
How timorously
My wishes climb
The overhanging if
Or when;
How perilously.

So. Let them be.
Let me not be
A while-keeper
Who keeps accounts with time.

Come again?
Gone!
On, anywhere—
As if hard-pressed,
As if in debt, in love
With then,
In fear of here;
Though everywhere
Is here, when there;
And presently
This "this" is all the rest.

Savings none?
None
Accountable.
Past hunger's past.
The left, the lost
(Amen)
Irrecoverable
Renounced as well;
The possible
Our modicum
For this spent life at last.

THE HIPPOPOTAMUS

T. S. Eliot

Similiter et omnes revereantur Diaconos, ut mandatum Jesu
Christi; et Episcopum, ut Jesum Christum, existentem filium Patris;
Presbyteros autem, ut concilium Dei et conjunctionem Apostolo-
rum. Sine his Ecclesia non vocatur; de quibus suadeo vos sic habeo.

S. IGNATII AD TRALLIANOS.

And when this epistle is read among you, cause that it be read
also in the church of the Laodiceans.

The broad-back hippopotamus
Rests on his belly in the mud;
Although he seems so firm to us
He is merely flesh and blood.

Flesh and blood is weak and frail,
Susceptible to nervous shock;
While the True Church can never fail
For it is based upon a rock.

The hippo's feeble steps may err
In compassing material ends,
While the True Church need never stir
To gather in its dividends.

The 'potamus can never reach
The mango on the mango-tree;
But fruits of pomegranate and peach
Refresh the Church from over sea.

At mating time the hippo's voice
Betrays inflexions hoarse and odd,
But every week we hear rejoice
The Church, at being one with God.

The hippopotamus's day
Is passed in sleep; at night he hunts;
God works in a mysterious way—
The Church can sleep and feed at once.

I saw the 'potamus take wing
Ascending from the damp savannas,
And quiring angels round him sing
The praise of God, in loud hosannas.

Blood of the Lamb shall wash him clean
And him shall heavenly arms enfold,
Among the saints he shall be seen
Performing on a harp of gold.

He shall be washed as white as snow,
By all the martyr'd virgins kist,
While the True Church remains below
Wrapt in the old miasmal mist.

YOU RISE UP

Paul Eluard
Translated by Wallace Fowlie

You rise up the water unfolds
You lie down the water opens

You are the water turned aside from its depths
You are the earth taking root
And on which everything is built

You make bubbles of silence in the desert of noises
You sing night hymns on the strings of the rainbow
You are everywhere you abolish all roads

You sacrifice time
To the eternal youth of the exact flame
Which unveils nature in reproducing it

Woman you put into the world a body always the same
Yours
You are resemblance.

MAN OF MY TIME

Salvatore Quasimodo
Translated by Allen Mandelbaum

You are still the one with the stone and the sling
man of my time. You were in the cockpit,
with the malign wings, the sundials of death,
—I have seen you—in the chariot of fire, at the gallows,
at the wheels of torture. I have seen you: it was you,
with your exact science persuaded to extermination,
without love, without Christ. Again, as always, you
have killed, as did your fathers kill, as did
the animals that saw you for the first time, kill.
And this blood smells as on the day
one brother told the other brother: "Let us
go into the fields." And that echo, chill, tenacious,
has reached down to you, within your day.
Forget, o sons, the clouds of blood
risen from the earth, forget the fathers:
their tombs sink down in ashes,
black birds, the wind, cover their heart.

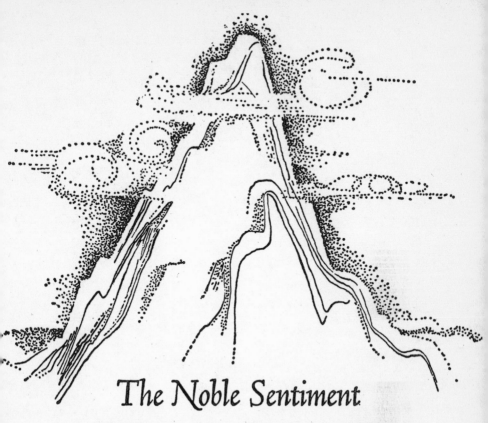

The Noble Sentiment

POEMS BY THE NOBEL LAUREATES FOR LITERATURE

The Nobel Prize has been no guarantee of immortality. René Sully Prudhomme and Frédéric Mistral are seldom read these days, and perhaps need not be. In the early days of the prize it was far too often awarded to provincial writers or those with the best literary lobbies. But the character of the prize has changed, especially since World War II. And poems like Pasternak's "Fresh Paint" and Yeats's "When You Are Old" and Gabriela Mistral's "Poem of the Son" will survive as long as man's thoughts turn in on himself in search of his place in his time.

Here are thirty-six poems by winners of the Nobel Prize for literature. All of them catch the ear. Many of them hold the mind.

To the best of our knowledge this is the first time poems by all the Nobel Prize winners who have written significant poetry have been published together.

HOME

Verner von Heidenstam
Translated by Charles Wharton Stork

I'm longing for the forest;
The pathway in the grasses,
The house that on the ness is.
What orchards hold such apples
Deep-hid from eager spying?
What grain, when zephyr dapples,
Can breathe so soft a sighing?
Where could I hope as well to slumber
When bells the hours of evening number?

Where do my memories tarry?
Where are my dead still living?
Where I, while gray and gaunt still,
With harsh, relentless finger
The years my fate are weaving?
I am a shade, and haunt still
The place where memories linger.
Oh, seek not near to hover,
Although the doors are fastened
And matted leaves now cover
The steps where winds have hastened
And dropped their withered quarry.
Let others' laughter carry,
And new floods, wilder, stronger,
Bear me, the moat o'erswelling,
To those that speak no longer.
I sit within there lonely,
Myself a memory only,—
That is my kingly dwelling.

Oh, say not that our elders,
Whose eyes are closed forever,
That those we fain would banish
And from our lives would sever,—
Say not their colors vanish
Like flowers and like grasses,

That we from hearts efface them
Like dust, when one would clear it
From ancient window-glasses.
In power they upraise them,
A host they of the spirit.
The whole white earth enshrouding,
Our thoughts too overclouding,
Whate'er our fate or fortune,
Thoughts that, like swallows crowding,
Fly home at evening duly.
A home! how firm its base is
By walls securely shielded,—
Our world—the one thing truly
We in this world have builded.

POEM OF THE SON

Gabriela Mistral
Translated by Langston Hughes

I

A son, a son, a son! I wanted a son of yours
and mine, in those distant days of burning bliss
when my bones would tremble at your least murmur
and my brow would tremble at your least murmur
and my brow would glow with a radiant mist.

I said a son, as a tree in spring
lifts its branches yearning toward the skies,
a son with innocent mien and anxious mouth,
and wondering, wide and Christ-like eyes.

His arms like a garland entwine around my neck,
the fertile river of my life is within him pent,
and from the depths of my being over all the hills
a sweet perfume spreads its gentle scent.

We look as we pass at a mother big with child,
whose lips are trembling and whose eyes are a prayer.
When deep in love we walk through the crowd,
the wonder of a babe's sweet eyes makes us stare.

Through sleepless nights full of joy and dreams
no fiery lust invaded my bed.
For him who would be born swaddled in song,
I hollowed my breasts to pillow his head.

The sun never seemed too warm to bathe him;
but my lap I hated as too rough a place,
My heart beat wildly at so wonderful a gift,
and tears of humility streamed down my face.

Of death's vile destruction I had no fear,
for the child's eyes would free your eyes from such doom,
and I would not mind walking beneath death's dark stare
in the brilliance of morning or at evening's gloom.

II

Now I am thirty years old, and my brow is streaked
with the precocious ashes of death. And slow tears
like eternal rain at the poles,
salty, bitter, and cold, water my years.

While the pine burns with a gentle flame,
musing, I think it would have been meet
that my son be born with my own weary mouth,
my bitter heart and my voice of defeat.

With your heart like a poisonous fruit,
and me whom your lips would again betray,
for forty moons he might not have slept on my breast;
and because he was yours, he might have gone away.

In what flowering orchards, beside what running waters
in what springtime might he have cleansed his blood of my sorrow,
though I wandered afar in gentler climes,
while it coursed through his veins in some mystical tomorrow?

The fear that some day from his mouth hot with hate
he might say to me, as I to my father did protest,
"Why was your weeping flesh so fertile
as to fill with nectar a mother's breast?"

I find bitter joy in that you sleep now
deep in a bed of earth, and I cradle no child,
for I sleep, too, with no cares, no remorse,
beneath my tangle of brambles wild.

Since I may no longer close my eyes
like a crazy woman I hear voices from outer space,
and with twisted mouth on torn knees I would kneel
if I saw him pass with my pain in his face.

To me God's respite never would be given:
through his innocent flesh the wicked wound me now:
for through all eternity my blood will cry aloud
in my son ecstatic of eye and brow.

Blessed be my breast in which kin is lost
and blessed be my belly in which they die!
The face of my mother will no longer cross the world
nor her voice in the wind change to sorrow's cry.

Forests decayed to ashes will rise a hundred times
to fall again a hundred times by axe or nature's blight.
But in the month of harvest I will fall to rise no more:
me and mine shall disappear in endless night.

As though I were paying the debt of a whole race,
like cells in a beehive, my breast fills with pain.
Each passing hour to me seems a lifetime,
a bitter river flowing seaward is each vein.

I am blind to the sun and blind to the wind
for which my poor dead ones so anxiously long.
And my lips are weary of fervent prayers that,
before I grow mute, my mouth pours into song.

I did not plant for my own granary, nor teach in hope
of loving arms' support when death I might meet
and my broken body sustain me no longer,
and my hand grope for the winding sheet.

I taught the children of others, trusting only in You
to fill my granary with grain divine.
Our Father Who art in heaven, lift up this beggar.
Should I die tonight, let me be Thine.

THEME'

Carl Spitteler
Translated by Margarete Münsterberg

Bell, my silver tonguéd bell,
Oh, thy secret prithee tell:
Dwellst where bats and night-owls roam,
Lonely in thy moldered home;
Tell me, whence thy solemn ring?
And who taught thee, pray, to sing?

When in gloomy shaft I lay,
Night of hell I saw alway.
In this tower high and free
Through the whirling winds I see
Human sorrow graced by soul.
And thou wonderst why I toll?

SNOWFALL

Giousé Carducci
Translated by G. A. Greene

Slowly flutters the snow from ash-coloured heavens in silence;
Sound or tumult of life rises not up from the town;

Not of herbseller the cry, nor rumorous rattle of wagons,
Not love's passionate song joyous in musical youth.

But, from the belfry swaying, hoarsely the hours thro' the evening
Moan like sighs from a world far from the light of our day.

Wandering song-birds beat at my tarnished window panes; friendly
Spirits returning are they, seeking and calling for me.

Soon, O belovèd ones, soon—be calm, heart ever undaunted—
Soon to the silence I come, soon in the shades to repose.

THE BIRD

Rabindranath Tagore

Though the evening comes with slow steps and has
    signalled for all songs to cease;
Though your companions have gone to their rest and
    you are tired;
Though fear broods in the dark and the face of the sky
    is veiled;
Yet, bird, O my bird, listen to me, do not close your
    wings.

That is not the gloom of the leaves of the forest, that is
    the sea swelling like a dark black smoke.
That is not the dance of the flowering jasmine, that is
    flashing foam.
Ah, where is the sunny green shore, where is your nest?
Bird, O my bird, listen to me, do not close your wings.

The lone night lies along your path, the dawn sleeps
    behind the shadowy hills.
The stars hold their breath counting the hours, the
    feeble moon swims the deep night.
Bird, O my bird, listen to me, do not close your wings.

There is no hope, no fear for you.
There is no word, no whisper, no cry.
There is no home, no bed of rest.
There is only your own pair of wings and the pathless
    sky.
Bird, O my bird, listen to me, do not close your wings.

WHEN YOU ARE OLD

William Butler Yeats

When you are old and gray and full of sleep,
And nodding by the fire, take down this book,
And slowly read, and dream of the soft look
Your eyes had once, and of their shadows deep;

How many loved your moments of glad grace,
And loved your beauty with love false or true;
But one man loved the pilgrim soul in you,
And loved the sorrows of your changing face.

And bending down beside the glowing bars,
Murmur, a little sadly, how love fled
And paced upon the mountains overhead
And hid his face amid a crowd of stars.

GALANTE GARDEN: I

Juan Ramón Jiménez
Translated by H. R. Hays

Spring morning!
She came to kiss me
Just as a morning skylark
Soared up from the furrow singing,
"Spring morning!"

I spoke to her of a white butterfly
That I saw in the footpath;
And she gave me a rose
And said, "How I love you!
Don't you know that I love you?"

So many kisses she cherished
On her red lips for me!
I was kissing her eyelids . . .
"My eyes are for you
And you for my red lips!"

The spring heavens
Were blue with peace and oblivion . . .
A morning skylark
Sang in the still sleeping garden . . .
Its voice was light and crystal
In the newplowed furrow . . .
Spring morning!

THE CONCLUSIVE VOYAGE'

Juan Ramón Jiménez
Translated by H. R. Hays

I shall go away. And the birds will still be there,
Singing,
And my garden will be there with its green tree
And its white well.

Each afternoon the sky will be blue and peaceful,
And the notes will ring out as this afternoon they ring out
From the bells of the belltower.

And those who love me will be dead,
And the village will renew itself each year,
And in the corner of my flowering, whitewashed garden,
My spirit shall wander nostalgically . . .

And I shall go away; and be alone, homeless, with no
Green tree, with no white well,
With no blue and peaceful sky,
And the birds will still be there, singing.

NEW LEAVES

Juan Ramón Jiménez
Translated by H. R. Hays

TO ISOLDITA ESPLÁ

Look how the golden children
Are climbing the silver poplars to the sky!
And they go, staring at the sky,
As they climb in the blue their eyes like pure dreams,
Look how the golden children
Are climbing up the silver poplars to the sky!
And the blue of their lovely
Eyes and the sky are touching . . . eyes and sky are one!
Look how the golden children
Are climbing the silver poplars to the sky!

RISPETTI: ON THE DEATH OF A CHILD

Paul Heyse
Translated by E. H. Mueller

I thought I heard a knock on the door,
And I jumped up as if you were here again,
Speaking to me, as you so often did,
In a coaxing tone: "Daddy, may I come in?"

When at eventide I walked along the steep seashore
I felt your small hand quite warm in mine.

And where the tide had rolled up stones,
I said aloud: "Look out that you don't fall!"

A YOUNG GIRL'S SONG

Paul Heyse
Translated by E. H. Mueller

Shall I love him,
Shall I let him go,
The one to whom my heart has secretly surrendered?
Or shall I teach myself
To hate him out and out?
Advise me well, but don't dissuade me!

To be sure, he is wild
And impetuous in manner,
But no one knows how much I love him.
He can plead with me
So convincingly—
Advise me well, but don't dissuade me!

I could have richer ones,
And wiser ones;
It would be good to have security.
But I begrudge this impetuous lad
To any other woman—
Advise me well, but don't dissuade me!

If I should let myself be swayed
Into making a worse choice,
It would be better to go to my grave.
But it is always wise
To listen to advice—
Advise me well, but don't dissuade me!

AN IRISH AIRMAN
FORESEES HIS DEATH
William Butler Yeats

I know that I shall meet my fate
Somewhere among the clouds above;
Those that I fight I do not hate,
Those that I guard I do not love;
My country is Kiltartan Cross,
My countrymen Kiltartan's poor,
No likely end could bring them loss
Or leave them happier than before.
Nor law, nor duty bade me fight,
Nor public men, nor cheering crowds,
A lonely impulse of delight
Drove to this tumult in the clouds;
I balanced all, brought all to mind,
The years to come seemed waste of breath,
A waste of breath the years behind
In balance with this life, this death.

FRESH PAINT
Boris Pasternak
Translated by Babette Deutsch

I should have seen the sign: "Fresh paint,"
But useless to advise
The careless soul, and memory's stained
With cheeks, calves, hands, lips, eyes.

More than all failure, all success,
I loved you, for your skill
In whitening the yellowed world
As white cosmetics will.

Listen, my dark, my friend: by God,
Whiter than madness or lamp shades
All will grow white somehow,
Or bandage on a brow.

THE HOLLOW MEN

Mistah Kurtz—he dead. A penny for the Old Guy

T. S. Eliot

I

We are the hollow men
We are the stuffed men
Leaning together
Headpiece filled with straw. Alas!
Our dried voices, when
We whisper together
Are quiet and meaningless
As wind in dry grass
Or rats' feet over broken glass
In our dry cellar

Shape without form, shade without colour,
Paralyzed force, gesture without motion;

Those who have crossed
With direct eyes, to death's other Kingdom
Remember us—if at all—not as lost
Violent souls, but only
As the hollow men
The stuffed men.

II

Eyes I dare not meet in dreams
In death's dream kingdom
These do not appear:
There, the eyes are
Sunlight on a broken column

There, is a tree swinging
And voices are
In the wind's singing
More distant and more solemn
Than a fading star.
Let me be no nearer
In death's dream kingdom
Let me also wear
Such deliberate disguises
Rat's coat, crowskin, crossed staves
In a field
Behaving as the wind behaves
No nearer—
Not that final meeting
In the twilight kingdom

III

This is the dead land
This is cactus land
Here the stone images
Are raised, here they receive
The supplication of a dead man's hand
Under the twinkle of a fading star.

Is it like this
In death's other kingdom
Waking alone
At the hour when we are
Trembling with tenderness
Lips that would kiss
Form prayers to broken stone.

IV

The eyes are not here
There are no eyes here
In this valley of dying stars
In this hollow valley
This broken jaw of our lost kingdoms
In this last of meeting places
We grope together
And avoid speech
Gathered on this beach of the tumid river

Sightless, unless
The eyes reappear
As the perpetual star
Multifoliate rose
Of death's twilight kingdom
The hope only
Of empty men.

v

Here we go round the prickly pear
Prickly pear prickly pear
Here we go round the prickly pear
At five o'clock in the morning.

Between the idea
And the reality
Between the motion
And the act
Falls the Shadow
                 For Thine is the Kingdom
Between the conception
And the creation
Between the emotion
And the response
Falls the Shadow
                 Life is very long
Between the desire
And the spasm
Between the potency
And the existence
Between the essence
And the descent
Falls the Shadow
                 For Thine is the Kingdom
For Thine is
Life is
For Thine is the

This is the way the world ends
This is the way the world ends
This is the way the world ends
Not with a bang but a whimper.

THE LAKE ISLE OF INNISFREE

William Butler Yeats

I will arise and go now, and go to Innisfree,
And a small cabin build there, of clay and wattles made;
Nine bean rows will I have there, a hive for the honey bee,
And live alone in the bee-loud glade.

And I shall have some peace there, for peace comes dropping slow,
Dropping from the veils of the morning to where the cricket sings;
There midnight's all a glimmer, and noon a purple glow,
And evening full of the linnet's wings.

I will arise and go now, for always, night and day,
I hear lake-water lapping with low sounds by the shore;
While I stand on the roadway, or on the pavements gray,
I hear it in the deep heart's core.

GUNGA DIN

Rudyard Kipling

You may talk o' gin an' beer
When you're quartered safe out 'ere,
An' you're sent to penny-fights an' Aldershot it;
But when it comes to slaughter
You will do your work on water,
An' you'll lick the bloomin' boots of 'im that's got it.
Now in Injia's sunny clime,
Where I used to spend my time
A-servin' of 'Er Majesty the Queen,
Of all them black-faced crew
The finest man I knew
Was our regimental bhisti, Gunga Din.

    He was "Din! Din! Din!
    You limpin' lump o' brick-dust, Gunga Din!
    Hi! slippey hitherao!
    Water! get it! Panee lao!
    You squidgy-nosed old idol, Gunga Din!"

The uniform 'e wore
Was nothin' much before,
An' rather less than 'arf o' that be'ind,
For a piece o' twisty rag
An' a goatskin water-bag
Was all the field-equipment 'e could find.
When the sweatin' troop-train lay
In a sidin' through the day,
Where the 'eat would make your bloomin' eye-brows crawl,
We shouted "Harry By!"
Till our throats were bricky-dry,
Then we wopped 'im 'cause 'e couldn't serve us all.

    It was "Din! Din! Din!
    You 'eathen, when the mischief 'ave you been?
    You put some juldee in it
    Or I'll marrow you this minute,
    If you don't fill up my helmet, Gunga Din!"

'E would dot an' carry one
Till the longest day was done;
An' 'e didn't seem to know the use o' fear.
If we charged or broke or cut,
You could bet your bloomin' nut,
'E'd be waitin' fifty paces right flank rear.
With 'is mussick on 'is back,
'E would skip with our attack,
An' watch us till the bugles made "Retire,"
An' for all 'is dirty 'ide
'E was white, clear white, inside
When 'e went to tend the wounded under fire!

    It was "Din! Din! Din!"
    With the bullets kickin' dust-spots on the green
    When the cartridges ran out,
    You could 'ear the front-files shout,
    "Hi! ammunition-mules an' Gunga Din!"

I sha'n't forget the night
When I dropped be'ind the fight
With a bullet where my belt-plate should 'a' been.
I was chokin' mad with thirst,

An' the man that spied me first
Was our good old grinnin', gruntin' Gunga Din.
'E lifted up my 'ead,
An' 'e plugged me where I bled,
An' 'e guv me 'arf-a-pint o' water—green:
It was crawlin' an' it stunk,
But of all the drinks I've drunk,
I'm gratefullest to one from Gunga Din.

    It was "Din! Din! Din!
    'Ere's a beggar with a bullet through 'is spleen
    'E's chawin' up the ground,
    An' 'e's kickin' all around:
    For Gawd's sake git the water, Gunga Din!"

'E carried me away
To where a dooli lay,
An' a bullet come an' drilled the beggar clean.
'E put me safe inside,
An' just before 'e died:
"I 'ope you liked your drink," sez Gunga Din.
So I'll meet 'im later on
At the place where 'e is gone—
Where it's always double drill an' no canteen;
'E'll be squattin' on the coals,
Givin' drink to pore damned souls,
An' I'll git a swig in hell from Gunga Din!

    Yes, Din! Din! Din!
    You Lazarushian-leather Gunga Din!
    Though I've belted you an' flayed you,
    By the livin' Gawd that made you,
    You're a better man than I am, Gunga Din!

THE MARES OF THE CAMARGUE
From *Mirèio*

Frédéric Mistral
Translated by George Meredith

A hundred mares, all white! their manes
Like mace-reed of the marshy plains
Thick-tufted, wavy, free o' the shears:
    And when the fiery squadron rears
    Bursting at speed, each mane appears
    Even as the white scarf of a fay
Floating upon their necks along the heavens away.

O race of humankind, take shame!
For never yet a hand could tame,
Nor bitter spur that rips the flanks subdue
    The mares of the Camargue. I have known,
    By treason snared, some captives shown;
    Expatriate from their native Rhone,
Led off, their saline pastures far from view;

And on a day, with prompt rebound,
They have flung their riders to the ground,
And at a single gallop, scouring free,
    Wide nostril'd to the wind, twice ten
    Of long marsh-leagues devour'd, and then,
    Back to the Vacarés again,
After ten years of slavery just to breathe salt sea.

For of this savage race unbent
The ocean is the element.
Of old escaped from Neptune's ear, full sure
    Still with the white foam fleck'd are they,
    And when the sea puffs black from gray,
    And ships part cables, loudly neigh
The stallions of Camargue, all joyful in the roar;

And keen as a whip they lash and crack
Their tails that drag the dust, and back
Scratch up the earth, and feel, entering their flesh, where he,

The God, drives deep his trident teeth,
Who in one horror, above, beneath,
Bids storm and watery deluge seethe,
And shatters to their depths the abysses of the sea.

THE RAIN'S ALREADY WITH US

Salvatore Quasimodo
Translated by Allen Mandelbaum

The rain's already with us
tossing silent air.
The swallows skim spent waters
close by the Lombard lakes,
fly like gulls at little fish;
beyond the garden enclosures, the scent of hay.

Again a year is burned,
without lament, without a cry
upraised to win us—suddenly—a day.

THE STRUGGLE

Sully Prudhomme
Translated by Arthur O'Shaughnessy

Nightly tormented by returning doubt,
I dare the sphinx with faith and unbelief;
And through lone hours when no sleep brings relief
The monster rises all my hopes to flout.

In a still agony, the light blown out,
I wrestle with the unknown; nor long nor brief
The night appears, my narrow couch of grief
Grown like the grave with Death walled round about.

Sometimes my mother, coming with her lamp,
Seeing my brow as with a death-sweat damp,
Asks, "Ah, what ails thee, Child? Hast thou no rest?"

And then I answer, touched by her look of yearning,
Holding my beating heart and forehead burning,
"Mother, I strove with God, and was hard prest."

HOW EASILY MEN'S CHEEKS ARE HOT

Verner von Heidenstam
Translated by Charles Wharton Stork

How easily men's cheeks are hot with wrath!
In haste, though sadly ignorant of the art,
The many judge the individual heart.
But every heart a secret chamber hath,
Thereto a door whose lock no key will turn.
What oil the lamp within that room doth burn
No man may know. But through the keyhole stream
Pale, slender rays of light, and by their gleam
We move about and wake, and fall asleep.
It leads us; to our journey's end we keep
Along the pathway pointed by its beam.

THE CAUCASUS

Boris Pasternak
Translated by Eugene M. Kayden

The Caucasus lay vast in light.
It seemed a rumpled bed, the glow
Of azure ice more fathomless
Than chasms of stagnant heat below.

In mists and out of sorts, it reared
The hatreds of its icy crests
In steady automatic action,
Like salvos from machine-gun nests.

And gazing at this beauty, seeing
Brigades of labor in a race
To win new triumphs, how I envied
The obstacles they had to face.

Oh, if we had their sort of luck!
If, out of time, this age of ours,
This plan, might scrutinize our labor,
As this gigantic mountain lowers!

Then day and night before my vision
Our plan would march, its heel upon
The substance of my prophecies,
Shaping my life and my renown.

No time for angry altercation,
No time another hour to give
To writing verses, but, in secret,
My poems then I would really live!

IMAGINED HAPPINESS

Erik Axel Karlfeldt
Translated by Charles Wharton Stork

From a poverty-shadowed life
  In the night of my lone distress
I sing unto you, my hoped-for wife,
  My treasure of queenliness.
I paint in my hours of dreaming
  With flying brush, till the lines
Of your haloed features are gleaming
  On a background of shadowy pines.

With pink of the cranberry bright
  Your wistful mouth I've expressed,
With soft mosses red and white
  Have hinted your throat and breast.
From birch-leaves in autumn turning
  I caught the right gold for your hair,
But your smile has a touch of yearning
  I never could capture there.

You dwell in a splendor of light,
    You float as on music of strings,
But you love the sigh of the wood's deep night
    And the song that the wild thicket sings.
From empty display that o'erpowers,
    From pleasures that cloy without cease,
You long for the grasses, the flowers,
    For silence, oblivion, and peace.

When your will is on fire some day
    And doubt may no more restrain,
You'll come of yourself on the fateful way
    You ne'er can retrace again.
I sing, I exult at the meeting,
    My glad heart leaps on its throne;
We melt at the passionate greeting
    For all of our lives into one.

From a poverty-shadowed life
    In the night of my lone distress
I proudly cry: "Would you be my wife,
    Then count not the more and less!"
Your beauty in that sweet hour
    Will richly adore our nest,
For happiness is your dower,
    Your morning-gift is rest.

BEAUTY IS MOST AT TWILIGHT'S CLOSE

Pär Lagerkvist
Translated by G. Kenneth Laycock

Beauty is most at twilight's close.
All the love the heavens dispose
Hovers aglimmer, agloom
Over the fields,
Over the earth house-strewn.

All is tenderness, all is caressed by hands.
The Lord himself blots out the distant lands.
All near, all far.
On loan to man
Are given all things that are.

All is mine, and all shall be taken from me,
In a little while all shall be taken from me.
Trees, clouds, the ground I pace.
I shall fare alone—
Nor track nor trace.

SYNNÖVE'S SONG

Björnstjerne Björnson
Translated by Charles Wharton Stork

Oh, thanks for all since the days long past
When we played about on the purple heather!
I thought that the merry times would last
Till we should grow old together.

I thought we should run on hand in hand
From the birches—and how we used to love them!—
To where the Solbakke houses stand,
And on to the church above them.

I waited many an eventide
And looked far off through the pines around me,
But shadows fell from the mountainside,
And you, oh you never found me.

I sat and waited, and often thought:
He'll surely dare it when dusk is falling.
But the twilight faded and then burnt out,
And the day was gone past recalling.

Poor eye, its wont it never forsook,
It never could get the trick o' turning;
It never knew anywhere else to look,
'Twas fixed in a deep-set yearning.

They tell of a place where peace may be:
It's in the kirk, as is rightly fitting.
But do not ask me to go and see—
He'd be right across from me sitting.

But still I know—and 'tis well and good—
Who let our farms be so near together,
And cut the opening in the wood
To look out on the bright spring weather.

But still I know—and 'tis right and fair—
Who built the kirk and its pointing spire,
And made the pews go pair and pair
Along the aisle to the choir.

THE GENTLE HILL

Salvatore Quasimodo
Translated by Allen Mandelbaum

Birds far-off and open in the evening
tremble on the river. And the rain insists
and the hissing of the poppies illumined
by the wind. Like everything remote
do you return to mind. The light green
of your dress is here among the plants
burnt by lightning-flashes where the gentle
hill of Ardenne rises and one hears
the kite-hawk on the fans of broom-corn.

Perhaps in my return deluded, I
confided in that flight of locked-in spirals,
the harshness, the defeated Christian pity,
and this naked pain of sadnesses.
You have a flower of coral in your hair.
But your face is an unchanging shadow;
(thus death does). From the darkened houses
of your borough, I hear the Adda and the rain,
or perhaps a quivering of human steps
upon the banks among the tender canes.

SHE WAS ALL THAT YOU LOVED

Halldór Laxness
Translated by Magnús Á. Árnason

She was all that you loved and cherished,
All that you yearned for and dreamed.
You sang her in verse all your wisdom,
You taught her all you esteemed.

I found in your heart's coverts hidden
The budding of truth and sight,
The emblem of all that is highest
In earthly life and light.

And guiltless we lived them together—
Those truths that the worlds unite:
From drama of pleasures inconstant
To saintly sins of delight.

THE COCOONING
From *Mirèio*
Frédéric Mistral
Translated by Harriet Waters Preston

When the crop is fair in the olive-yard,
  And the earthen jars are ready
For the golden oil from the barrels poured,
  And the big cart rocks unsteady
With its tower of gathered sheaves, and strains
And groans on its way through fields and lanes:

When brawny and bare as an old athlete
  Comes Bacchus the dance a-leading,
And the laborers all, with juice-dyed feet,
  The vintage of Crau are treading,
And the good wine pours from the brimful presses,
And the ruby foam in the vats increases;

When under the leaves of the Spanish broom
　　The clear silk-worms are holden,
And artist each, in a tiny loom,
　　Weaving a web of golden,
Fine, frail cells out of sunlight spun,
Where they creep and sleep by the million,—

Glad is Provence on a day like that,
　　'Tis the time of jest and laughter:
The Ferigoulet and the Baume Muscat
　　They quaff, and they sing thereafter
And lads and lasses, their toils between,
Dance to the tinkling tambourine.

TORA'S SONG

Knut Hamsun

Translated by Charles Wharton Stork

Worldly possessions? 'twas easy to find them,
For nothing there was that he owned on earth.
Faults did he have? you could scarcely mind them,
But ne'er I'll forget his heartsome mirth.

Dances he'd dance that were wild and furious,
But always he used me tenderly.
Often his words would be proud, imperious;
Gently he won what he gained of me.

Soft was the touch of his arm's caressing,
Blue as a lake was his steadfast eye.
Songs would he sing without ever ceasing
Even to the day when he had to die.

Now have my days grown aweary longing,
Death is unkind to leave me lone.
Thoughts so many the while come thronging—
And yet after all I have but one.

THE BOY AND THE FLUTE

Björnstjerne Björnson
Translated by Sir Edmund Gosse

Through the forest the boy wends all day long:
For there he has heard such a wonderful song.
He carved him a flute of the willow-tree,
And tried what the tune within it might be.
The tune came out of it sad and gay;
But while he listen'd it pass' away.
He fell asleep, and once more it sung,
And over his forehead it lovingly hung.

He thought he would catch it, and wildly woke;
And the tune in the pale night faded and broke.
"O God! my God! take me up to Thee!
For the tune Thou hast made is consuming me."
And the Lord God said: "'Tis a friend divine,
Though never one hour shalt thou hold it thine.
Yet all other music is poor and thin
By the side of this which thou never shalt win!"

O, LET ME KISS—

Karl Gjellerup
Translated by Charles Wharton Stork

O, let me reverently kiss thine eye,
That sends a greeting in its radiant glance
As from another world to comfort me!
And would that in our life together I
May clear away whatever griefs and cares
Obscure its beams. If such may be my lot,
O, let me reckon the most secret part
Of my life's labor as its flower and crown,
Since there is someone worthier far than I,
More precious— O, how far more precious than
My flesh-encumbered, transitory self—
For whom my life, however it may teem
With petty faults, will not have been in vain.

A PAIR

Karl Gjellerup
Translated by Charles Wharton Stork

Sink the world! Can that dismay us?
Let Old Night resume her reign!
I am Eros, thou art Chaos.
Lo! the world is born again.

A BATHING GIRL

Johannes V. Jensen
Translated by Charles Wharton Stork

Even, I think, when you're bathing,
Girl, you make love to the billows,
Innocent-hearted as they are,
Practising ever caresses.

With tickling girl-hands you catch at
The curly heads of the breakers,
As, you remember, Europa
Riding (How fearsome!) the bull.

What are those lithe swimming antics,
What but incipient embraces?
Why do you turn on your back, too,
When comes the wave, whitely seething?

Kissed on your whole lovely body,
Tumbled about by the billows,
You are reborn of the foam—
Oh, but your feet in the air, though!

Ask not for grace with your legs!
That has brought many to ruin.
No, turn your back to the spoiler—
Not that that always will save you.

Ocean beleaguers you, bather,
Like a vast buffalo herd;
When was so little a thing
Striven for so mightily? Seldom.

When, too, you stand in your shift
Out in the breeze,
Surely some god of air
Smiles at such ill-covered limbs.

These are not evil thoughts;
I love you.
And the salt taste on your lips,
That is my soul, my darling!

FELLOW-CITIZENS

Verner von Heidenstam
Translated by Charles Wharton Stork

As sure as we have a fatherland
We are heirs to it one with another,
By common right in an equal band
The rich and his needy brother.
Let each have his voice as we did of old
When a shield was the freeman's measure,
And not all be weighed like sacks of gold
By a merchant counting his treasure.

We fought for our homes together when
Our coast by the foeman was blighted.
It was not alone the gentlemen
Drew sword when the beacons were lighted.
Not only the gentlemen sank to earth
But also the faithful yeomen;
'Tis a blot on our flag that we reckon worth
By wealth, and poor men are no men.

'Tis a shame to do as we oft have done,—
Give strangers the highest places,
But beat our own doors with many a stone
And publish our own disgraces.
We are weary of bleeding by our own knife,
When the heart from the head we sever;
We would be as one folk with a single life,
Which we are and shall be forever.

THE CHILD OF PEACE

Selma Lagerlof
Translated by Charles Wharton Stork

Peace, the one-time radiant goddess,
Now sits bent with heavy sorrow;
For the wicked war-troll, snatching
From its crib her lovely infant,
Left another brat as changeling,
Cross, claw-fingered, and mis-shapen,
Thirsting after blood and tear-streams,
Hungering, too, for death and ravage.
Peace, ah woe is thee, poor mother!

These two courses hast thou, goddess:
Fling the troll-child from its cradle,
Leave it on the public highway,
Let it grow into a savage,
Free from all restraint of nurture
Till it gains the strength of manhood;
Or adopt it to your bosom,
Take it to your mother bosom!

Yield not to the fit of anger,
But caress the changeling infant,
Tame it, Peace, with kind thoughts tame it,
Mould its nature with your mildness,
Till it lose its claws and tushes,
And at last some radiant morning
Be transformed into the lost one
And you sit there blind with gladness,
With your own child in your bosom.

A VAGRANT

Erik Axel Karlfeldt
Translated by Charles Wharton Stork

"Who are you and whence do you come?"
I will not and cannot reply,
I am no man's son and I have no home,
No son shall I leave when I die.
A stranger from far am I.

"What's your religion, what is your creed?"
I only know this: I know naught.
And if I have missed the right path, indeed
My error I've never been taught.
But God first and last I have sought.

"How is your life?" It is storm and pain,
A hard, endless battle-drive;
A glow that is quenched, a hope made vain,
And clouds that with sunbeams strive,
But still I am glad I'm alive.

THE LAST WORDS

Maurice Maeterlinck
Translated by Frederick York Powell

And if he ever should come back,
    What am I to say?
—Tell him that I watch'd for him
    All my life away.

And if he should ask me more,
    Nor know my face again?
—Speak gently as a sister speaks,
    He may be in pain.

If he ask me where you are,
  How shall I reply?
—Then give him my golden ring,
  Very silently.

And if he should want to know
  Why the hall stands bare?
—Then show him the burnt-out lamp
  And the door ajar.

And if he should ask me then
  How you fell asleep?
—Tell him that I smiled and died.
  Do not let him weep.

Life Sketches

POEMS FROM EXPERIENCE

The great lady of American poetry, Marianne Moore, once said that the job of poetry is to depict "real toads in imaginary gardens."

The poems which follow sketch the real life implied by Miss Moore's metaphor—birth, death, and the experiences which join the two ends together. This is poetry of contrasts—Melville Cane's view of the political summit, W. H. Auden's search for Atlantis, John Betjeman's vision of the "communal canteens," Alfred Noyes's war between pity and death. There is nothing alien to poetry except ignorance.

Not all of human experience lies waiting in these poems; that is not their ambition. But enough of life's force runs through them to persuade you they are about the real thing.

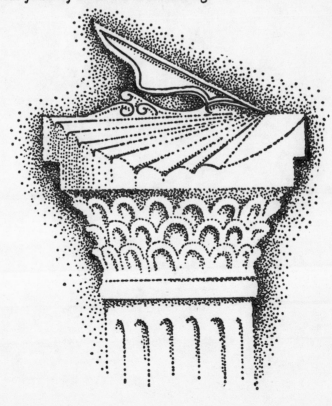

ODE TO A MODEL

Vladimir Nabokov

I have followed you model,
in magazine ads through all seasons,
from dead leaf on the sod
to red leaf on the breeze,

from your lily-white armpit
to the tip of your butterfly eyelash,
charming and pitiful,
silly and stylish.

Or in kneesocks and tartan
standing there like some fabulous symbol,
parted feet pointing outward
—pedal form of akimbo.

On a lawn, in a parody
of Spring and its cherry-tree,
near a vase and a parapet,
virgin practising archery.

Ballerina, black-masked,
near a parapet of alabaster.
"Can one—somebody asked—
rhyme 'star' and 'disaster'?"

Can one picture a blackbird
as the negative of a small firebird?
Can a record, run backward,
turn 'repaid' into 'diaper'?

Can one marry a model?
Kill your past, make you real, raise a family,
by removing you bodily
from back numbers of Sham?

OUT OF MY STUDY WINDOW
Reed Whittemore

It is late afternoon. Out of my study window
The icicles lengthen, the sun descends, and the world
I am left in, lined with unpainted plaster,
Begins to resemble a cave in a dirty glacier.
I was in such a cave once, in Switzerland. Now, feeling ill,
I remember only that in it I got a chill
And sneezed my way the length of the Rhine thereafter.

In a few minutes friends will be coming for cocktails. The chatter
Of cigaret smoke and alcohol
Will warm us up some; darkness will hide the icicles;
And perhaps if the fire is hot and the lights are bright
And someone has news about someone we all dislike,
The evening will pass without thought of what is the matter
With all of us, burrowing here in our winter hole.

Keats. Tennyson.
Most of the poets have warm, sunny lands tucked away
In their serried works where galoshes, woodpiles, aspirin
And the like are never required, and melancholy
Is induced by a surfeit of jolly,
Joshing occasions on coral beaches
Rather than gray day after gray day.

If I had talent to make such a place I would not,
I think, scribble about it but would just
Move in, settle down and endeavor to blot
From my memory all the aforesaid icicles,
Letting the future of literature go for heat
On earth, green trees for man, and the sweet
Ease of a life held in tropical trust.

For though I am told that the northern races are stronger,
And that our absurdly labelled temperate zones
Produce minds, bodies and souls that live better and longer,
I have not a shred of evidence here in my study
To document such tomfoolery; and, if I had,
One look out my window would shortly persuade
Me that cold doth bitch, not brace my bones.

Thus runs my winter logic, logic I don't
Respect very much, knowing that weather
Is man's best excuse for saying he won't,
As he looks from his window and sees his deathly complaint
Hanging down from the eaves, falling out of the clouds,
When in fact it is what he in all months breeds
In spleen, heart and mind, all inside, all grieving together.

It is darker now. I am better for making this show
Of rhymes, humor and icicles.
The friends I spoke of above have arrived below,
And await the drinks I must mix, meanwhile discussing
A cold wave coming from Canada, and cussing.
I think I had best go down; I will tell them an icicle
Is something about which to be illogical.

ALPINE VIEW

Melville Cane

The Chiefs of State marched up the hill
Until they reached the summit.
A fact which leads one to conclude:
The higher up the altitude,
The swifter down the plummet.

ATLANTIS

W. H. Auden

Being set on the idea
    Of getting to Atlantis,
You have discovered of course
    Only the Ship of Fools is
Making the voyage this year,
As gales of abnormal force

Are predicted, and that you
Must therefore be ready to
Behave absurdly enough
To pass for one of The Boys,
At least appearing to love
Hard liquor, horseplay and noise.

Should storms, as may well happen,
Drive you to anchor a week
In some old harbour-city
Of Ionia, then speak
With her witty scholars, men
Who have proved there cannot be
Such a place as Atlantis:
Learn their logic, but notice
How its subtlety betrays
Their enormous simple grief;
Thus they shall teach you the ways
To doubt that you may believe.

If, later, you run aground
Among the headlands of Thrace,
Where with torches all night long
A naked barbaric race
Leaps frenziedly to the sound
Of conch and dissonant gong;
On that stony savage shore
Strip off your clothes and dance, for
Unless you are capable
Of forgetting completely
About Atlantis, you will
Never finish your journey.

Again, should you come to gay
Carthage or Corinth, take part
In their endless gaiety;
And if in some bar a tart,
As she strokes your hair, should say
"This is Atlantis, dearie,"
Listen with attentiveness
To her life-story: unless

You become acquainted now
 With each refuge that tries to
Counterfeit Atlantis, how
 Will you recognise the true?

Assuming you beach at last
 Near Atlantis, and begin
The terrible trek inland
 Through squalid woods and frozen
Tundras where all are soon lost;
If, forsaken then, you stand,
 Stone and snow, silence and air,
 Dismissal everywhere,
O remember the great dead
 And honour the fate you are,
Travelling and tormented,
 Dialectic and bizarre.

Stagger onward rejoicing;
 And even then if, perhaps
Having actually got
 To the last col, you collapse
With all Atlantis shining
Below you yet you cannot
 Descend, you should still be proud
 Even to have been allowed
Just to peep at Atlantis
 In a poetic vision:
Give thanks and lie down in peace,
 Having seen your salvation.

All the little household gods
 Have started crying, but say
Good-bye now, and put to sea.
 Farewell, my dear, farewell: may
Hermes, master of the roads,
And the four dwarf Kabiri,
 Protect and serve you always;
 And may the Ancient of Days
Provide for all you must do
 His invisible guidance,
Lifting up, dear, upon you
 The light of His countenance.

when any mortal
E. E. Cummings

when any mortal(even the most odd)

can justify the ways of man to God
i'll think it strange that normal mortals can

not justify the ways of God to man

THE FISH
Elizabeth Bishop

I caught a tremendous fish
and held him beside the boat
half out of water, with my hook
fast in a corner of his mouth.
He didn't fight.
He hadn't fought at all.
He hung a grunting weight,
battered and venerable
and homely. Here and there
his brown skin hung in strips
like ancient wall-paper:
and its pattern of darker brown
was like wall-paper:
shapes like full-blown roses
stained and lost through age.
He was speckled with barnacles,
fine rosettes of lime,
and infested
with tiny white sea-lice,
and underneath two or three
rags of green weed hung down.
While his gills were breathing in
the terrible oxygen
—the frightening gills,
fresh and crisp with blood,

that can cut so badly—
I thought of the coarse white flesh
packed in like feathers,
the big bones and the little bones,
the dramatic reds and blacks
of his shiny entrails,
and the pink swim-bladder
like a big peony.
I looked into his eyes
which were far larger than mine
but shallower, and yellowed,
the irises backed and packed
with tarnished tinfoil
seen through the lenses
of old scratched isinglass.
They shifted a little, but not
to return my stare.
—It was more like the tipping
of an object toward the light.
I admired his sullen face,
the mechanism of his jaw,
and then I saw
that from his lower lip
—if you could call it a lip—
grim, wet, and weapon-like,
hung five old pieces of fish-line,
or four and a wire leader
with the swivel still attached,
with all their five big hooks
grown firmly in his mouth.
A green line, frayed at the end
where he broke it, two heavier lines,
and a fine black thread
still crimped from the strain and snap
when it broke and he got away.
Like medals with their ribbons
frayed and wavering,
a five-haired beard of wisdom
trailing from his aching jaw.
I stared and stared

and victory filled up
the little rented boat,
from the pool of bilge
where oil had spread a rainbow
around the rusted engine
to the bailer rusted orange,
the sun-cracked thwarts,
the oarlocks on their strings,
the gunnels—until everything
was rainbow, rainbow, rainbow!
And I let the fish go.

POLONIUS' ADVICE TO LAERTES
From *Hamlet*
William Shakespeare

There,—my blessing with you!
And these few precepts in thy memory
See thou character. —Give thy thoughts no tongue,
Nor any unproportion'd thought his act.
Be thou familiar, but by no means vulgar.
The friends thou hast, and their adoption tried,
Grapple them to thy soul with hoops of steel;
But do not dull thy palm with entertainment
Of each new-hatched, unfledged comrade. Beware
Of entrance to a quarrel; but being in,
Bear't that the opposed may beware of thee.
Give every man thine ear, but few thy voice:
Take each man's censure, but reserve thy judgment.
Costly thy habit as thy purse can buy,
But not expressed in fancy; rich, not gaudy:
For the apparel oft proclaims the man.
Neither a borrower nor a lender be,
For loan oft loses both itself and friend,
And borrowing dulls the edge of husbandry.
This above all: to thine own self be true,
And it must follow, as the night the day,
Thou canst not then be false to any man.

From THE CASTLE OF CHILLON

Lord Byron

Eternal Spirit of the chainless Mind!
Brightest in dungeons, Liberty, thou art,—
For there thy habitation is the heart—
The heart which love of Thee alone can bind;

And when thy sons to fetters are consign'd,
To fetters, and the damp vault's dayless gloom,
Their country conquers with their martyrdom,
And Freedom's fame finds wings on every wind.

Chillon! thy prison is a holy place
And thy sad floor an altar, for 'twas trod,
Until his very steps have left a trace

Worn as if thy cold pavement were a sod,
By Bonnivard! May none those marks efface!
For they appeal from tyranny to God.

CAVALRY CROSSING A FORD

Walt Whitman

A line in long array where they wind betwixt green islands,
They take a serpentine course, their arms flash in the sun—hark to
the musical clank,
Behold the silvery river, in it the splashing horses loitering stop to
drink,
Behold the brown-faced men, each group, each person a picture, the
negligent rest on the saddles,
Some emerge on the opposite bank, others are just entering the ford
—while,
Scarlet and blue and snowy white,
The guidon flags flutter gayly in the wind.

IN FLANDERS FIELDS

John McCrae

IN FLANDERS FIELDS the poppies blow
Between the crosses, row on row,
   That mark our place; and in the sky
   The larks, still bravely singing, fly
Scarce heard amid the guns below.

We are the Dead. Short days ago
We lived, felt dawn, saw sunset glow,
   Loved and were loved, and now we lie
   In Flanders fields.

Take up our quarrel with the foe:
To you from failing hands we throw
   The torch; be yours to hold it high.
   If ye break faith with us who die
We shall not sleep, though poppies grow
   In Flanders fields.

I HAVE A RENDEZVOUS WITH DEATH

Alan Seeger

I have a rendezvous with Death
At some disputed barricade,
When Spring comes back with rustling shade
And apple-blossoms fill the air—
I have a rendezvous with Death
When Spring brings back blue days and fair.

It may be he shall take my hand
And lead me into his dark land
And close my eyes and quench my breath—
It may be I shall pass him still.

I have a rendezvous with Death
On some scarred slope of battered hill,
When Spring comes round again this year
And the first meadow-flowers appear.

God knows 'twere better to be deep
Pillowed in silk and scented down,
Where Love throbs out in blissful sleep,
Pulse nigh to pulse, and breath to breath,
Where hushed awakenings are dear . . .
But I've a rendezvous with Death
At midnight in some flaming town,
When Spring trips north again this year,
And I to my pledged word am true,
I shall not fail that rendezvous.

I'M NOBODY! WHO ARE YOU?

Emily Dickinson

I'm nobody! Who are you?
Are you nobody, too?
Then there's a pair of us—don't tell!
They'd banish us, you know.

How dreary to be somebody!
How public, like a frog,
To tell your name the livelong day
To an admiring bog!

TRIAD

Adelaide Crapsey

These be
Three silent things:
The falling snow . . . the hour
Before the dawn . . . the mouth of one
Just dead.

EVOLUTION

John Banister Tabb

Out of the dusk a shadow,
Then, a spark;
Out of the cloud a silence,
Then, a lark;
Out of the heart a rapture,
Then, a pain;
Out of the dead, cold ashes,
Life again.

MAGIC

Thomas Wolfe

And who shall say—
Whatever disenchantment follows—
That we ever forget magic,
Or that we can ever betray,
On this leaden earth,
The apple-tree, the singing,
And the gold?

CAPTAIN KELLY LETS HIS
DAUGHTER GO
TO BE A NUN

Thomas Butler Feeney, S.J.

Tiffany, Tiffany,
What are you doing
Deep in the mines
And under the sea?
Come out of that, Tiffany,
Out of the caverns,
Out of the ocean
And listen to me!

I own a jewel
Blanche as the moonlight,
Pearl as a sunset
Star on a hill;
Billions of bullion
Never could buy her,
Only the Gold
Who is God ever will.

A FLOWER GIVEN TO MY DAUGHTER

James Joyce

Frail the white rose and frail are
Her hands that gave
Whose soul is sere and paler
Than time's wan wave.

Rosefrail and fair—yet frailest
A wonder wild
In gentle eyes thou veilest,
My blueveined child.

THE SOLDIER

Rupert Brooke

If I should die, think only this of me:
    That there's some corner of a foreign field
That is for ever England. There shall be
    In that rich earth a richer dust concealed;
A dust whom England bore, shaped, made aware,
    Gave, once, her flowers to love, her ways to roam,
A body of England's, breathing English air,
    Washed by the rivers, blest by suns of home.

And think, this heart, all evil shed away,
     A pulse in the eternal mind, no less
     Gives somewhere back the thoughts by England given;
Her sights and sounds; dreams happy as her day;
     And laughter, learnt of friends; and gentleness,
          In hearts at peace, under an English heaven.

WITHOUT MORE WEIGHT

Giuseppe Ungaretti
Translated by Allen Mandelbaum

For a God that would smile like a child,
So many cries of sparrows,
Many dances in the branches,

A soul would shed its heaviness,
The meadows wear such tenderness,
Such chasteness in the eyes relive,

The hands like leaves
Entrance in air . . .

Who still would fear, who judge?

DEATH IN LEAMINGTON

John Betjeman

She died in the upstairs bedroom
     By the light of the ev'ning star
That shone through the plate glass window
     From over Leamington Spa.

Beside her the lonely crochet
     Lay patiently and unstirred,
But the fingers that would have work'd it
     Were dead as the spoken word.

And Nurse came in with the tea-things
  Breast high 'mid the stands and chairs—
But Nurse was alone with her own little soul,
  And the things were alone with theirs.

She bolted the big round window,
  She let the blinds unroll,
She set a match to the mantle,
  She covered the fire with coal.

And "Tea!" she said in a tiny voice
  "Wake up! It's nearly five."
Oh! Chintzy, chintzy cheeriness,
  Half dead and half alive!

Do you know that the stucco is peeling?
  Do you know that the heart will stop?
From those yellow Italianate arches
  Do you hear the plaster drop?

Nurse looked at the silent bedstead,
  At the gray, decaying face,
As the calm of a Leamington ev'ning
  Drifted into the place.

She moved the table of bottles
  Away from the bed to the wall;
And tiptoeing gently over the stairs
  Turned down the gas in the hall.

LAUGH AND BE MERRY
John Masefield

Laugh and be merry, remember, better the world with a song,
Better the world with a blow in the teeth of a wrong.
Laugh, for the time is brief, a thread the length of a span.
Laugh, and be proud to belong to the old proud pageant of man.

Laugh and be merry: remember, in olden time,
God made Heaven and Earth for joy He took in a rhyme,
Made them, and filled them full with the strong red wine of His mirth,
The splendid joy of the stars: the joy of the earth.

So we must laugh and drink from the deep blue cup of the sky,
Join the jubilant song of the great stars sweeping by,
Laugh, and battle, and work, and drink of the wine outpoured
In the dear green earth, the sign of the joy of the Lord.

Laugh and be merry together, like brothers akin,
Guesting awhile in the rooms of a beautiful inn,
Glad till the dancing stops, and the lilt of the music ends.
Laugh till the game is played; and be you merry, my friends.

THE LISTENERS

Walter de la Mare

"Is there anybody there?" said the Traveller,
    Knocking on the moonlit door;
And his horse in the silence champed the grasses
    Of the forest's ferny floor:
And a bird flew up out of the turret,
    Above the Traveller's head:
And he smote upon the door again a second time;
    "Is there anybody there?" he said.
But no one descended to the Traveller;
    No head from the leaf-fringed sill
Leaned over and looked into his gray eyes,
    Where he stood perplexed and still.
But only a host of phantom listeners
    That dwelt in the lone house then
Stood listening in the quiet of the moonlight
    To that voice from the world of men:
Stood thronging the faint moonbeams on the dark stair,
    That goes down to the empty hall,
Hearkening in an air stirred and shaken
    By the lonely Traveller's call.

And he felt in his heart their strangeness,
  Their stillness answering his cry,
While his horse moved, cropping the dark turf,
  'Neath the starred and leafy sky;
For he suddenly smote on the door, even
  Louder, and lifted his head:—
"Tell them I came, and no one answered,
  That I kept my word," he said.
Never the least stir made the listeners,
  Though every word he spake
Fell echoing through the shadowiness of the still house
  From the one man left awake:
Ay, they heard his foot upon the stirrup,
  And the sound of iron on stone,
And how the silence surged softly backward,
  When the plunging hoofs were gone.

TREE, TREE . . .

Federico Garcia Lorca

Tree, tree,
dry and green.

The girl of beautiful face
goes gathering olives.
The wind, that suitor of towers,
Grasps her round the waist.
Four riders have passed
on Andalusian ponies,
With suits of azure and green,
and long dark cloaks.
"Come to Cordoba, lass."
The girl pays no heed.
Three young bullfighters have passed,
their waists are slender,
their suits orange-coloured,
their swords of antique silver.
"Come to Seville, lass."

The girl pays no heed.
When the evening became
purple, with diffused light,
a youth passed by bringing
roses and myrtles of the moon.
"Come to Granada, lass."
But the girl pays no heed.
The girl of beautiful face
still goes on gathering olives,
with the gray arm of the wind
encircling her waist.

Tree, tree,
dry and green.

THE LAMB

William Blake

Little Lamb, who made thee?
Dost thou know who made thee,
Gave thee life, and bade thee feed
By the stream and o'er the mead;
Gave thee clothing of delight,
Softest clothing, woolly, bright;
Gave thee such a tender voice,
Making all the vales rejoice?
  Little Lamb, who made thee?
  Dost thou know who made thee?

Little Lamb, I'll tell thee,
Little Lamb, I'll tell thee;
He is called by thy name,
For He calls Himself a Lamb.
He is meek, and He is mild;
He became a little child.
I a child, and thou a lamb,
We are called by His name.
  Little Lamb, God bless thee!
  Little Lamb, God bless thee.

THE PLANSTER'S VISION

John Betjeman

Cut down that timber! Bells, too many and strong,
　　Pouring their music through the branches bare,
　　From moon-white church-towers down the windy air
Have pealed the centuries out with Evensong.
Remove those cottages, a huddled throng!
　　Too many babies have been born in there,
　　Too many coffins, bumping down the stair,
Carried the old their garden paths along.

I have a Vision of The Future, chum,
　　The workers' flats in fields of soya beans
　　Tower up like silver pensils, score on score:
And Surging Millions hear the Challenge come
　　From microphones in communal canteens
　　"No Right! No Wrong! All's perfect, evermore."

THE LONG HILL

Sara Teasdale

I must have passed the crest a while ago
And now I am going down—
Strange to have crossed the crest and not to know,
But the brambles were always catching the hem of my gown.

All the morning I thought how proud I should be
To stand there straight as a queen,
Wrapped in the wind and the sun with the world under me—
But the air was dull, there was little I could have seen.

It was nearly level along the beaten track
And the brambles caught in my gown—
But it's no use now to think of turning back,
The rest of the way will be only going down.

A HOSPITAL

Alfred Noyes

Within these walls, Pity will war with Death,
Conquer and fail, and conquer yet again.
Here broken life on life will fight for breath.
Grave eyes will watch, and hearts grow numb with pain;

Till the new hope that makes the eyes grow blind
Breathes, and the long suspense breaks down in tears;
And quiet skill, content to serve its kind,
Turns to new conflicts, through uncounted years.

Here knowledge like a heavenly lamp shall shine,
And wondering children's faces, peaked and wise,
Look up at strangers' faces and divine
The unchanging love that looks through changing eyes.

For Love that left high heaven to dwell with men
Looks, through men's eyes, on His own children then.

THE RAINY DAY

Henry Wadsworth Longfellow

The day is cold, and dark, and dreary;
It rains, and the wind is never weary;
The vine still clings to the moldering wall,
But at every gust the dead leaves fall,
    And the day is dark and dreary.

My life is cold, and dark, and dreary;
It rains, and the wind is never weary;
My thoughts still cling to the moldering Past,
But the hopes of youth fall thick in the blast
    And the days are dark and dreary.

Be still, sad heart! and cease repining;
Behind the clouds is the sun still shining;
    Thy fate is the common fate of all,
Into each life some rain must fall,
    Some days must be dark and dreary.

MINIVER CHEEVY

Edwin Arlington Robinson

Miniver Cheevy, child of scorn,
Grew lean while he assailed the seasons;
He wept that he was ever born,
And he had reasons.

Miniver loved the days of old
When swords were bright and steeds were prancing;
The vision of a warrior bold
Would set him dancing.

Miniver sighed for what was not,
And dreamed, and rested from his labors;
He dreamed of Thebes and Camelot,
And Priam's neighbors.

Miniver mourned the ripe renown
That made so many a name so fragrant;
He mourned Romance, now on the town,
And Art, a vagrant.

Miniver loved the Medici,
Albeit he had never seen one;
He would have sinned incessantly
Could he have been one.

Miniver cursed the commonplace,
And eyed a khaki suit with loathing;
He missed the medieval grace
Of iron clothing.

Miniver scorned the gold he sought,
But sore annoyed was he without it;
Miniver thought, and thought, and thought,
And thought about it.

Miniver Cheevy, born too late,
Scratched his head and kept on thinking;
Miniver coughed, and called it fate,
And kept on drinking.

From RABBI BEN EZRA

Robert Browning

Grow old along with me!
The best is yet to be,
The last of life for which the first was made;
Our times are in His hand
Who saith: "A whole I planned—
Youth shows but half; trust God, see all nor be afraid."

PRELUDES

T. S. Eliot

I

The winter evening settles down
With smell of steaks in passageways.
Six o'clock.
The burnt-out ends of smoky days.
And now a gusty shower wraps
The grimy scraps
Of withered leaves about your feet
And newspapers from vacant lots;
The showers beat
On broken blinds and chimney-pots,
And at the corner of the street
A lonely cab-horse steams and stamps.
And then the lighting of the lamps.

II

The morning comes to consciousness
Of faint stale smells of beer
From the sawdust-trampled street
With all its muddy feet that press
To early coffee-stands.
With the other masquerades
That time resumes,
One thinks of all the hands
That are raising dingy shades
In a thousand furnished rooms.

III

You tossed a blanket from the bed,
You lay upon your back, and waited;
You dozed, and watched the night revealing
The thousand sordid images
Of which your soul was constituted;
They flickered against the ceiling.
And when all the world came back
And the light crept up between the shutters
And you heard the sparrows in the gutters,
You had such a vision of the street
As the street hardly understands;
Sitting along the bed's edge, where
You curled the papers from your hair,
Or clasped the yellow soles of feet
In the palms of both soiled hands.

IV

His soul stretched tight across the skies
That fade behind a city block,
Or trampled by insistent feet
At four and five and six o'clock;
And short square fingers stuffing pipes,
And evening newspapers, and eyes
Assured of certain certainties,
The conscience of a blackened street
Impatient to assume the world.

I am moved by fancies that are curled
Around these images, and cling:
The notion of some infinitely gentle
Infinitely suffering thing.

Wipe your hand across your mouth, and laugh;
The worlds revolve like ancient women
Gathering fuel in vacant lots.

MR. FLOOD'S PARTY

Edwin Arlington Robinson

Old Eben Flood, climbing alone one night
Over the hill between the town below
And the forsaken upland hermitage
That held as much as he should ever know
On earth again of home, paused warily.
The road was his with not a native near;
And Eben, having leisure, said aloud,
For no man else in Tilbury Town to hear:

'Well, Mr. Flood, we have the harvest moon
Again, and we may not have many more;
The bird is on the wing, the poet says,
And you and I have said it here before.
Drink to the bird.' He raised up to the light
The jug that he had gone so far to fill,
And answered huskily: 'Well, Mr. Flood,
Since you propose it, I believe I will.'

Alone, as if enduring to the end
A valiant armour of scarred hopes outworn,
He stood there in the middle of the road
Like Roland's ghost winding a silent horn.
Below him, in the town among the trees,
Where friends of other days had honoured him,
A phantom salutation of the dead
Rang thinly till old Eben's eyes were dim.

Then, as a mother lays her sleeping child
Down tenderly, fearing it may awake,
He set the jug down slowly at his feet
With trembling care, knowing that most things break;
And only when assured that on firm earth
It stood, as the uncertain lives of men
Assuredly did not, he paced away,
And with his hand extended paused again:

'Well, Mr. Flood, we have not met like this
In a long time; and many a change has come
To both of us, I fear, since last it was
We had a drop together. Welcome home!'
Convivially returning with himself,
Again he raised the jug up to the light;
And with an acquiescent quaver said:
'Well, Mr. Flood, if you insist, I might.

'Only a very little, Mr. Flood—
For auld lang syne. No more, sir; that will do.'
So, for the time, apparently it did,
And Eben evidently thought so too;
For soon amid the silver loneliness
Of night he lifted up his voice and sang,
Secure, with only two moons listening,
Until the whole harmonious landscape rang—

'For auld lang syne.' The weary throat gave out,
The last word wavered; and the song being done,
He raised again the jug regretfully
And shook his head, and was again alone.
There was not much that was ahead of him,
And there was nothing in the town below—
Where strangers would have shut the many doors
That many friends had opened long ago.

WHEN DEATH TO EITHER SHALL COME

Robert Bridges

When Death to either shall come,—
        I pray it be first to me,—
Be happy as ever at home,
        If so, as I wish, it be.

Possess thy heart, my own;
        And sing to the child on thy knee,
Or read to thyself alone
        The songs that I made for thee.

EPIGRAM
Sir William Jones

On parent knees, a naked new-born child,
Weeping thou sat'st while all around thee smiled:
So live, that sinking to thy life's last sleep,
Calm thou may'st smile, whilst all around thee weep.

KINDLY UNHITCH THAT STAR, BUDDY
Ogden Nash

I hardly suppose I know anybody who wouldn't rather
    be a success than a failure,
Just as I suppose every piece of crabgrass in the garden
    would much rather be an azalea,
And in celestial circles all the run-of-the-mill angels
    would rather be archangels or at least cherubim and
    seraphim,
And in the legal world all the little process-servers hope
    to grow up into great big bailiffim and sheriffim.
Indeed, everybody wants to be a wow,
But not everybody knows exactly how.
Some people think they will eventually wear diamonds
    instead of rhinestones
Only by everlastingly keeping their noses to their ghrinestones.
And other people think they will be able to put in more
    time at Palm Beach and the Ritz
By not paying too much attention to attendance at the
    office but rather in being brilliant by starts and fits.
Some people after a full day's work sit up all night getting
    a college education by correspondence,
While others seem to think they'll get just as far by de-
    voting their evenings to the study of the difference
    in temperament between brunettance and blondance.
Some stake their all on luck,
And others put their faith in their ability to pass the
    buck.

In short, the world is filled with people trying to
  achieve success,
And half of them think they'll get it by saying No and
  half of them by saying Yes,
And if all the ones who say No said Yes, and vice versa,
  such is the fate of humanity that ninety-nine per cent
  of them still wouldn't be any better off than they
  were before.
Which perhaps is just as well because if everybody was
  a success nobody could be contemptuous of anybody
  else and everybody would start in all over again trying to be a bigger success than everybody else so
  they would have somebody to be contemptuous of
  and so on forevermore,
Because when people start hitching their wagons to a
  star,
That's the way they are.

THE FATHERLAND

James Russell Lowell

Where is the true man's fatherland?
    Is it where he by chance is born?
    Doth not the yearning spirit scorn
In such scant borders to be spanned?
Oh, yes! his fatherland must be
As the blue heaven wide and free!

Is it alone where freedom is,
    Where God is God and man is man?
    Doth he not claim a broader span
For the soul's love of home than this?
Oh, yes, his fatherland must be
As the blue heaven wide and free!

Where'er a human heart doth wear
    Joy's myrtle-wreath or sorrow's gyves,
    Where'er a human spirit strives
After a life more true and fair,
There is the true man's birthplace grand,
His is a world-wide fatherland!

Where'er a single slave doth pine,
    Where'er one man may help another,—
      Thank God for such a birthright, brother,—
That spot of earth is thine and mine!
There is the true man's birthplace grand,
His is a world-wide fatherland!

RIGHTEOUS ANGER

James Stephens

The lanky hank of a she in the inn over there
Nearly killed me for asking the loan of a glass of beer:
May the devil grip the whey-faced slut by the hair,
And beat bad manners out of her skin for a year.

That parboiled imp, with the hardest jaw you will see
On virtue's path, and a voice that would rasp the dead,
Came roaring and raging the minute she looked at me,
And threw me out of the house on the back of my head!

If I asked her master he'd give me a cask a day;
But she with the beer at hand, not a gill would arrange!
May she marry a ghost and bear him a kitten and may
The High King of Glory permit her to get the mange.

NANCY HANKS

Rosemary Benét

If Nancy Hanks
Came back as a ghost,
Seeking news
Of what she loved most,
She'd ask first,
"Where's my son?
What's happened to Abe?
What's he done?

"Poor little Abe,
Left all alone
Except for Tom,
Who's a rolling stone;
He was only nine
The year I died.
I remember still
How hard he cried.

"Scraping along
In a little shack
With hardly a shirt
To cover his back,
And a prairie wind
To blow him down,
Or pinching times
If he went to town.

"You wouldn't know
About my son?
Did he grow tall?
Did he have fun?
Did he learn to read?
Did he get to town?
Do you know his name?
Did he get on?"

VICTORY IN DEFEAT

Edwin Markham

Defeat may serve as well as victory
To shake the soul and let the glory out.
When the great oak is straining in the wind,
The boughs drink in new beauty, and the trunk
Sends down a deeper root on the windward side.
Only the soul that knows the mighty grief
Can know the mighty rapture. Sorrows come
To stretch our spaces in the heart for joy.

THE OLD STOIC

Emily Brontë

Riches I hold in light esteem,
And love I laugh to scorn;
And lust of fame was but a dream,
That vanished with the morn:

And if I pray, the only prayer
That moves my lips for me
Is, "Leave the heart that now I bear,
And give me liberty!"

Yes, as my swift days near the goal,
'Tis all that I implore;
In life and death a chainless soul,
With courage to endure.

THERE IS NO FRIGATE LIKE A BOOK

Emily Dickinson

There is no frigate like a book
    To take us lands away,
Nor any coursers like a page
    Of prancing poetry.
This traverse may the poorest take
    Without oppress of toll;
How frugal is the chariot
    That bears a human soul!

THE GOLF LINKS

Sarah N. Cleghorn

The golf links lie so near the mill
That almost every day
The laboring children can look out
And see the men at play.

VICE

Alexander Pope

Vice is a monster of so frightful mien,
As to be hated, needs but to be seen;
Yet seen too oft, familiar with her face,
We first endure, then pity, then embrace.

THE MAN HE KILLED

Thomas Hardy

'Had he and I but met
By some old ancient inn,
We should have sat us down to wet
Right many a nipperkin!

'But ranged as infantry,
And staring face to face,
I shot at him as he at me,
And killed him in his place.

'I shot him dead because—
Because he was my foe,
Just so: my foe of course he was;
That's clear enough; although

'He thought he'd 'list, perhaps,
Off-hand like—just as I—
Was out of work—had sold his traps—
No other reason why.

'Yes; quaint and curious war is!
You shoot a fellow down
You'd treat if met where any bar is,
Or help to half-a-crown.'

From HAMLET

William Shakespeare

To be, or not to be: that is the question:
Whether 'tis nobler in the mind to suffer
The slings and arrows of outrageous fortune,
Or to take arms against a sea of troubles,
And by opposing end them? To die: to sleep;
No more; and, by a sleep to say we end
The heart-ache and the thousand natural shocks
That flesh is heir to, 'tis a consummation
Devoutly to be wished. To die, to sleep;
To sleep: perchance to dream: aye, there's the rub;
For in that sleep of death what dreams may come
When we have shuffled off this mortal coil,
Must give us pause. There's the respect
That makes calamity of so long life;
For who would bear the whips and scorns of time,
The oppressor's wrong, the proud man's contumely,
The pangs of disprized love, the law's delay,
The insolence of office, and the spurns
That patient merit of the unworthy takes,
When he himself might his quietus make

With a bare bodkin? who would fardels bear,
To grunt and sweat under a weary life,
But that the dread of something after death,
The undiscovered country from whose bourn
No traveller returns, puzzles the will,
And makes us rather bear those ills we have
Than fly to others that we know not of?
Thus conscience does make cowards of us all;
And thus the native hue of resolution
Is sicklied o'er with the pale cast of thought,
And enterprises of great pith and moment
With this regard their currents turn awry,
And lose the name of action.

MIGNON

Johann Wolfgang von Goethe
Translated by Edgar A. Bowring

Know'st thou the land where the fair citron blows,
Where the bright orange midst the foliage glows,
Where soft winds greet us from the azure skies,
Where silent myrtles, stately laurels rise,
Know'st thou it well?
      'Tis there, 'tis there,
That I with thee, beloved one, would repair!

Know'st thou the house? On columns rests its pile,
Its halls are gleaming, and its chambers smile,
And marble statues stand and gaze on me:
"Poor child! what sorrow hath befallen thee?"
Know'st thou it well?
      'Tis there, 'tis there,
That I with thee, protector, would repair!

Know'st thou the mountain, and its cloudy bridge?
The mule can scarcely find the misty ridge;
In caverns dwells the dragon's olden brood,
The frowning crag obstructs the raging flood.
Know'st thou it well?
      'Tis there, 'tis there,
Our path lies—Father—thither, oh repair!

THE PIPE

Sir John Squire

An author's favourite pipe am I,
My Kaffir woman's countenance
Tells the beholder at a glance
My master smokes incessantly.

If he is mournful or in pain
I smoke as does the ploughman's cot
When the good wife prepares the pot
Before her spouse comes home again.

I bind his soul and rock her well
In the blue twisting skein which slips
And rises from my fiery lips

And weave a very potent spell
Which soothes his heart in its distress
And heals his spirit's weariness.

A SAIL

Mikhail Lermontov
Translated by Avrahm Yarmolinsky

A far sail shimmers, white and lonely,
Through the blue haze above the foam.
What does it seek in foreign harbors?
What has it left behind at home?

The billows romp, and the wind whistles.
The rigging swings, the tall mast creaks.
It is not happiness he flees from,
Alas, it is not joy he seeks!

Below, the sea, like blue light flowing,
Above, the sun shines without cease,
But it is storm the rebel asks for,
As though in storm were peace.

LESSONS OF THE WAR: NAMING OF PARTS

Henry Reed

Today we have naming of parts. Yesterday,
We had daily cleaning. And tomorrow morning,
We shall have what to do after firing. But today,
Today we have naming of parts. Japonica
Glistens like coral in all of the neighbouring gardens,
 And today we have naming of parts.

This is the lower sling swivel. And this
Is the upper sling swivel, whose use you will see,
When you are given your slings. And this is the piling swivel,
Which in your case you have not got. The branches
Hold in the gardens their silent, eloquent gestures,
 Which in our case we have not got.

This is the safety-catch, which is always released
With an easy flick of the thumb. And please do not let me
See anyone using his finger. You can do it quite easy
If you have any strength in your thumb. The blossoms
Are fragile and motionless, never letting anyone see
 Any of them using their finger.

And this you can see is the bolt. The purpose of this
Is to open the breech, as you see. We can slide it
Rapidly backwards and forwards: we call this
Easing the spring. And rapidly backwards and forwards
The early bees are assaulting and fumbling the flowers:
 They call it easing the Spring.

They call it easing the Spring: it is perfectly easy
If you have any strength in your thumb: like the bolt,
And the breech, and the cocking-piece, and the point of
  balance,
Which in our case we have not got; and the almond-blossom
Silent in all of the gardens and the bees going backwards
  and forwards,
For today we have naming of parts.

TO MY NEW MISTRESS
Beverly Bowie

Pain is my familiar, now.
She sits with me and smiles,
Watching the grimace form along the nerve-ends.
She comes upon the hour, politely,
With a knock,
Entering only as the last wisp
Of drug vanishes wraithlike
Through the window.

We lie together, matching spasm for spasm,
One another's worst,
Coupled in a crescendo we can
Not avoid or interrupt,
Until in the last passages
Of our peculiar lust we sense
The returning mist of mercy,
And then, spent and perhaps apologetic,
She steals away.
For awhile.

MY LIFE CLOSED TWICE BEFORE ITS CLOSE
Emily Dickinson

My life closed twice before its close;
It yet remains to see
If Immortality unveil
A third event to me,

So huge, so hopeless to conceive,
As these that twice befell.
Parting is all we know of heaven,
And all we need of hell.

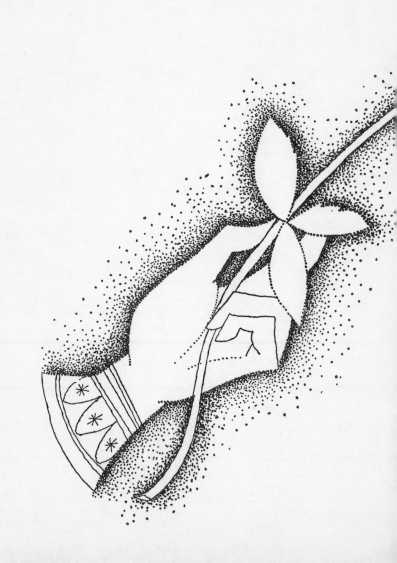

The Eternal Passion

POEMS ABOUT LOVE FOUND AND LOST

Although the idea of romantic love and the idealization of woman only dates back to the Dark Ages and the beginnings of chivalry, the attraction of man to woman and woman to man is at least as ancient in literature as the book of Genesis. There woman is made from man and given to him as a helper. But the relationship has been infinitely more complex than that, and from the tangle of emotions we call love has come poetry of beauty, pathos and dignity. Art intensifies experience, elevates it to a new plane of meaning. This happens when the poet speaks of love.

THE CAT

Charles Baudelaire
Translated by Roy Campbell

Come, my fine cat, against my loving heart;
Sheathe your sharp claws, and settle.
And let my eyes into your pupils dart
Where agate sparks with metal.

Now while my fingertips caress at leisure
Your head and wiry curves,
And that my hand's elated with the pleasure
Of your electric nerves,

I think about my woman—how her glances
Like yours, dear beast, deep-down
And cold, can cut and wound one as with lances;
Then, too, she has that vagrant
And subtle air of danger that makes fragrant
Her body, lithe and brown.

LYRICS

James Agee

No doubt left. Enough deceiving.
Now I know you do not love.
Now you know I do not love.
Now we know we do not love.
No more doubt. No more deceiving.

Yet there is pity in us for each other
And better times are almost fresh as true.
The dog returns. And the man to his mother.
And tides. And you to me. And I to you.
And we are cowardly kind the cruelest way,
Feeling the cliff unmorsel from our heels
And knowing balance gone, we smile, and stay
A little, whirling our arms like desperate wheels.

Not met and marred with the year's whole turn of grief,
But easily on the mercy of the morning
Fell this still folded leaf:
Small that never Summer spread
Demented on the dusty heat;
And sweet that never Fall
Wrung sere and tarnished red;
Safe now that never knew
Stunning Winter's bitter blue
It fell fair in the fair season:

Therefore with reason
Dress all in cheer and lightly put away
    With music and glad will
This little child that cheated the long day
    Of the long day's ill:
Who knows this breathing joy, heavy on us all,
    Never, never, never.

I loitered weeping with my bride for gladness
Her walking side against and both embracing
Through the brash brightening rain that now the season changes
White on the fallen air that now my fallen
                    the fallen girl her grave effaces.

JENNY KISSED ME

Leigh Hunt

Jenny kissed me when we met,
Jumping from the chair she sat in;
Time, you thief, who love to get
Sweets into your list, put that in!
Say I'm weary, say I'm sad,
Say that health and wealth have missed me,
Say I'm growing old, but add,
Jenny kissed me.

IT DROPPED SO LOW IN MY REGARD
Emily Dickinson

It dropped so low in my regard
    I heard it hit the ground,
And go to pieces on the stones
    At bottom of my mind;

Yet blamed the fate that fractured, less
    Than I reviled myself
For entertaining plated wares
    Upon my silver shelf.

LETTER: THE JAPANESE,
TO HER HUSBAND AT WAR
William Walsh

The bird you caught me, with blue feathers,
sang once and died of bars. That Fall
you crossed the north bridge
binding your sleeves. Cold
cracked the doorstone; gone to weeds now.
But I have kept the north gate free of them,
with waiting.
            Four times,
the pear tree spilled its ice shells
and four times, white flowers
since you pulled me down pears
to eat them.
            Every year,
the young boys paint new kites.
(You said the sky bloomed dragons.)
Our hands knew the pull of winds
so high up, you could only see them.
We crossed our glazed lines to cut them.

The pear tree droops with Autumn.
Drops its fruit; no one to eat them.
Where they fall the air sickens
in the rain, in the hot season.

At the north gate I watch for you
loosing your sleeves.

ACT II

Katherine Davis

The curtain rises on Act II.
Read your actor's lines; discover
How to be the perfect lover.
Rehearse the tender scenes;
Speak your part with conjured fervour,
But forgive me if your fond caress
Fails miserably to move me.

My pulse and brain
Re-live Act I
When a wild, impassioned gypsy
Came to me on instant wings
And wooed me with the muted strings
Of gypsy violins;
Dark eyes flashing,
Mouth on fire,
Desire exploding
On desire.

Act II seems just a little dull,
Secure in safe, pre-traveled ruts,
So uninspired
That my mind shuts
And sees my real love once again
In a circle of light,
With the sun on his hair,
And joy with him,
Singing of springtime.

And Rûth said, Intreat me not to leave
thee, or to return from following after thee:
for whither thou goest, I will go; and where
thou lodgest, I will lodge: thy people shall be
my people, and thy God my God:

Where thou diest, will I die, and there
will I be buried: the LORD do so to me, and
more also, if ought but death part thee and
me.

SONG

Oliver Goldsmith

When lovely woman stoops to folly
    And finds too late that men betray,
What charm can soothe her melancholy?
    What art can wash her guilt away?

The only art her guilt to cover,
    To hide her shame from every eye,
To give repentance to her lover,
    And wring his bosom, is—to die.

APOLOGY FOR YOUTH

Sister M. Madeleva, C.S.C.

Stand at my window;
watch them pass;
a lass and a lad,
a lad and a lass.

This is a way
to go to school,
learning an olden,
golden rule.

They seek for wisdom
in a book;
then they look up
and look—and look.

And wonder, wonder
if, after all,
wisdom is so
reciprocal.

They ask for beauty,
ask for truth
who have no thought
to ask for youth.

Theirs are the earth,
the sea, the sky;
they sing; they dance,
they float; they fly.

Why do they hurry,
hurry so?
Can they or will they
or do they know

They will earn some love;
they will learn some truth,
but never learn
nor earn back youth.

Stand at my window,
lad and lass;
let not this youth,
this young love pass.

Hold the wonder;
love the lore
you would one day change
the slow years for.

SONNET CXVI

William Shakespeare

Let me not to the marriage of true minds
Admit impediments. Love is not love
Which alters when it alteration finds,
Or bends with the remover to remove:
O, no! it is an ever-fixed mark,
That looks on tempests and is never shaken;
It is the star to every wand'ring bark,
Whose worth's unknown, although his height be taken.

Love's not Time's fool, though rosy lips and cheeks
Within his bending sickle's compass come;
Love alters not with his brief hours and weeks,
But bears it out even to the edge of doom:—
If this be error and upon me proved,
I never writ, nor no man ever loved.

SONG TO CELIA

Ben Johnson

Drink to me only with thine eyes,
    And I will pledge with mine;
Or leave a kiss but in the cup,
    And I'll not look for wine.
The thirst that from the soul doth rise
    Doth ask a drink divine;
But might I of Jove's nectar sup,
    I would not change for thine.

I sent thee late a rosy wreath,
    Not so much honoring thee
As giving it a hope that there
    It could not withered be.
But thou thereon didst only breathe,
    And sent'st it back to me;
Since when it grows, and smells, I swear,
    Not of itself but thee.

Song from AGLAURA

Sir John Suckling

Why so pale and wan, fond lover?
    Prithee, why so pale?
Will, when looking well can't move her,
    Looking ill prevail?
    Prithee, why so pale?

Why so dull and mute, young sinner?
    Prithee, why so mute?
Will, when speaking well can't win her,
    Saying nothing do 't?
    Prithee, why so mute?

Quit, quit for shame! This will not move;
    This cannot take her.
If of herself she will not love,
    Nothing can make her:
    The devil take her!

POET TO HIS LOVE

Maxwell Bodenheim

An old silver church in a forest
Is my love for you.
The trees around it
Are words that I have stolen from your heart.
An old silver bell, the last smile you gave,
Hangs at the top of my church.
It rings only when you come through the forest
And stand beside it.
And then it has no need for ringing,
For your voice takes its place.

A DECADE

Amy Lowell

When you came, you were like red wine and honey,
And the taste of you burnt my mouth with its sweetness.
Now you are like morning bread,
Smooth and pleasant.
I hardly taste you at all, for I know your savor;
But I am completely nourished.

I SHALL NOT CARE

Sara Teasdale

When I am dead and over me bright April
    Shakes out her rain-drenched hair,
Though you should lean above me broken-hearted,
    I shall not care.

I shall have peace, as leafy trees are peaceful
    When rain bends down the bough;
And I shall be more silent and cold-hearted
    Than you are now.

POEM IN PROSE

Archibald MacLeish

This poem is for my wife
I have made it plainly and honestly
The mark is on it
Like the burl on the knife

I have not made it for praise
She has no more need for praise
Than summer has
On the bright days

In all that becomes a woman
Her words and her ways are beautiful
Love's lovely duty
The well-swept room

Wherever she is there is sun
And time and a sweet air
Peace is there
Work done

There are always curtains and flowers
And candles and baked bread
And a cloth spread
And a clean house

Her voice when she sings is a voice
At dawn by a freshening sea
Where the wave leaps in the
Wind and rejoices

Wherever she is it is now
It is here where the apples are
Here in the stars
In the quick hour

The greatest and richest good—
My own life to live—
This she has given me

If giver could

AFTER LONG SILENCE

William Butler Yeats

Speech after long silence; it is right,
All other lovers being estranged or dead,
Unfriendly lamplight hid under its shade,
The curtains drawn upon unfriendly night,
That we descant and yet again descant
Upon the supreme theme of Art and Song:
Bodily decrepitude is wisdom; young
We loved each other and were ignorant.

SONNET XXXVIII
From *Sonnets from the Portuguese*
Elizabeth Barrett Browning

First time he kissed me, he but only kissed
The fingers of this hand wherewith I write;
And ever since, it grew more clean and white,
Slow to world-greetings, quick with its "Oh, list,"
When the angels speak. A ring of amethyst
I could not wear here, plainer to my sight,
Than that first kiss. The second passed in height
The first, and sought the forehead, and half missed,
Half falling on the hair. O beyond meed!
That was the chrism of love, which love's own crown,
With sanctifying sweetness, did precede.
The third upon my lips was folded down
In perfect, purple state; since when, indeed,
I have been proud, and said, "My love, my own!"

MEETING AT NIGHT
Robert Browning

The gray sea and the long black land;
And the yellow half-moon large and low;
And the startled little waves that leap
In fiery ringlets from their sleep,
As I gain the cove with pushing prow,
And quench its speed in the slushy sand.

Then a mile of warm sea-scented beach;
Three fields to cross till a farm appears;
A tap at the pane, the quick sharp scratch
And blue spirt of a lighted match,
And a voice less loud, through its joys and fears,
Than the two hearts beating each to each!

WHEN I WAS ONE-AND-TWENTY

A. E. Housman

When I was one-and-twenty
I heard a wise man say,
"Give crowns and pounds and guineas
But not your heart away;
Give pearls away and rubies
But keep your fancy free."
But I was one-and-twenty,
No use to talk to me.

When I was one-and-twenty
I heard him say again,
"The heart out of the bosom
Was never given in vain;
'Tis paid with sighs a plenty
And sold for endless rue."
And I am two-and-twenty,
And oh, 'tis true, 'tis true.

PAUL

James Wright

I used to see her in the door,
Lifting up her hand to wave
To citizens, or pass the hour
With neighboring wives who did not have
Anything more than time to say.

I used to see her in the door,
Simple and quiet woman, slim;
And so, I think, Paul cared the more
The night they carried her from him,
The night they carried her away.

The doctor did not even ask
For any neighborly advice;
He knew he had a simple task,
And it was obvious from his eyes
There was not anything to say.

The doctor had a word for Paul;
He said that she was resting now,
And would not wake, and that was all.
And then he walked into the snow,
Into the snow he walked away.

And did Paul shriek and curse the air,
And did he pummel with his fist
Against the wall, or tear his hair
And rush outside to bite the mist
That did not have a thing to say?

He sat upon her ruffled bed
And did not even look at me.
She was lovely, she was dead.
Some sparrows chirruped on a tree
Outside, and then they flew away.

THE GARRET

Ezra Pound

Come, let us pity those who are better off than we are.
Come, my friend, and remember
    that the rich have butlers and no friends,
And we have friends and no butlers.
Come, let us pity the married and the unmarried.

Dawn enters with little feet
    like a gilded Pavlova,
And I am near my desire.
Nor has life in it aught better
Than this hour of clear coolness,
    the hour of waking together.

THE BLINDED SOLDIER
TO HIS LOVE

Alfred Noyes

I did not know you then.
I cannot see you now;
But let my hands again
Feel your sweet hair and brow.
Your eyes are grey, I am told,
Your hair a tawny gold.

Yet, if of these I tire,
I shall not need to stray.
Your eyes shall feed my fire
With brown or blue for grey;
And your deep hair shall be
As mutable as the sea.

Let forms and colours flow
Like clouds around a star.
I clasp the soul and know
How vain those day-dreams are;
Dreams from these eyes withdrawn
Beyond all thought of dawn.

But what is dawn to me?
In Love's Arabian night,
What lover cares to see
The unwelcome morning light?
With you, O sweetest friend,
My night shall never end.

TO LUCASTA, ON GOING
TO THE WARS

Richard Lovelace

Tell me not, Sweet, I am unkind,
     That from the nunnery
Of thy chaste breast and quiet mind
     To war and arms I fly.

True, a new mistress now I chase,
    The first foe in the field;
And with a stronger faith embrace
    A sword, a horse, a shield.

Yet this inconstancy is such
    As thou too shalt adore;
I could not love thee, Dear, so much,
    Loved I not Honor more.

ANNABEL LEE

Edgar Allan Poe

It was many and many a year ago,
    In a kingdom by the sea
That a maiden there lived whom you may know
    By the name of Annabel Lee;—
And this maiden she lived with no other thought
    Than to love and be loved by me.

I was a child and she was a child,
    In this kingdom by the sea,
But we loved with a love that was more than love—
    I and my Annabel Lee—
With a love that the winged seraphs in Heaven
    Coveted her and me.

And this was the reason that, long ago,
    In this kingdom by the sea,
A wind blew out of a cloud, chilling
    My beautiful Annabel Lee;
So that her high-born kinsmen came
    And bore her away from me,
To shut her up in a sepulcher
    In this kingdom by the sea.

The angels, not half so happy in Heaven,
    Went envying her and me:—
Yes!—that was the reason (as all men know,
    In this kingdom by the sea)
That the wind came out of the cloud, by night,
    Chilling and killing my Annabel Lee.

But our love it was stronger by far than the love
    Of those who were older than we—
    Of many far wiser than we—
And neither the angels in Heaven above,
    Nor the demons down under the sea,
Can ever dissever my soul from the soul
    Of the beautiful Annabel Lee:—

For the moon never beams without bringing me dreams
    Of the beautiful Annabel Lee;
And the stars never rise but I feel the bright eyes
    Of the beautiful Annabel Lee;
And so, all the night-tide, I lie down by the side
Of my darling,—my darling,—my life and my bride,
    In the sepulcher there by the sea—
    In her tomb by the sounding sea.

THE QUARREL

Conrad Aiken

Suddenly, after the quarrel, while we waited,
Disheartened, silent, with downcast looks, nor stirred
Eyelid nor finger, hopeless both, yet hoping
Against all hope to unsay the sundering word:

While the room's stillness deepened, deepened about us,
And each of us crept his thought's way to discover
How, with as little sound as the fall of a leaf,
The shadow had fallen, and lover quarrelled with lover;

And while, in the quiet, I marvelled—alas, alas—
At your deep beauty, your tragic beauty, torn
As the pale flower is torn by the wanton sparrow—
This beauty, pitied and loved, and now forsworn;

It was then, when the instant darkened to its darkest,—
When faith was lost with hope, and the rain conspired
To strike its gay arpeggios against our heartstrings,—
When love no longer dared, and scarcely desired:

It was then that suddenly, in the neighbor's room,
The music started: that brave quartette of strings
Breaking out of the stillness, as out of our stillness,
Like the indomitable heart of life that sings

When all is lost; and startled from our sorrow,
Tranced from our grief by the diviner grief,
We raised remembering eyes, each looked at other,
Blinded with tears of joy; and another leaf

Fell silently as that first; and in the instant
The shadow had gone, our quarrel became absurd;
And we rose, to the angelic voices of the music,
        And I touched your hand, and we kissed, without a word.

BELIEVE ME, IF ALL THOSE ENDEARING
YOUNG CHARMS

Thomas Moore

Believe me, if all those endearing young charms,
Which I gaze on so fondly to-day,
Were to change by to-morrow, and fleet in my arms,
Like fairy-gifts fading away,
Thou wouldst still be adored, as this moment thou art,
Let thy loveliness fade as it will,
And around the dear ruin each wish of my heart
Would entwine itself verdantly still.

It is not while beauty and youth are thine own,
And thy cheeks unprofaned by a tear,
That the fervor and faith of a soul may be known,
To which time will but make thee more dear!
No, the heart that has truly loved never forgets,
But as truly loves on to the close,
As the sunflower turns to her god when he sets
The same look which she turned when he rose!

THE INDIAN SERENADE

Percy Bysshe Shelley

I arise from dreams of thee
In the first sweet sleep of night,
When the winds are breathing low,
And the stars are shining bright:
I arise from dreams of thee,
And a spirit in my feet
Hath led me—who knows how?
To thy chamber window, Sweet!

The wandering airs they faint
On the dark, the silent stream—
The Champak odors fail
Like sweet thoughts in a dream;
The nightingale's complaint,
It dies upon her heart;—
As I must on thine,
Oh, beloved as thou art!

Oh lift me from the grass!—
I die! I faint! I fail!
Let thy love in kisses rain
On my lips and eyelids pale.
My cheek is cold and white, alas!
My hearts beats loud and fast;—
Oh! press it to thine own again,
Where it will break at last.

'TIS THE LAST ROSE OF SUMMER

Thomas Moore

'Tis the last rose of summer,
Left blooming alone;
All her lovely companions
Are faded and gone;
No flower of her kindred,
No rose-bud is nigh,
To reflect back her blushes,
Or give sigh for sigh.

I'll not leave thee, thou lone one!
To pine on the stem;
Since the lovely are sleeping,
Go, sleep thou with them.
Thus kindly I scatter
Thy leaves o'er the bed
Where thy mates of the garden
Lie scentless and dead.

So soon may I follow,
When friendships decay,
And from Love's shining circle
The gems drop away.
When true hearts lie withered,
And fond ones are flown,
O who would inhabit
This bleak world alone?

NON SUM QUALIS ERAM BONAE SUB REGNO CYNARAE

Ernest Dowson

Last night ah, yesternight, betwixt her lips and mine
There fell thy shadow, Cynara! thy breath was shed
Upon my soul between the kisses and the wine;
And I was desolate and sick of an old passion,
   Yea, I was desolate and bowed my head:
I have been faithful to thee, Cynara! in my fashion.

All night upon mine heart I felt her warm heart beat,
Night-long within mine arms in love and sleep she lay;
Surely the kisses of her bought red mouth were sweet;
But I was desolate and sick of an old passion,
    When I awoke and found the dawn was gray:
I have been faithful to thee, Cynara! in my fashion.

I have forgot much, Cynara! gone with the wind,
Flung roses, roses riotously with the throng,
Dancing, to put thy pale, lost lilies out of mind;
But I was desolate and sick of an old passion,
    Yea, all the time, because the dance was long:
I have been faithful to thee, Cynara! in my fashion.

I cried for madder music and for stronger wine,
But when the feast is finished and the lamps expire,
Then falls thy shadow, Cynara! the night is thine;
And I am desolate and sick of an old passion,
    Yea hungry for the lips of my desire:
I have been faithful to thee, Cynara! in my fashion.

SONNET XVIII

William Shakespeare

Shall I compare thee to a Summer's day?
Thou art more lovely and more temperate:
Rough winds do shake the darling buds of May,
And Summer's lease hath all too short a date:
Sometimes too hot the eye of heaven shines,
And often is his gold complexion dimm'd;
And every fair from fair sometime declines,
By chance or nature's changing course untrimm'd:
But thy eternal Summer shall not fade
Nor lose possession of that fair thou owest;
Nor shall Death brag thou wanderest in his shade,
When in eternal lines to time thou growest:
So long as men can breathe, or eyes can see,
So long lives this, and this gives life to thee.

A WHITE ROSE

John Boyle O'Reilly

The red rose whispers of passion,
And the white rose breathes of love;
Oh, the red rose is a falcon,
And the white rose is a dove.

But I send you a cream white rosebud
With a flush on its petal tips;
For the love that is purest and sweetest
Has a kiss of desire on the lips.

AN IMMORALITY

Ezra Pound

Sing we for love and idleness,
Naught else is worth the having.
Though I have been in many a land,
There is naught else in living.

And I would rather have my sweet,
Though rose-leaves die of grieving,
Than do high deeds in Hungary
To pass all men's believing.

DIVINELY SUPERFLUOUS BEAUTY

Robinson Jeffers

The storm-dances of gulls, the barking game of seals,
Over and under the ocean . . .
Divinely superfluous beauty
Rules the games, presides over destinies, makes trees grow
And hills tower, waves fall.

The incredible beauty of joy
Stars with fire the joining of lips, O let our loves too
Be joined, there is not a maiden
Burns and thirsts for love
More than my blood for you, by the shore of seals while the wings
Weave like a web in the air
Divinely superfluous beauty.

TO HIS COY MISTRESS
Andrew Marvell

Had we but World enough, and Time,
This coyness Lady were no crime.
We would sit down, and think which way
To walk, and pass our long Loves Day.
Thou by the Indian Ganges side
Should'st Rubies find: I by the Tide
Of Humber would complain. I would
Love you ten years before the Flood:
And you should if you please refuse
Till the Conversion of the Jews.
My vegetable Love should grow
Vaster than Empires, and more slow.
An hundred years should go to praise
Thine Eyes, and on thy Forehead Gaze.
Two hundred to adore each Breast:
But thirty thousand to the rest.
An Age at least to every part,
And the last Age should show your Heart.
For Lady you deserve this State;
Nor would I love at lower rate.

But at my back I alwaies hear
Times winged Charriot hurrying near:
And yonder all before us lye
Desarts of vast Eternity.
Thy Beauty shall no more be found;
Nor, in thy marble Vault, shall sound

My echoing Song: then Worms shall try
That long preserv'd Virginity:
And your quaint Honour turn to dust;
And into ashes all my Lust.
The Grave's a fine and private place,
But none I think do there embrace.

Now therefore, while the youthful hew
Sits on thy skin like morning dew
And while thy willing Soul transpires
At every pore with instant Fires,
Now let us sport us while we may;
And now, like am'rous birds of prey,
Rather at once our Time devour,
Than languish in his slow-chapt pow'r.
Let us roll all our Strength, and all
Our sweetness, up into one Ball:
And tear our Pleasures with rough strife,
Thorough the Iron gates of Life.
Thus, though we cannot make our Sun
Stand still, yet we will make him run.

AFTER TWO YEARS

Richard Aldington

She is all so slight
And tender and white
As a May morning.
She walks without hood
At dusk. It is good
To hear her sing.

It is God's will
That I shall love her still
As He loves Mary,
And night and day
I will go forth to pray
That she love me.

She is as gold
Lovely, and far more cold.
Do thou pray with me,
For if I win grace
To kiss twice her face
God has done well to me.

SONG OF SOLOMON 2:8-13

The voice of my beloved! behold, he
cometh leaping upon the mountains,
skipping upon the hills.

My beloved is like a roe or a young hart:
behold, he standeth behind our wall, he
looketh forth at the windows, shewing
himself through the lattice.

My beloved spake, and said unto me,
Rise up, my love, my fair one, and come away.

For, lo, the winter is past, the rain is over
and gone;

The flowers appear on the earth; the time
of singing of birds is come, and the voice
of the turtle is heard in our land;

The fig tree putteth forth her green figs,
and the vines with the tender grape give a good
smell. Arise, my love, my fair one, and
come away.

From THE RUBAIYAT OF OMAR KHAYYAM
Edward FitzGerald

Ah Love! could you and I with Him conspire
To grasp this sorry Scheme of Things entire,
Would not we shatter it to bits—and then
Remold it nearer to the Heart's desire!

SONNET XXIX

William Shakespeare

When, in disgrace with Fortune and men's eyes,
I all alone beweep my outcast state,
And trouble deaf heaven with my bootless cries,
And look upon myself, and curse my fate,
Wishing me like to one more rich in hope,
Featured like him, like him with friends possest,
Desiring this man's art and that man's scope,
With what I most enjoy contented least;
Yet in these thoughts myself almost despising—
Haply I think on thee: and then my state,
Like to the lark at break of day arising
From sullen earth, sings hymns at Heaven's gate;
For thy sweet love rememb'red such wealth brings
That then I scorn to change my state with Kings.

SHE CAME OUT OF THE FROST

Alexander Blok

Translated by Avrahm Yarmolinsky

She came out of the frost,
Her cheeks glowing,
And filled the room with
Freshness of air and perfume,
A ringing voice
And chatter
Utterly disrespectful
Of serious pursuits.

She proceeded to drop
A fat volume of an art review
On the floor
And suddenly
My room
Began to look fearfully crowded.

All this was somewhat annoying
And rather absurd.

She asked me, however,
To read Macbeth to her.
When I came to: "The earth hath bubbles . . ."
(I cannot say it without agitation),
I noticed she too was agitated
And was staring out of the window.
It appears that a large spotted tomcat
Was cautiously crawling
Along the edge of the roof
After two doves that were billing.

I got angry, chiefly
Because the doves, not we, were kissing,
And the days of Paolo and Francesca were gone.

HOW DO I LOVE THEE?

From *Sonnets from the Portuguese*

Elizabeth Barrett Browning

How do I love thee? Let me count the ways.
I love thee to the depth and breadth and height
My soul can reach, when feeling out of sight
For the ends of Being and ideal Grace.
I love thee to the level of everyday's
Most quiet need, by sun and candle-light.
I love thee freely, as men strive for Right;
I love thee purely, as they turn from Praise.
I love thee with the passion put to use
In my old griefs, and with my childhood's faith.
I love thee with a love I seemed to lose
With my lost saints,—I love thee with the breadth,
Smiles, tears, of all my life! —and, if God choose,
I shall but love thee better after death.

URBAN ROSES

Ted Isaac

Each morning I lift my blind to stare
Into the concrete garden where
The love we've planted in each other's grown
Tangled and wiry, rooted in stone;

Not softly yielding as flowers grow,
But coarse and spiked with thorns as though
Proof to the world that roots can claw
Through scars of the earth to rock and draw
Strength from granite and stonily
Hold back the world from you and me.

MY HEART, MY HEART
IS MOURNFUL

Heinrich Heine
Translated by James Thomson

My heart, my heart is mournful,
    Yet joyously shines the May;
I stand by the linden leaning,
    High on the bastion gray.

The blue town-moat thereunder
    Glides peacefully along,
A boy in a boat is angling,
    And whistling a careless song.

Beyond, like a well-known picture,
    All small and fair, are strewed
Houses and gardens and people,
    Oxen and meadows and wood.

The maidens bleach the linen,
    And dance in the grass for glee;
The mill-wheel scatters diamonds,
    Its far hum reaches me.

Upon the hoary tower
    A sentry-box stands low;
A youth in his coat of scarlet
    There passes to and fro.

He trifles with his musket,
    Which gleams in the sunshine red,
He shoulders and presents it,—
    I would he shot me dead!

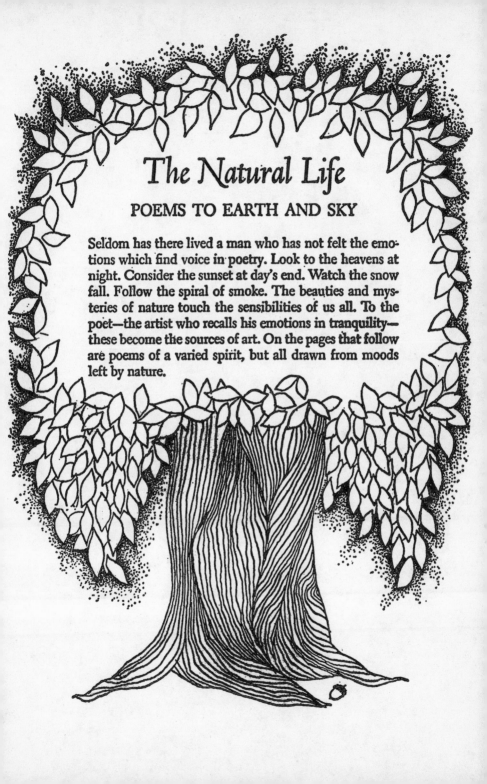

The Natural Life

POEMS TO EARTH AND SKY

Seldom has there lived a man who has not felt the emotions which find voice in poetry. Look to the heavens at night. Consider the sunset at day's end. Watch the snow fall. Follow the spiral of smoke. The beauties and mysteries of nature touch the sensibilities of us all. To the poet—the artist who recalls his emotions in tranquility—these become the sources of art. On the pages that follow are poems of a varied spirit, but all drawn from moods left by nature.

FLOWER IN THE CRANNIED WALL

Alfred, Lord Tennyson

Flower in the crannied wall,
I pluck you out of the crannies,
I hold you here, root and all, in my hand,
Little flower—but *if* I could understand
What you are, root and all, and all in all,
I should know what God and man is.

BIRCHES

Robert Frost

When I see birches bend to left and right
Across the lines of straighter darker trees,
I like to think some boy's been swinging them.
But swinging doesn't bend them down to stay.
Ice-storms do that. Often you must have seen them
Loaded with ice a sunny winter morning
After a rain. They click upon themselves
As the breeze rises, and turn many-colored
As the stir cracks and crazes their enamel.
Soon the sun's warmth makes them shed crystal shells
Shattering and avalanching on the snow-crust—
Such heaps of broken glass to sweep away
You'd think the inner dome of heaven had fallen.
They are dragged to the withered bracken by the load,
And they seem not to break; though once they are bowed
So low for long, they never right themselves:
You may see their trunks arching in the woods
Years afterwards, trailing their leaves on the ground
Like girls on hands and knees that throw their hair
Before them over their heads to dry in the sun.
But I was going to say when Truth broke in
With all her matter-of-fact about the ice-storm
I should prefer to have some boy bend them
As he went out and in to fetch the cows—

Some boy too far from town to learn baseball,
Whose only play was what he found himself,
Summer or winter, and could play alone.
One by one he subdued his father's trees
By riding them down over and over again
Until he took the stiffness out of them,
And not one but hung limp, not one was left
For him to conquer. He learned all there was
To learn about not launching out too soon
And so not carrying the tree away
Clear to the ground. He always kept his poise
To the top branches, climbing carefully
With the same pains you use to fill a cup
Up to the brim, and even above the brim.
Then he flung outward, feet first, with a swish,
Kicking his way down through the air to the ground.
So was I once myself a swinger of birches.
And so I dream of going back to be.
It's when I'm weary of considerations,
And life is too much like a pathless wood
Where your face burns and tickles with the cobwebs
Broken across it, and one eye is weeping
From a twig's having lashed across it open.
I'd like to get away from earth awhile
And then come back to it and begin over.
May no fate willfully misunderstand me
And half grant what I wish and snatch me away
Not to return. Earth's the right place for love:
I don't know where it's likely to go better.
I'd like to go by climbing a birch tree,
And climb black branches up a snow-white trunk
Toward heaven, till the tree could bear no more,
But dipped its top and set me down again.
That would be good both going and coming back.
One could do worse than be a swinger of birches.

FOR CITY SPRING

Stephen Vincent Benét

Now grimy April comes again,
Maketh bloom the fire-escapes,
Maketh silvers in the rain,
Maketh winter coats and capes
Suddenly all worn and shabby
Like the fur of winter bears,
Maketh kittens, maketh baby,
Maketh kissing on the stairs.
Maketh bug crawl out of crack,
Maketh ticklings down the back
As if sunlight stroked the spine
To a hurdy-gurdy's whine
And the shower ran white wine.

April, April, sing cuckoo,
April, April, maketh new
Mouse and cockroach, man and wife,
Everything with blood and life;
Bloweth, groweth, flourisheth,
Danceth in a ragged skirt
On the very stoop of Death
And will take no mortal hurt.
Maketh dogs to whine and bound,
Maketh cats to caterwaul,
Maketh lovers, all around,
Whisper in the hall.

On, and when the night comes down
And the shrieking of the town
Settles to the steady roar
Of a long sea-beaten shore,
April hieth, April spieth
Everywhere a lover lieth,
Bringeth sweetness, bringeth fever,
Will not stop at "I would liever,"
Will not heed, "Now God a mercy!"
Turneth Moral topsy-versy,

Bringeth he and she to bed,
Bringeth ill to maidenhead,
Bringeth joyance in its stead.
By May, by May, she lieth sped,
Yet still we praise that crocus head,
April!

SILVER

Walter de la Mare

Slowly, silently, now the moon
Walks the night in her silver shoon;
This way, and that, she peers, and sees
Silver fruit upon silver trees;
One by one the casements catch
Her beams beneath the silvery thatch;
Couched in his kennel, like a log,
With paws of silver sleeps the dog;
From their shadowy cote the white breasts peep
Of doves in a silver-feathered sleep;
A harvest mouse goes scampering by,
With silver claws, and silver eye;
And moveless fish in the water gleam,
By silver reeds in a silver stream.

NIGHT CLOUDS

Amy Lowell

The white mares of the moon rush along the sky
Beating their golden hoofs upon the glass Heavens;
The white mares of the moon are all standing on their hind legs
Pawing at the green porcelain doors of the remote Heavens.
Fly, mares!
Strain your utmost,
Scatter the milky dust of stars,
Or the tiger sun will leap upon you and destroy you
With one lick of his vermillion tongue.

Song from PIPPA PASSES
Robert Browning

The year's at the spring,
And day's at the morn;
Morning's at seven;
The hill-side's dew-pearled;
The lark's on the wing;
The snail's on the thorn;
God's in His Heaven—
All's right with the world!

DO YOU FEAR THE WIND?
Hamlin Garland

Do you fear the force of the wind,
The slash of the rain?
Go face them and fight them,
Be savage again.
Go hungry and cold like the wolf,
  Go wade like the crane:
The palms of your hands will thicken,
The skin of your cheek will tan,
You'll grow ragged and weary and swarthy,
  But you'll walk like a man!

SONG OF JANUARY
Gerta Kennedy

Brash and bare and whistling cold
now's the moment to be bold.
When the meridian is low,
the children frost their pies with snow,
and grasp the bristling winter gale
for swords, to slice the dragon's tail.

Now purge the rancor from our bones,
the cold's our cross, reprieves, atones,
bleaches clean the blood-stained grief,
hardens wrath into belief.
Old north, tyrannical and pure,
blow on our flesh your crystal cure.

SO THIS IS AUTUMN

W. W. *Watt*

Now far and near on field and hill
We watch the death of chlorophyll
As earl autumn rushes in
With xanthophyll and carotin.
I hold that ignorance is bliss,
Considering the fact that this
Is how a botanist perceives
The colorings of autumn leaves.

AUTUMN

Emily Dickinson

The morns are meeker than they were,
The nuts are getting brown;
The berry's cheek is plumper,
The rose is out of town.

The maple wears a gayer scarf,
The field a scarlet gown.
Lest I should be old-fashioned,
I'll put a trinket on.

WINTER LANDSCAPE

John Berryman

The three men coming down the winter hill
In brown, with tall poles and a pack of hounds
At heel, through the arrangement of the trees,
Past the five figures at the burning straw,
Returning cold and silent to their town,

Returning to the drifted snow, the rink
Lively with children, to the older men,
The long companions they can never reach,
The blue light, men with ladders, by the church
The sledge and shadow in the twilit street,

Are not aware that in the sandy time
To come, the evil waste of history
Outstretched, they will be seen upon the brow
Of that same hill: when all their company
Will have been irrecoverably lost,

These men, this particular three in brown
Witnessed by birds will keep the scene and say
By their configuration with the trees,
The small bridge, the red houses and the fire,
What place, what time, what morning occasion

Sent them into the wood, a pack of hounds
At heel and the tall poles upon their shoulders,
Thence to return as now we see them and
Ankle-deep in snow down the winter hill
Descend while three birds watch and the fourth flies.

THE WANDERER

Eugene Field

Upon a mountain height, far from the sea,
  I found a shell,
And to my listening ear the lonely thing
Ever a song of ocean seemed to sing,
  Ever a tale of ocean seemed to tell.

How came the shell upon the mountain height?
   Ah, who can say
Whether there dropped by some too careless hand,
Or whether there cast when ocean swept the land,
   Ere the Eternal ordained the Day?

Strange, was it not? Far from its native deep,
   One song it sang,—
Sang of the awful mysteries of the tide,
Sang of the misty sea, profound and wide,—
   Ever with echoes of the ocean rang.

And as the shell upon the mountain height
   Sings of the sea,
So do I ever, leagues and leagues away,—
So do I ever, wandering where I may,—
   Sing O my home! sing O my home! of thee.

TO THE LADY-BIRD

Old English Song

Lady-bird! Lady-bird! fly away home;
   The field-mouse is gone to her nest,
The daisies have shut up their sweet sleepy eyes,
   And the bees and the birds are at rest.

Lady-bird! Lady-bird! fly away home;
   The glow-worm is lighting her lamp,
The dew's falling fast, and your fine speckled
     wings
Will be wet with the close-clinging damp.

Lady-bird! Lady-bird! fly away home;
   The fairy-bells tinkle afar;
Make haste, or they'll catch you, and harness you
     fast,
With a cobweb, to Oberon's car.

THE DOUBLE TREE

Winfield Townley Scott

I do not know why. It is not only
In the April sun the flowered apricot tree—
It is more the shadow of the tree against the wall
The shadow of flowered branches that sets the tree
There in the April sun and on the earth,
Fan coral within the soft sea of spring.
Sparrow and the shadow of sparrow fly
Into the double tree, create it there
So dimensional it must be believed.
What sun objectifies, like us, is real
For this little while in the sun's season.

BLADES OF GRASS

Stephen Crane

In Heaven,
Some little blades of grass
Stood before God.
"What did you do?"
Then all save one of the little blades
Began eagerly to relate
The merits of their lives.
This one stayed a small way behind,
Ashamed.
Presently, God said,
"And what did you do?"
The little blade answered, "Oh, my Lord,
Memory is bitter to me,
For, if I did good deeds,
I know not of them."
Then God, in all His splendor,
Arose from His throne.
"Oh, best little blade of grass!" He said.

SUDDEN FROST

David Wagoner

Pale light tatters the stones beyond the hemlock,
And, like a thorn, the call of the killdeer
Curves through the many winds; and what was bleak
Is stark in the dawn, as mist plumes colder.
The ferret hungers in the high whins; like water
In a pose, the thatch of knuckle-grass has frozen
Across the hare's burrow, and none may enter.
O the crow cracks at the earth; it will not loosen.
Underfoot, the wasp lies hollow, its brilliant husk
Arched to pierce, like the killdeer, all who threaten
To live; and above, the leaves of the hemlock whisk
Like the sound of wasps, as, maundering and uncertain,
In an air already greyed to the thinnest light,
The thinnest noise, the first snow falls too late.

THE WINDHOVER

Gerard Manley Hopkins

I caught this morning morning's minion, kingdom of daylight's
dauphin, dapple-dawn-drawn Falcon, in his riding
Of the rolling level underneath him steady air, and striding
High there, how he rung upon the rein of a wimpling wing
In his ecstasy! then off, off forth on swing,
As a skate's heel sweeps smooth on a bow-bend: the hurl and gliding
Rebuffed the big wind. My heart in hiding
Stirred for a bird,—the achieve of, the mastery of the thing!

Brute beauty and valour and act, oh, air, pride, plume, here
Buckle! And the fire that breaks from thee then, a billion
Times told lovelier, more dangerous, O my chevalier!
No wonder of it: shéer plod makes plough down sillion
Shine, and blue-bleak embers, ah my dear,
Fall, gall themselves, and gash gold-vermilion.

242

I WANDERED LONELY AS A CLOUD

William Wordsworth

I wandered lonely as a cloud
   That floats on high o'er vales and hills,
When all at once I saw a crowd,
   A host of golden daffodils;
Beside the lake, beneath the trees,
Fluttering and dancing in the breeze.

Continuous as the stars that shine
   And twinkle on the milky way,
They stretched in never-ending line
   Along the margin of a bay:
Ten thousand saw I at a glance,
Tossing their heads in sprightly dance.

The waves beside them danced; but they
   Out-did the sparkling waves in glee:
A poet could not but be gay,
   In such a jocund company:
I gazed—and gazed—but little thought
What wealth the show to me had brought.

For oft, when on my couch I lie
   In vacant or in pensive mood,
They flash upon that inward eye
   Which is the bliss of solitude;
And then my heart with pleasure fills,
And dances with the daffodils.

THE RETURN

Edna St. Vincent Millay

Earth does not understand her child,
Who from the loud gregarious town
Returns, depleted and defiled,
To the still woods, to fling him down.

Earth can not count the sons she bore:
The wounded lynx, the wounded man
Come trailing blood unto her door;
She shelters both as best she can.

But she is early up and out,
To trim the year or strip its bones;
She has no time to stand about
Talking of him in undertones

Who has no aim but to forget,
Be left in peace, be lying thus
For days, for years, for centuries yet,
Unshaven and anonymous;

Who, marked for failure, dulled by grief,
Has traded in his wife and friend
For this warm ledge, this alder leaf:
Comfort that does not comprehend.

A THING OF BEAUTY
John Keats

A thing of beauty is a joy for ever:
Its loveliness increases; it will never
Pass into nothingness; but still will keep
A bower quiet for us, and a sleep
Full of sweet dreams, and health, and quiet breathing.
Therefore, on every morrow, are we wreathing
A flowery band to bind us to the earth,
Spite of despondence, of the inhuman dearth
Of noble natures, of the gloomy days,
Of all the unhealthy and o'er-darkened ways
Made for our searching: yes, in spite of all,
Some shape of beauty moves away the pall
From our dark spirits. Such the sun, the moon,
Trees old and young, sprouting a shady boon
For simple sheep; and such are daffodils
With the green world they live in; and clear rills

That for themselves a cooling covert make
'Gainst the hot season; the mid-forest brake,
Rich with a sprinkling of fair musk-rose blooms:
And such too is the grandeur of the dooms
We have imagined for the mighty dead;
All lovely tales that we have heard or read:
And endless fountain of immortal drink,
Pouring unto us from the heaven's brink.
Nor do we merely feel these essences
For one short hour; no, even as the trees
That whisper round a temple become soon
Dear as the temple's self, so does the moon,
The passion poesy, glories infinite,
Haunt us till they become a cheering light
Unto our souls, and bound to us so fast,
That, whether there be shine, or gloom o'ercast,
They always must be with us, or we die.

SEA FEVER

John Masefield

I must go down to the seas again, to the lonely sea and the sky,
And all I ask is a tall ship and a star to steer her by;
And the wheel's kick and the wind's song and the white sail's shaking,
And a gray mist on the sea's face, and a gray dawn breaking.

I must go down to the seas again, for the call of the running tide
Is a wild call and a clear call that may not be denied;
And all I ask is a windy day with the white clouds flying,
And the flung spray and the blown spume, and the sea gulls crying.

I must go down to the seas again, to the vagrant gipsy life,
To the gull's way and the whale's way where the wind's like a whetted
    knife;
And all I ask is a merry yarn from a laughing fellow-rover,
And quiet sleep and a sweet dream when the long trick's over.

FOG

Carl Sandburg

The fog comes
on little cat feet.

It sits looking
over harbor and city
on silent haunches
and then, moves on.

FORMER BARN LOT

Mark Van Doren

Once there was a fence here,
  And the grass came and tried—
Leaning from the pasture—
  To get inside.

But colt feet trampled it,
  Turning it brown;
Until the farmer moved
  And the fence fell down;

Then any bird saw,
  Under the wire,
Grass nibbling inward
  Like green fire.

GLYCINE'S SONG

Samuel Taylor Coleridge

A sunny shaft did I behold,
From sky to earth it slanted:
And poised therein a bird so bold—
Sweet bird, thou wert enchanted!

He sank, he rose, he twinkled, he troll'd
Within that shaft of sunny mist;
His eyes of fire, his beak of gold,
All else of amethyst!

And thus he sang: 'Adieu! adieu!
Love's dreams prove seldom true.
The blossoms, they make no delay:
The sparking dew-drops will not stay.
   Sweet month of May,
     We must away;
     Far, far away!
      To-day! to-day!'

FERN HILL

Dylan Thomas

Now as I was young and easy under the apple boughs
About the lilting house and happy as the grass was green,
   The night above the dingle starry,
     Golden in the heydays of his eyes,
And honoured among wagons I was prince of the apple towns
And once below a time I lordly had the trees and leaves
   Trail with daisies and barley
   Down the rivers of the windfall light.

And as I was green and carefree, famous among the barns
About the happy yard and singing as the farm was home,
   In the sun that is young once only,
     Time let me play and be
     Golden in the mercy of his means,
And green and golden I was huntsman and herdsman, the calves
Sang to my horn, the foxes on the hills barked clear and cold,
   And the sabbath rang slowly
   In the pebbles of the holy streams.

All the sun long it was running, it was lovely, the hayfields
High as the house, the tunes from the chimneys, it was air
And playing, lovely and watery
And fire green as grass.
And nightly under the simple stars
As I rode to sleep the owls were bearing the farm away,
All the moon long I heard, blessed among stables, the nightjars
Flying with the ricks, and the horses
Flashing into the dark.

And then to awake, and the farm, like a wanderer white
With the dew, come back, the cock on his shoulder: it was all
Shinging, it was Adam and maiden,
The sky gathered again
And the sun grew round that very day.
So it must have been after the birth of the simple light
In the first, spinning place, the spellbound horses walking warm
Out of the whinnying green stable
    On to the fields of praise.

And honoured among foxes and pheasants by the gay house
Under the new made clouds and happy as the heart was long,
In the sun born over and over,
I ran my heedless ways,
My wishes raced through the house-high hay
And nothing I cared, at my sky blue trades, that time allows
In all his tuneful turning so few and such morning songs
Before the children green and golden
    Followed him out of grace,

Nothing I cared, in the lamb white days, that time would take me
Up to the swallow thronged loft by the shadow of my hand,
In the moon that is always rising,
Nor that riding to sleep
I should hear him fly with the high fields
And wake to the farm forever fled from the childless land.
Oh as I was young and easy in the mercy of his means,
Time held me green and dying
    Though I sang in my chains like the sea.

THE HARBOR

Carl Sandburg

Passing through huddled and ugly walls,
By doorways where women haggard
Looked from their hunger-deep eyes,
Haunted with shadows of hunger-hands,
Out from the huddled ugly walls,
I came sudden, at the city's edge,
On a blue burst of lake—
Long lake waves breaking under the sun
On a spray-flung curve of shore;
And a fluttering storm of gulls,
Masses of great gray wings
And flying white bellies
Veering and wheeling free in the open.

SONNET

Richard Wilbur

The winter deepening, the hay all in,
The barn fat with cattle, the apple-crop
Conveyed to market or the fragrant bin,
He thinks the time has come to make a stop,

And sinks half-grudging in his firelit seat,
Though with his heavy body's full consent,
In what would be the posture of defeat,
But for that look of rigorous content.

Outside, the night dives down like one great crow
Against his cast-off clothing where it stands
Up to the knees in miles of hustled snow,

Flapping and jumping like a kind of fire,
And floating skyward its abandoned hands
In gestures of invincible desire.

VELVET SHOES

Elinor Wylie

Let us walk in the white snow
    In a soundless space;
With footsteps quiet and slow,
    At a tranquil pace,
Under veils of white lace.

I shall go shod in silk,
    And you in wool,
White as white cow's milk,
    More beautiful
Than breast of gull.

We shall walk through the still town
    In a windless peace;
We shall step upon white down,
    Upon silver fleece,
    Upon softer than these.

We shall walk in velvet shoes:
    Wherever we go
Silence will fall like dews
    On white silence below.
    We shall walk in the snow.

INDIAN SUMMER

Wilfred Campbell

Along the line of smoky hills
    The crimson forest stands,
And all the day the blue-jay calls
    Throughout the autumn lands.

Now by the brook the maple leans
    With all his glory spread,
And all the sumachs on the hills
    Have turned their green to red.

Now by great marshes wrapt in mist,
   Or past some river's mouth,
Throughout the long, still autumn day
   Wild birds are flying south.

THE OAK

Alfred, Lord Tennyson

Live thy Life,
   Young and old,
Like yon oak,
Bright in spring,
   Living gold;

Summer-rich
   Then; and then
Autumn-changed,
Soberer-hued
   Gold again.

All his leaves
   Fallen at length,
Look, he stands,
Trunk and bough,
   Naked strength.

BEACH HOUSE

Mary Rita Hurley

Drive the pilings deep!
Safe from the sweep
Of the sea,
Or foamy fingers
Coming at high tide
Will search out
Every weakness,
Every flaw.

Even so,
Along the shore
There'll always be
Driftwood
At low tide:
A rotting spar,
The splintered jag
Of mast,
A fishing float
Or flag—
Grayed harbingers
Of fate,
Long dead reminders
That the sea
Can wait.

NIGHTINGALES

Robert Bridges

Beautiful must be the mountains whence ye come,
And bright in the fruitful valleys the streams wherefrom
    Ye learn your song:
Where are those starry woods? O might I wander there,
    Among the flowers, which in that heavenly air
        Bloom the year long!

Nay, barren are those mountains and spent the streams:
Our song is the voice of desire, that haunts our dreams,
    A throe of the heart,
Whose pining visions dim, forbidden hopes profound,
    No dying cadence nor long sigh can sound,
        For all our art.

Alone, aloud in the raptured ear of men
We pour our dark nocturnal secret; and then,
    As night is withdrawn
From these sweet-springing meads and bursting boughs of May,
Dream, while the innumerable choir of day
    Welcome the dawn.

ANIMALS

Walt Whitman

I think I could turn and live with animals, they are so placid and self-
 contained;
I stand and look at them long and long.
They do not sweat and whine about their condition;
They do not lie awake in the dark and weep for their sins;
They do not make me sick discussing their duty to God;
Not one is dissatisfied—not one is demented with the mania of
 owning things;
Not one kneels to another, nor to his kind that lived thousands of
 years ago;
Not one is respectable or industrious over the whole earth.

THE SNOW

Emily Dickinson

It sifts from leaden sieves,
It powders all the wood,
It fills with alabaster wool
The wrinkles of the road.

It makes an even face
Of mountain and of plain,—
Unbroken forehead from the east
Unto the east again.

It reaches to the fence,
It wraps it, rail by rail,
Till it is lost in fleeces;
It flings a crystal veil

On stump and stack and stem,—
The summer's empty room,
Acres of seams where harvests were,
Recordless, but for them.

It ruffles wrists of posts,
As ankles of a queen,—
Then stills its artisans like ghosts,
Denying they have been.

HAZE

Henry David Thoreau

Woof of the sun, ethereal gauze,
Woven of Nature's richest stuffs,
Visible heat, air-water, and dry sea,
Last conquest of the eye;
Toil of the day displayed, sun-dust,
Aerial surf upon the shores of earth,
Ethereal estuary, firth of light,
Breakers of air, billows of heat,
Fine summer spray on inland seas;
Bird of the sun, transparent-winged,
Owlet of noon, soft-pinioned,
From heath or stubble rising without song,—
Establish thy serenity o'er the fields.

FABLE

Ralph Waldo Emerson

The mountain and the squirrel
Had a quarrel;
And the former called the latter "Little Prig."
Bun replied,
"You are doubtless very big;
But all sorts of things and weather
Must be taken in together
To make up a year
And a sphere.

And I think it's no disgrace
To occupy my place.
If I'm not so large as you,
You are not so small as I,
And not half so spry.
I'll not deny you make
A very pretty squirrel track;
Talents differ: all is well and wisely put;
If I cannot carry forests on my back,
Neither can you crack a nut."

IN A WOOD
From *The Woodlanders*
Thomas Hardy

Pale beech and pine so blue,
   Set in one clay,
Bough to bough cannot you
   Live out your day?
When the rains skim and skip,
Why mar sweet comradeship,
Blighting with poison-drip
   Neighbourly spray?

Heart-halt and spirit-lame,
   City-opprest,
Unto this wood I came
   As to a nest;
Dreaming that sylvan peace
Offered the harrowed ease—
Nature a soft release
   From men's unrest.

But, having entered in,
   Great growths and small
Show them to men akin—
   Combatants all!
Sycamore shoulders oak,
Bines the slim sapling yoke,
Ivy-spun altars choke
   Elms stout and tall.

Touches from ash, O wych,
   Sting you like scorn!
You, too, brave hollies, twitch
   Sidelong from thorn.
Even the rank poplars bear
Lothly a rival's air,
Cankering in black despair.
   If overborne.

Since, then, no grace I find
   Taught me of trees,
Turn I back to my kind,
   Worthy as these.
There at least smiles abound,
There discourse trills around,
There, now and then, are found
   Life-loyalties.

LEAVES

Sara Teasdale

One by one, like leaves from a tree,
All my faiths have forsaken me;
But the stars above my head
Burn in white and delicate red,
And beneath my feet the earth
Brings the sturdy grass to birth.
I who was content to be
But a silken-singing tree,
But a rustle of delight
In the wistful heart of night—
I have lost the leaves that knew
Touch of rain and weight of dew.
Blinded by a leafy crown,
I looked neither up nor down—
But the little leaves that die
Have left me room to see the sky;
Now for the first time I know
Stars above and earth below.

SPRING

William Blake

Sound the flute!
Now it's mute.
Birds delight
Day and Night;
Nightingale
In the dale,
Lark in Sky,
Merrily,
Merrily, merrily, to welcome in the Year.

Little Boy,
Full of joy:
Little Girl,
Sweet and small;
Cock does crow,
So do you;
Merry voice,
Infant noise,
Merrily, merrily, to welcome in the Year.

Little Lamb
Here I am;
Come and lick
My white neck;
Let me pull
Your soft Wool;
Let me kiss
Your soft face;
Merrily, merrily, we welcome in the Year.

SONG OF MAY MORNING

John Milton

Now the bright morning-star, day's harbinger,
Comes dancing from the east, and leads with her
The flowery May, who from her green lap throws

The yellow cowslip, and the pale primrose.
Hail, bounteous May, that dost inspire
Mirth, and youth, and warm desire:
Woods and groves are of thy dressing,
Hill and dale doth boast thy blessing.
Thus we salute thee with our early song,
And welcome thee, and wish thee long.

TO PRIMROSES
Filled With Morning Dew.
Robert Herrick

Why do ye weep, sweet babes? Can tears
Speak grief in you,
Who were but born
Just as the modest morn
Teemed her refreshing dew?
Alas! ye have not known that shower
That mars a flower:
Nor felt the unkind
Breath of a blasting wind;
Nor are ye worn with years;
Or warped as we,
Who think it strange to see
Such pretty flowers, like to orphans young.
Speaking by tears before ye have a tongue.

Speak, whimpering younglings, and make known
The reason why
Ye droop and weep.
Is it for want of sleep,
Or childish lullaby?
Or that ye have not seen as yet
The violet?
Or brought a kiss
From that sweetheart to this?
No, no; this sorrow shown
By your tears shed,
Would have this lecture read:
That things of greatest, so of meanest worth,
Conceived with grief are, and with tears brought forth.

MY HEART LEAPS UP

William Wordsworth

My heart leaps up when I behold
   A rainbow in the sky:
So was it when my life began,
So is it now I am a man,
So be it when I shall grow old
   Or let me die!
The Child is father of the Man:
And I could wish my days to be
Bound each to each by natural piety.

THE RIVALS

James Stephens

I heard a bird at dawn
Singing sweetly on a tree,
That the dew was on the lawn,
And the wind was on the lea;
But I didn't listen to him,
For he didn't sing to me!

I didn't listen to him,
For he didn't sing to me
That the dew was on the lawn,
And the wind was on the lea!
I was singing at the time,
Just as prettily as he!

I was singing all the time,
Just as prettily as he,
About the dew upon the lawn,
And the wind upon the lea!
So I didn't listen to him,
As he sang upon a tree!

LITTLE AIR

Stéphane Mallarmé
Translated by Roger Fry

Just a solitude
Without the swan and quay
Mirrors its loneliness
In the look which I turned

Here from the glitter
Too high to touch
In which the sky's streaked
With sunset golds

But languidly coasts
Like white linen doffed
Some shy bird it plunges
Exulting beside

In the billow become you
Your nude jubilation

TO A SNOWFLAKE

Francis Thompson

What heart could have thought you?—
Past our devisal
(O filigree petal!)
Fashioned so purely,
Fragilely, surely,
From what Paradisal
Imagineless metal,
Too costly for cost?
Who hammered you, wrought you,
From argentine vapour?—
'God was my shaper.
Passing surmisal,
He hammered, He wrought me,
From curled silver vapour,
To lust of His mind:—

Thou could'st not have thought me!
So purely, so palely,
Tinily, surely,
Mightily, frailly,
Insculped and embossed,
With His hammer of wind,
And His graver of frost.'

BARTER

Marie Blake

I will exchange a city for a sunset,
The tramp of legions for a wind's wild cry;
And all the braggart thrusts of steel triumphant
For one far summit, blue against the sky.

THE WEST WIND

John Masefield

It's a warm wind, the west wind, full of birds' cries;
I never hear the west wind but tears are in my eyes.
For it comes from the west lands, the old brown hills,
And April's in the west wind, and daffodils.

It's a fine land, the west land, for hearts as tired as mine,
Apple orchards blossom there, and the air's like wine.
There is cool green grass there, where men may lie at rest,
And the thrushes are in song there, fluting from the nest.

"Will ye not come home, brother? ye have been long away,
It's April, and blossom time, and white is the may;
And bright is the sun, brother, and warm is the rain,—
Will ye not come home, brother, home to us again?

"The young corn is green, brother, where the rabbits run,
It's blue sky, and white clouds, and warm rain and sun.
It's song to man's soul, brother, fire to man's brain,
To hear the wild bees and see the merry spring again.

"Larks are singing in the west, brother, above the green wheat,
So will ye not come home, brother, and rest your tired feet?
I've a balm for bruised hearts, brother, sleep for aching eyes,"
Says the warm wind, the west wind, full of birds' cries.

It's the white road westwards is the road I must tread
To the green grass, the cool grass, and rest for heart and head,
To the violets and the warm hearts and the thrushes' song,
In the fine land, the west land, the land where I belong.

WHO HAS SEEN THE WIND?

Christina Rossetti

Who has seen the wind?
  Neither I nor you:
But when the leaves hang trembling,
  The wind is passing through.

Who has seen the wind?
  Neither you nor I:
But when the trees bow down their heads,
  The wind is passing by.

WINTER NIGHT

Robert Fitzgerald

The grey day left the dusk in doubt.
Now it is dark.
Nightfall and no stars are out,
But this black wind will set its mark
Like anger on the souls that stir
From chimney side or sepulcher.

From hill to pasture moans the snow.
The farms hug tight
Their shaking ribs against the blow.
There is no mercy in this night
Nor scruple to its wrath. The dead
Sleep light this wind being overhead.

THE SNOW FALL

Archibald MacLeish

Quietness clings to the air.
Quietness gathers the bell
To a great distance.
Listen!
This is the snow.
This is the slow
Chime
The snow
Makes.
It encloses us.
Time in the snow is alone:
Time in the snow is at last,
Is past.

A WEIGHTLESS ELEMENT

Gottfried Benn
Translated by Christopher Middleton

When like wistaria against this wall
around you rings a weightless element
then is the time that you lament
being not rich and inexhaustible,

not like the blossom, or like the light:
in rays arriving, changing its design,
acting on forms akin to it
that, ringed in single ecstasy, entwine,

the single velvet ground where things repose,
so lush, so undivided, and
with time according, self-confined,
go not the way lamenting goes.

GRASS

Carl Sandburg

Pile the bodies high at Austerlitz and Waterloo.
Shovel them under and let me work—
              I am the grass; I cover all.
And pile them high at Gettysburg
And pile them high at Ypres and Verdun.
Shovel them under and let me work.
Two years, ten years, and passengers ask the conductor:
              What place is this?
              Where are we now?

              I am the grass.
              Let me work.

THE ELEPHANT IS SLOW TO MATE

D. H. Lawrence

The elephant, the huge old beast is slow to mate;
he finds a female, they show no haste they wait

for the sympathy in their vast shy hearts slowly, slowly to rouse
as they loiter along the river-beds and drink and browse

and dash in panic through the brake of forest with the herd,
and sleep in massive silence, and wake together, without a word.

So slowly the great hot elephant hearts grow full of desire,
and the great beasts mate in secret at last, hiding their fire.

Oldest they are and the wisest of beasts so they know at last
how to wait for the loneliest of feasts for the full repast.

They do not snatch, they do not tear; their massive blood
moves as the moon-tides, near, more near till they touch in flood.

In the American Grain

POEMS IN OUR HISTORY

Patriotism generally makes poor poetry. The poet's loyalties are to art and to humanity. And these have no particular nationality. But like his less articulate fellow man the poet is shaped by the land he is given to, and be he Bengali or American the place of his home finds a place in his poetry. The native American influence can be perceived only dimly in some poetry—Eliot's or Pound's. Other poets (some, like Bertolt Brecht, from other lands) have consciously addressed themselves to the American experience. The image they have given us is beautiful and ugly, uplifting and depressing, but always changing and alive. Here is a short selection of these poems written in the American grain.

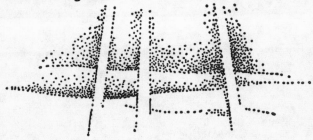

TO THE WESTERN WORLD
Louis Simpson

A siren sang, and Europe turned away
From the high castle and the shepherd's crook.
Three caravels went sailing to Cathay
On the strange ocean, and the captains shook
Their banners out across the Mexique Bay.

And in our early days we did the same.
Remembering our fathers in their wreck
We crossed the sea from Palos where they came
And saw, enormous to the little deck,
A shore in silence waiting for a name.

The treasures of Cathay were never found.
In this America, this wilderness
Where the axe echoes with a lonely sound,
The generations labor to possess
And grave by grave we civilize the ground.

A MAN SAW A BALL
OF GOLD IN THE SKY
Stephen Crane

A man saw a ball of gold in
        the sky;
He climbed for it,
And eventually he achieved
        it—
It was clay.

Now this is the strange part:
When the man went to the
        earth
And looked again,
Lo, there was the ball of gold.
Now this is the strange part:
It was a ball of gold.
Ay, by the heavens, it was a
        ball of gold.

THE INDIAN BURYING GROUND

Philip Freneau

In spite of all the learned have said,
　　I still my old opinion keep;
The posture, that we give the dead,
　　Points out the soul's eternal sleep.

Not so the ancients of these lands—
　　The Indian, when from life released,
Again is seated with his friends,
　　And shares again the joyous feast.

His imaged birds, and painted bowl,
　　And venison, for a journey dressed,
Bespeak the nature of the soul,
　　Activity, that knows no rest.

His bow, for action ready bent,
　　And arrows, with a head of stone,
Can only mean that life is spent,
　　And not the old ideas gone.

Thou, stranger, that shalt come this way,
　　No fraud upon the dead commit—
Observe the swelling turf, and say
　　They do not lie, but here they sit.

Here still a lofty rock remains,
　　On which the curious eye may trace
(Now wasted, half, by wearing rains)
　　The fancies of a ruder race.

Here still an aged elm aspires,
　　Beneath whose far-projecting shade
(And which the shepherd still admires)
　　The children of the forest played!

There oft a restless Indian queen
　　(Pale Shebah, with her braided hair)
And many a barbarous form is seen
　　To chide the man that lingers there.

By midnight moons, o'er moistening dews;
  In habit for the chase arrayed,
The hunter still the deer pursues,
  The hunter and the deer, a shade!

And long shall timorous fancy see
  The painted chief, and pointed spear,
And Reason's self shall bow the knee
  To shadows and delusions here.

THE JAZZ OF THIS HOTEL

Vachel Lindsay

Why do I curse the jazz of this hotel?
I like the slower tom-toms of the sea;
I like the slower tom-toms of the thunder;
I like the more deliberate dancing knee
Of outdoor love, of outdoor talk and wonder.
I like the slower deeper violin
Of the wind across the fields of Indian corn;
I like the far more ancient violoncello
Of whittling loafers telling stories mellow
Down at the village grocery in the sun;
I like the slower bells that ring for church
Across the Indiana landscape old.
Therefore I curse the jazz of this hotel
That seems so hot, but is so hard and cold.

THE FORGOTTEN CITY

William Carlos Williams

When I was coming down from the country
with my mother, the day of the storm,
trees were across the road and small branches
kept rattling on the roof of the car.

There was ten feet or more of water
making the parkways impassable with the wind
bringing more rain in sheets. Brown torrents
gushed up through new sluiceways in the
valley floor so that I had to take any road
I could find bearing to the south and west,
to get back to the city. I passed through
extraordinary places, as vivid as any
I ever saw where the storm had broken
the barrier and let through
a strange commonplace: Long, deserted avenues
with unrecognized names at the corners and
drunken looking people with completely
foreign manners. Monuments, institutions
and in one place a large body of water
startled me with an acre or more of hot
jets spouting up symmetrically over it. Parks.
I had no idea where I was and promised
myself I would some day go back to study
this curious and industrious people who lived
in these apartments, at these sharp
corners and turns of intersecting avenues
with so little apparent communication
with an outside world. How did they get
cut off this way from representation in our
newspapers and other means of publicity
when so near the metropolis, so closely
surrounded by the familiar and the famous.

ROUGE BOUQUET

Joyce Kilmer

In a wood they call the Rouge Bouquet
There is a new-made grave to-day,
Built by never a spade nor pick
Yet covered with earth ten metres thick.

There lie many fighting men,
    Dead in their youthful prime,
Never to laugh nor love again
    Nor taste the Summertime.
For Death came flying through the air
And stopped his flight at the dugout stair,
Touched his prey and left them there,
    Clay to clay.
He hid their bodies stealthily
In the soil of the land they fought to free
    And fled away.
Now over the grave abrupt and clear
    Three volleys ring;
And perhaps their brave young spirits hear
    The bugle sing:
"Go to sleep!
Slumber well where the shell screamed and fell.
Let your rifles rest on the muddy floor,
You will not need them any more.
Danger's past;
Now at last,
Go to sleep!"
There is on earth no worthier grave
To hold the bodies of the brave
Than this place of pain and pride
Where they nobly fought and nobly died.
Never fear but in the skies
    Saints and angels stand
Smiling with their holy eyes
    On this new-come band.
St. Michael's sword darts through the air
And touches the aureole on his hair
As he sees them stand saluting there,
    His stalwart sons:
And Patrick, Bridgid, Columkill
Rejoice that in veins of warriors still
    The Gael's blood runs.
And up to Heaven's doorway floats,
    From the wood called Rouge Bouquet,
A delicate cloud of bugle notes

That softly say:
"Farewell! Farewell.
Comrades true, born anew, peace to you!
Your souls shall be where the heroes are
And your memory shine like the morning-star.
Brave and dear,
Shield us here.
Farewell!"

ABRAHAM LINCOLN WALKS AT MIDNIGHT

Vachel Lindsay

(In Springfield, Illinois)
It is portentous, and a thing of state
That here at midnight, in our little town
A mourning figure walks, and will not rest,
Near the old court-house pacing up and down,

Or by his homestead, or in shadowed yards
He lingers where his children used to play,
Or through the market, on the well-worn stones
He stalks until the dawn-stars burn away.

A bronzed, lank man! His suit of ancient black,
A famous high top-hat and plain worn shawl
Make him the quaint great figure that men love,
The prairie-lawyer, master of us all.

He cannot sleep upon his hillside now.
He is among us:—as in times before!
And we who toss and lie awake for long
Breathe deep, and start, to see him pass the door.

His head is bowed. He thinks on men and kings.
Yes, when the sick world cries, how can he sleep?
Too many peasants fight, they know not why,
Too many homesteads in black terror weep.

The sins of all the war-lords burn his heart.
He sees the dreadnaughts scouring every main.
He carries on his shawl-wrapped shoulders now
The bitterness, the folly and the pain.

He cannot rest until a spirit-dawn
Shall come;—the shining hope of Europe free:
The league of sober folk, the Workers' Earth,
Bringing long peace to Cornland, Alp and Sea.

It breaks his heart that kings must murder still,
That all his hours of travail here for men
Seem yet in vain. And who will bring white peace
That he may sleep upon his hill again?

THE HILL ABOVE THE MINE

Malcolm Cowley

Nobody comes to the graveyard on the hill,
sprawled on the ash-gray slope above the mine,
where coke-oven fumes drift heavily by day
and creeping fires at night; nobody stirs
here by the crumbled wall, where headstones loom
among the blackberry vines, nobody walks
in the blue starlight under the cedar branches
twisted and black against the moon, or speaks
except the unquiet company of the dead,

and one who calls the roll:
                    "Ezekiel Cowley?"
Dead.

        "Laban and Uriah Evans?"
                    Dead.

"Jasper McCullough, your three wives, your thirty
children, of whom four bastards?"
                    Dead, all dead,

sleeping under the brambles in the starlight
above the unpainted cabins and the mine.

What have you seen, O dead?
       "We saw our woods
butchered, flames curling in the maple tops,
white ashes drifting, a railroad in the valley
bridging the creek, and mine shafts under the hill.
We saw our farms lie fallow and houses grow
all summer in the flowerless meadows. Rats
all winter gnawed the last husks in the barn.
In spring the waters rose, crept through the fields
and stripped them bare of soil, while on the hill
we waited and stood firm."

       Wait on, O dead!
The waters still shall rise, the hills fold in,
the tombs open to heaven, and you shall ride
eastward on a rain wind, spurring the thunder,
your white bones drifting like herons across the moon.

Rhymes from A BOOK OF AMERICANS

Stephen Vincent Benét
(With Rosemary Benét)

1.

Thomas Jefferson 1743–1826

Thomas Jefferson
What do you say
Under the gravestone
Hidden away?

"I was a giver,
I was a moulder,
I was a builder
With a strong shoulder."

Six feet and over,
Large-boned and ruddy,
The eyes grey-hazel
But bright with study.

The big hands clever
With pen and fiddle
And ready, ever,
For any riddle.

From buying empires,
To planting 'taters,
From Declarations
To trick dumb-waiters.

"I liked the people
The sweat and crowd of them,
Trusted them always
And spoke aloud of them.

"I liked all learning
And wished to share it
Abroad like pollen
For all who merit.

"I liked queer gadgets
And secret shelves,
And helping nations
To rule themselves."

2.

John Quincy Adams 1767–1848

When President John Quincy
Set out to take a swim,
He'd hang his Presidential clothes
Upon a hickory limb
And bound in the Potomac
Like a dolphin on the swell.
—He was extremely dignified
But rather plump, as well.
And when Supreme Court Justices
Remarked, from a canoe,
"Our Presidents don't do such things."
He merely said, "I do."
He never asked what people thought
But gave them tit for tat.
The Adamses have always been
Remarkably like that.

3.

Daniel Boone 1797–1879

When Daniel Boone goes by at night
The phantom deer arise
And all lost, wild America
Is burning in their eyes.

MILLIONS ARE LEARNING HOW

James Agee

From now on kill America out of your mind.
America is dead these hundred years.
You've better work to do, and things to find:
  Waste neither time nor tears.

See, rather, all the millions and all the land
Mutually shapen as a child of love.
As individual as a hand
  And to be thought highly of.

The wrinkling mountains stay: the master stream
Still soils the Gulf a hundred amber miles:
A people as a creature in a dream
  Not yet awakened, smiles.

Those poisons which were low along the air
Like mists, like mists are lifting. Even now,
Thousands are breathing health in, here and there:
  Millions are learning how.

HOMESICK BLUES

Langston Hughes

De railroad bridge's
A sad song in de air.
De railroad bridge's
A sad song in de air.
Ever' time de trains pass
I wants to go somewhere.

I went down to de station;
Ma heart was in ma mouth.
Went down to de station;
Heart was in ma mouth.
Lookin' for a box car
To roll me to de South.

Homesick blues, Lawd,
'S a terrible thing to have.
Homesick blues is
A terrible thing to have.
To keep from cryin'
I opens ma mouth an' laughs.

JOHN SUTTER

Yvor Winters

I was the patriarch of the shining land,
Of the blond summer and metallic grain;
Men vanished at the motion of my hand,
And when I beckoned they would come again.

The earth grew dense with grain at my desire;
The shade was deepened at the springs and streams;
Moving in dust that clung like pillared fire,
The gathering herds grew heavy in my dreams.

Across the mountains, naked from the heights,
Down to the valley broken settlers came,
And in my houses feasted through the nights,
Rebuilt their sinews and assumed a name.

In my clear rivers my own men discerned
The motive for the ruin and the crime—
Gold heavier than earth, a wealth unearned,
Loot, for two decades, from the heart of Time.

Metal, intrinsic value, deep and dense,
Preanimate, inimitable, still,
Real, but an evil with no human sense,
Dispersed the mind to concentrate the will.

Grained by alchemic change, the human kind
Turned from themselves to rivers and to rocks;
With dynamite broke metal unrefined;
Measured their moods by geologic shocks.

With knives they dug the metal out of stone;
Turned rivers back, for gold through ages piled,
Drove knives to hearts, and faced the gold alone;
Valley and river ruined and reviled;

Reviled and ruined me, my servant slew,
Strangled him from the fig tree by my door.
When they had done what fury bade them do,
I was cursing a beggar, stripped and sore.

What end impersonal, what breathless age,
Incontinent of quiet and of years,
What calm catastrophe will yet assuage
This final drouth of penitential tears?

ODE FOR THE AMERICAN DEAD IN KOREA

Thomas McGrath

1.

God love you now, if no one else will ever,
Corpse in the paddy, or dead on a high hill
In the fine and ruinous summer of a war
You never wanted. All your false flags were
Of bravery and ignorance, like grade school maps:
Colors of countries you would never see—
Until that weekend in eternity
When, laughing, well armed, perfectly ready to kill
The world and your brother, the safe commanders sent
You into your future. Oh, dead on a hill,
Dead in a paddy, leeched and tumbled to
A tomb of footnotes. We mourn a changeling: you:
Handselled to poverty and drummed to war
By distinguished masters whom you never knew.

The bee that spins his metal from the sun,
The shy mole drifting like a miner ghost
Through midnight earth—all happy creatures run
As strict as trains on rails the circuits of
Blind instinct. Happy in your summer follies,
You mined a culture that was mined for war:
The state to mold you, church to bless, and always
The elders to confirm you in your ignorance.
No scholar put your thinking cap on nor
Warned that in dead seas fishes died in schools
Before inventing legs to walk the land.
The rulers stuck a tennis racket in your hand,
An Ark against the flood. In time of change
Courage is not enough: the blind mole dies,
And you on your hill, who did not know the rules.

3.

Wet in the windy counties of the dawn
The lone crow skirls his draggled passage home:
And God (whose sparrows fall aslant his gaze,
Like grace or confetti) blinks and he is gone,
And you are gone. Your scarecrow valor grows
And rusts like early lilac while the rose
Blooms in Dakota and the stock exchange
Flowers. Roses, rents, all things conspire
To crown your death with wreaths of living fire.
And the public mourners come: the politic tear
Is cast in the Forum. But, in another year,
We will mourn you, whose fossil courage fills
The limestone histories: brave: ignorant: amazed:
Dead in the rice paddies, dead on the nameless hills.

ANNE RUTLEDGE

Edgar Lee Masters

Out of me unworthy and unknown
The vibrations of deathless music:
"With malice toward none, with charity for all."
Out of me the forgiveness of millions toward millions,

And the beneficent face of a nation
Shining with justice and truth.
I am Anne Rutledge who sleeps beneath these weeds,
Beloved in life of Abraham Lincoln,
Wedded to him, not through union,
But through separation.
Bloom forever, O Republic,
From the dust of my bosom!

THE CREATION
A Negro Sermon
James Weldon Johnson

And God stepped out on space,
And He looked around and said:
I'm lonely—
I'll make me a world.

And far as the eye of God could see
Darkness covered everything,
Blacker than a hundred midnights
Down in cypress swamp.

Then God smiled,
And the light broke,
And the darkness rolled up on one side,
And the light stood shining on the other,
And God said: That's good!

Then God reached out and took the light in His hands,
And God rolled the light around in His hands
Until He made the sun;
And He set that sun a-blazing in the heavens.
And the light that was left from making the sun
God gathered it up in a shining ball
And flung it against the darkness,
Spangling the night with the moon and stars.
Then down between
The darkness and the light
He hurled the world;
And God said: That's good!

Then God himself stepped down—
And the sun was on His right hand,
And the moon was on His left;
The stars were clustered about His head,
And the earth was under His feet.
And God walked, and where He trod
His footsteps hollowed the valleys out
And bulged the mountains up.

Then He stopped and looked and saw
That the earth was hot and barren.
So God stepped over to the edge of the world
And He spat out the seven seas—
He batted His eyes, and the lightnings flashed—
He clapped His hands, and the thunders rolled—
And the waters above the earth came down,
The cooling waters came down.

Then the green grass sprouted,
And the little red flowers blossomed,
The pine tree pointed his finger to the sky,
And the oak spread out his arms,
The lakes cuddled down in the hollows of the ground,
The rivers ran down to the sea;
And God smiled again,
And the rainbow appeared,
And curled itself around His shoulder.

Then God raised His arm and He waved His hand
Over the sea and over the land,
And He said: Bring forth! Bring forth!
And quicker than God could drop His hand,
Fishes and fowls
And beasts and birds
Swam the rivers and the seas,
Roamed the forests and the woods,
And split the air with their wings.
And God said: That's good!

Then God walked around,
And God looked around
On all that He had made.
He looked at His sun,
And He looked at His moon,
And He looked at His little stars;
He looked on His world
With all its living things,
And God said: I'm lonely still.

Then God sat down
On the side of a hill where He could think;
By a deep wide river He sat down;
With His head in His hands,
God thought and thought,
Till He thought: I'll make me a man!

Up from the bed of the river
God scooped the clay;
And by the bank of the river
He kneeled Him down;
And there the great God Almighty
Who lit the sun and fixed it in the sky,
Who flung the stars to the most far corner of the night,
Who rounded the earth in the middle of His hand;
The Great God,
Like a mammy bending over her baby,
Kneeled down in the dust
Toiling over a lump of clay
Till He shaped it in His own image;

Then into it He blew the breath of life,
And man became a living soul.
Amen. Amen.

I WENT TO THE CITY
Kenneth Patchen

I went to the city
And there I did weep,
Men a-crowin' like asses,
And livin' like sheep.
Oh, can't hold the han' of my love!
Can't hold her little white han'!
Yes, I went to the city,
And there I did bitterly cry,
Men out of touch with the earth,
And with never a glance at the sky.
Oh, can't hold the han' of my love!
Can't hold her pure little han'!

TO BROOKLYN BRIDGE
Hart Crane

How many dawns, chill from his rippling rest
The seagull's wings shall dip and pivot him,
Shedding white rings of tumult, building high
Over the chained bay waters Liberty—

Then, with inviolate curve, forsake our eyes
As apparitional as sails that cross
Some page of figures to be filed away;
—Till elevators drop us from our day . . .

I think of cinemas, panoramic sleights
With multitudes bent toward some flashing scene
Never disclosed, but hastened to again,
Foretold to other eyes on the same screen;

And Thee, across the harbour, silver-paced
As though the sun took step of thee, yet left
Some motion ever unspent in thy stride,—
Implicity thy freedom staying thee!

Out of some subway scuttle, cell or loft
A bedlamite speeds to thy parapets,
Tilting there momently, shrill shirt ballooning,
A jest falls from the speechless caravan.

Down Wall, from girder into street noon leaks,
A rip-tooth of the sky's acetylene;
All afternoon the cloud-flown derricks turn . . .
Thy cables breathe the North Atlantic still.

And obscure as that heaven of the Jews,
Thy guerdon . . . Accolade thou dost bestow
Of anonymity time cannot raise:
Vibrant reprieve and pardon thou dost show.

O harp and altar, of the fury fused,
(How could mere toil align thy choiring strings!)
Terrific threshold of the prophet's pledge,
Prayer of pariah, and the lover's cry,—

Again the traffic lights that skim thy swift
Unfractioned idiom, immaculate sigh of stars,
Beading thy path—condense eternity:
And we have seen night lifted in thine arms.

Under thy shadow by the piers I waited;
Only in darkness is thy shadow clear.
The City's fiery parcels all undone,
Already snow submerges an iron year . . .

O Sleepless as the river under thee,
Vaulting the sea, the prairies' dreaming sod,
Unto us lowliest sometime sweep, descend
And of the curveship lend a myth to God.

A GREEN AND PLEASANT LAND

John Peale Bishop

It was strange, O strange
That all this rose
Out of our forests:

Foundries exuding
A new sky: constant sunsets,
Suffocations of smoked cloud.

The fishes died;
Landscapes of slag, acids corroded
The green stream.

Engineers invented
Rapid metallic streams,
Sierras of anthracite, sulphur dawns,

Inhabited by sturdy grimaces
Of grime; besotted men
Who moved their muscles to another's mind.

CHILDREN OF LIGHT

Robert Lowell

Our Fathers wrung their bread from stocks and stones
And fenced their gardens with the Redman's bones;
Embarking from the Nether Land of Holland,
Pilgrims unhouseled by Geneva's night,
You planted here the Serpent's seeds of light;
And here the pivoting searchlights probe to shock
The riotous glass houses built on rock,
And candles gutter in a hall of mirrors,
And light is where the ancient blood of Cain
Is burning, burning the unburied grain.

CHICAGO

Carl Sandburg

Hog Butcher for the World,
Tool Maker, Stacker of Wheat,
Player with Railroads and the Nation's Freight Handler;
Stormy, husky, brawling,
City of the Big Shoulders:

They tell me you are wicked and I believe them, for I have seen your painted women under the gas lamps luring the farm boys.

And they tell me you are crooked and I answer: Yes, it is true I have seen the gunman kill and go free to kill again.

And they tell me you are brutal and my reply is: On the faces of women and children I have seen the marks of wanton hunger.

And having answered so I turn once more to those who sneer at this my city, and I give them back the sneer and say to them:

Come and show me another city with lifted head singing so proud to be alive and coarse and strong and cunning.

Flinging magnetic curses amid the toil of piling job on job, here is a tall bold slugger set vivid against the little soft cities;

Fierce as a dog with tongue lapping for action, cunning as a savage pitted against the wilderness,

    Bareheaded,

    Shoveling,

    Wrecking,

    Planning

    Building, breaking, rebuilding,

Under the smoke, dust all over his mouth, laughing with white teeth,

Under the terrible burden of destiny laughing as a young man laughs,

Laughing even as an ignorant fighter laughs who has never lost a battle,

Bragging and laughing that under his wrist is the pulse, and under his ribs the heart of the people,

            Laughing!

Laughing the stormy, husky, brawling laughter of Youth, half-naked, sweating, proud to be Hog Butcher, Tool Maker, Stacker of Wheat, Player with Railroads and Freight Handler to the Nation.

TO MAKE A PRAIRIE

Emily Dickinson

To make a prairie it takes a clover
    and one bee,—
One clover, and a bee,
And revery.
The revery alone will do
If bees are few.

OLD IRONSIDES

Oliver Wendell Holmes

Ay, tear her tattered ensign down!
    Long has it waved on high,
And many an eye has danced to see
    That banner in the sky;
Beneath it rung the battle shout,
    And burst the cannon's roar;—
The meteor of the ocean air
    Shall sweep the clouds no more.

Her deck, once red with heroes' blood,
    Where knelt the vanquished foe,
When winds were hurrying o'er the flood,
    And waves were white below,
No more shall feel the victor's tread,
    Or know the conquered knee;—
The harpies of the shore shall pluck
    The eagle of the sea!

Oh, better that her shattered hulk
    Should sink beneath the wave;
Her thunders shook the mighty deep,
    And there should be her grave;
Nail to the mast her holy flag,
    Set every threadbare sail,
And give her to the god of storms,
    The lightning and the gale!

THE VILLAGE BLACKSMITH

Henry Wadsworth Longfellow

Under a spreading chestnut-tree
    The village smithy stands;
The smith, a mighty man is he,
    With large and sinewy hands;
And the muscles of his brawny arms
    Are strong as iron bands.

His hair is crisp, and black, and long,
    His face is like the tan;
His brow is wet with honest sweat,
    He earns whate'er he can,
And looks the whole world in the face,
    For he owes not any man.

Week in, week out, from morn till night,
    You can hear his bellows blow;
You can hear him swing his heavy sledge
    With measured beat and slow,
Like a sexton ringing the village bell,
    When the evening sun is low.

And children coming home from school
    Look in at the open door;
They love to see the flaming forge,
    And hear the bellows roar,
And catch the burning sparks that fly
    Like chaff from a threshing-floor.

He goes on Sunday to the church,
    And sits among his boys;
He hears the parson pray and preach,
    He hears his daughter's voice,
Singing in the village choir,
    And it makes his heart rejoice.

It sounds to him like her mother's voice,
    Singing in Paradise!
He needs must think of her once more,
    How in the grave she lies;
And with his hard, rough hand he wipes
    A tear out of his eyes.

Toiling,—rejoicing,—sorrowing,
    Onward through life he goes;
Each morning sees some task begin,
    Each evening sees it close;
Something attempted, something done,
    Has earned a night's repose.

Thanks, thanks to thee, my worthy friend,
  For the lesson thou hast taught!
Thus at the flaming forge of life
  Our fortunes must be wrought;
Thus on its sounding anvil shaped
  Each burning deed and thought!

O CAPTAIN! MY CAPTAIN!

Walt Whitman

O Captain! my Captain! our fearful trip is done,
The ship has weather'd every rack, the prize we sought is won,
The port is near, the bells I hear, the people all exulting,
While follow eyes the steady keel, the vessel grim and daring;
  But O my heart! heart! heart!
    O the bleeding drops of red,
      Where on the deck my Captain lies,
      Fallen cold and dead.

O Captain! my Captain! rise up and hear the bells;
Rise up—for you the flag is flung—for you the bugle trills,
For you bouquets and ribbon'd wreaths—for you the shores
  a-crowding,
For you they call, the swaying mass, their eager faces turning;
  Here Captain! dear father!
    This arm beneath your head!
      It is some dream that on the deck,
      You've fallen cold and dead.

My Captain does not answer, his lips are pale and still,
My father does not feel my arm, he has no pulse nor will,
The ship is anchor'd safe and sound, its voyage closed and done,
From fearful trip the victor ship comes in with object won;
  Exult O shores, and ring O bells!
    But I with mournful tread,
      Walk the deck my Captain lies,
      Fallen cold and dead.

THE NEW COLOSSUS

Emma Lazarus

Not like the brazen giant of Greek fame,
With conquering limbs astride from land to land;
Here at our sea-washed, sunset gates shall stand
A mighty woman with a torch, whose flame
Is the imprisoned lightning, and her name
Mother of Exiles. From her beacon-hand
Glows world-wide welcome; her mild eyes command
The air-bridged harbor that twin cities frame.
"Keep, ancient lands, your storied pomp!" cries she
With silent lips. "Give me your tired, your poor,
Your huddled masses yearning to breathe free,
The wretched refuse of your teeming shore,
Send these, the homeless, tempest-tost to me,
I lift my lamp beside the golden door."

THE GREEN MOUNTAIN BOYS

William Cullen Bryant

Here we halt our march, and pitch our tent,
   On the rugged forest ground,
And light our fire with the branches rent,
   By winds from the beeches round,
Wild storms have torn this ancient wood,
   But a wilder is at hand,
With hail of iron and rain of blood,
   To sweep and scath the land.

How the dark waste rings with voices shrill,
   That startle the sleeping bird,
Tomorrow eve must the voice be still,
   And the step must fall unheard.
The Briton lies by the blue Champlain,
   In Ticonderoga's towers,
And ere the sun rise twice again,
   The towers and the lake are ours.

Fill up the bowl from the brook that glides,
  Where the fireflies light the brake;
A ruddier juice the Briton hides,
  In his fortress by the lake.
Build high the fire, till the panther leap
  From his lofty perch in fright,
And we'll strengthen our weary arms with sleep,
  For the deeds of tomorrow night.

THE PASTURE

Robert Frost

I'm going out to clean the pasture spring;
I'll only stop to rake the leaves away
(And wait to watch the water clear, I may):
I sha'n't be gone long. —You come too.

I'm going out to fetch the little calf
That's standing by the mother. It's so young,
It totters when she licks it with her tongue.
I sha'n't be gone long. —You come too.

SKYSCRAPER

Carl Sandburg

By day the skyscraper looms in the smoke and sun and has a soul.
Prairie and valley, streets of the city, pour people into it and they
  mingle, among its twenty floors and are poured out again back to
  the streets, prairies and valleys.
It is the men and women, boys and girls so poured in and out all day
  that give the building a soul of dreams and thoughts and memories.
(Dumped in the sea or fixed in a desert, who would care for the
  building or speak its name or ask a policeman the way to it?)

Elevators slide on their cables and tubes catch letters and parcels and iron pipes carry gas and water in and sewage out.

Wires climb with secrets, carry light and carry words, and tell terrors and profits and loves—curses of men grappling plans of business and questions of women in plots of love.

Hour by hour the caissons reach down to the rock of the earth and hold the building to a turning planet.

Hour by hour the girders play as ribs and reach out and hold together the stone walls and floors.

Hour by hour the hand of the mason and the stuff of the mortar clinch the pieces and parts to the shape an architect voted.

Hour by hour the sun and the rain, the air and the rust, and the press of time turning into centuries, play on the building inside and out and use it.

Men who sunk the pilings and mixed the mortar are laid in graves where the wind whistles a wild song without words,

And so are men who strung the wires and fixed the pipes and tubes and those who saw it rise floor by floor.

Souls of them all are here, even the hod carrier begging at back doors hundreds of miles away and the bricklayer who went to state's prison for shooting another man while drunk.

(One man fell from a girder and broke his neck at the end of a straight plunge—he is here—his soul has gone into the stones of the building.)

On the office doors from tier to tier—hundreds of names and each name standing for a face written across a dead child, a passionate lover, a driving ambition for a million dollar business or a lobster's ease of life.

Behind the signs on the doors they work and the walls tell nothing from room to room.

Ten-dollar-a-week stenographers take letters from corporation officers, lawyers, efficiency engineers, and tons of letters go bundled from the building to all ends of the earth.

Smiles and tears of each office girl go into the soul of the building just the same as the master-men who rule the building.

Hands of clocks turn to noon hours and each floor empties its men and some women who go away and eat and come back to work.

Toward the end of the afternoon all work slackens and all jobs go slower as the people feel day closing on them.

One by one the floors are emptied . . . The uniformed elevator men are gone. Pails clang . . . Scrubbers work, talking in foreign tongues. Broom and water and mop clean from the floors human dust and spit, and machine grime of the day.

Spelled in electric fire on the roof are words telling miles of houses and people where to buy a thing for money. The sign speaks till midnight.

Darkness on the hallways. Voices echo. Silence holds . . . Watchmen walk slow from floor to floor and try the doors. Revolvers bulge from their hip pockets . . . Steel safes stand in corners. Money is stacked in them.

A young watchman leans at a window and sees the lights of barges butting their way across a harbor, nets of red and white lanterns in a railroad yard, and a span of glooms splashed with lines of white and blurs of crosses and clusters over the sleeping city.

By night the skycraper looms in the smoke and the stars and has a soul.

I HEAR AMERICA SINGING

Walt Whitman

I hear America singing, the varied carols I hear,
Those of mechanics, each one singing his as it should be blithe and strong,
The carpenter singing his as he measures his plank or beam,
The mason singing his as he makes ready for work, or leaves off work,
The boatman singing what belongs to him in his boat, the deckhand singing on the steamboat deck,
The shoemaker singing as he sits on his bench, the hatter singing as he stands,
The wood-cutter's song, the ploughboy's on his way in the morning, or at noon intermission or at sundown,

The delicious singing of the mother, or of the young wife at work, or
    of the girl sewing or washing,
Each singing what belongs to him or her and to none else,
The day what belongs to the day—at night the party of young fellows,
    robust, friendly,
Singing with open mouths their strong melodious songs.

COAL FOR MIKE

Bertolt Brecht

I have heard how in Ohio
At the beginning of this century
A woman lived in Bidwell,
Mary McCoy, widow of a brakeman,
By the name of Mike McCoy,
Lived in poverty.

But every night from the thundering trains of the Wheeling Railroad
The brakemen heaved some lumps of coal
Over the picket fence into the potato patch,
Shouting briefly in harsh voices:
For Mike!

And every night
As the lumps of coal for Mike
Crashed against the rear wall of the hut
The old woman arose, crept,
Drunk with sleep, into an overcoat and heaped
The lumps of coal to one side,
The lumps of coal,
Gift of the brakemen to Mike, dead
But not forgotten.

And she arose so long before daybreak and heaped
Her gifts away from the eyes of the world so that
The men would not get into trouble
With the Wheeling Railroad.

This poem is dedicated to the comrades
Of the brakeman Mike McCoy
(Died from a weakness of the lungs
On an Ohio coal train)
For comradeship.

EFFORTLESSLY DEMOCRATIC SANTA FE TRAIL

Martha Baird

The Santa Fe Trail,
Broad and long,
Went through Kansas,
Four hundred miles.
To whom did the Santa Fe Trail belong?
It belonged to those who used it,
And it treated all alike.
It was just as broad and long for the little dog trotting beside the
    wagon, as for the man who drove the wagon, and for the man who
    owned the whole wagon train.
It was just as broad and long for all of them:
And sunflowers grew up on both sides of it:
Blessing it.

HYMN SUNG AT THE COMPLETION OF THE
CONCORD MONUMENT APRIL 19, 1836

Ralph Waldo Emerson

By the rude bridge that arched the flood,
    Their flag to April's breeze unfurled,
Here once the embattled farmers stood,
    And fired the shot heard round the world.

The foe long since in silence slept;
    Alike the conqueror silent sleeps;
And Time the ruined bridge has swept
    Down the dark stream which seaward creeps.

On this green bank, by this soft stream,
   We set to-day a votive stone;
That memory may their deed redeem,
   When, like our sires, our sons are gone.

Spirit, that made these heroes dare
   To die, or leave their children free,
Bid Time and Nature gently spare
   The shaft we raise to them and thee.

THE SOLDIER WALKS UNDER
THE TREES OF THE UNIVERSITY

Randall Jarrell

The walls have been shaded for so many years
By the green magnificence of these great lives
Their bricks are darkened till the end of time.
(Small touching whites in the perpetual
Darkness that saturates the unwalled world;
Saved from the sky by leaves, and from the earth by stone)
The pupils trust like flowers to the shades
And interminable twilight of these latitudes.

In our zone innocence is born in banks
And cultured in colonies the rich have sown:
The one is spared here what the many share
To write the histories that others are.
The oak escapes the storm that broke the reeds,
They read here; they read, too, of reeds,
Of storms; and are, almost, sublime
In their read ignorance of everything.

The poor are always—somewhere, but not here;
We learn of them where they and Guilt subsist
With Death and Evil: in books, in books, in books.
Ah, sweet to contemplate the causes, not the things!
The soul learns fortitude in libraries,
Enduring the patience in another's pain,
And pity for the lives we do not change:
All that the world would be, if it were real.

When will the boughs break blazing from these trees,
The darkened walls float heavenward like soot?
The days when men say: "Where we look is fire—
The iron branches flower in my veins?"
In that night even to be rich is difficult,
The world is something even books believe,
The bombs fall all year long among the states,
And the blood is black upon the unturned leaves.

THE SPELL OF THE YUKON
Robert W. Service

I wanted the gold, and I sought it;
   I scrabbled and mucked like a slave.
Was it famine or scurvy—I fought it;
   I hurled my youth into a grave.
I wanted the gold, and I got it—
   Came out with a fortune last fall—
Yet somehow life's not what I thought it,
   And somehow the gold isn't all.

No! There's the land. (Have you seen it?)
   It's the cussedest land that I know,
From the big, dizzy mountains that screen it
   To the deep, deathlike valleys below.
Some say God was tired when He made it;
   Some say it's a fine land to shun;
Maybe; but there's some as would trade it
   For no land on earth—and I'm one.

You come to get rich (damned good reason);
   You feel like an exile at first;
You hate it like hell for a season,
   And then you are worse than the worst.
It grips you like some kinds of sinning;
   It twists you from foe to a friend;
It seems it's been since the beginning;
   It seems it will be to the end.

I've stood in some mighty-mouthed hollow
　　That's plumb-full of hush to the brim;
I've watched the big, husky sun wallow
　　In crimson and gold, and grow dim,
Till the moon set the pearly peaks gleaming,
　　And the stars tumbled out, neck and crop;
And I've thought that I surely was dreaming,
　　With the peace o' the world piled on top.

The summer—no sweeter was ever;
　　The sunshiny woods all athrill;
The grayling aleap in the river,
　　The bighorn asleep on the hill.
The strong life that never knows harness;
　　The wilds where the caribou call;
The freshness, the freedom, the farness—
　　O God! how I'm stuck on it all.

The winter! the brightness that blinds you,
　　The white land locked tight as a drum,
The cold fear that follows and finds you,
　　The silence that bludgeons you dumb.
The snows that are older than history,
　　The woods where the weird shadows slant;
The stillness, the moonlight, the mystery,
　　I've bade 'em good-bye—but I can't.

There's a land where the mountains are nameless,
　　And the rivers all run God knows where;
There are lives that are erring and aimless,
　　And deaths that just hang by a hair;
There are hardships that nobody reckons;
　　There are valleys unpeopled and still;
There's a land—oh, it beckons and beckons,
　　And I want to go back—and I will.

They're making my money diminish;
　　I'm sick of the taste of champagne.
Thank God! when I'm skinned to a finish
　　I'll pike to the Yukon again.
I'll fight—and you bet it's no sham-fight;
　　It's hell!—but I've been there before;
And it's better than this by a damsite—
　　So me for the Yukon once more.

There's gold, and it's haunting and haunting;
    It's luring me on as of old;
Yet it isn't the gold that I'm wanting
    So much as just finding the gold.
It's the great, big, broad land 'way up yonder,
    It's the forests where silence has lease;
It's the beauty that thrills me with wonder,
    It's the stillness that fills me with peace.

A MODERN ROMANCE

Paul Engle

Come live with me and be my wife
And we will lead a packaged life,
Where food, drink, fun, all things save pain
Come neatly wrapped in cellophane.

I am the All-American boy,
Certified as fit for joy,
Elected (best of all the breed)
Hairline most likely to recede.
My parchment scroll to verify
Is stamped in gold and witnessed by
Secretary-Treasurer of
Americans Hundred Per Cent For Love.

You are the All-American girl,
Red toe to artificial curl,
Who passed all tests from skipping rope
And using only Cuddly Soap
To making fire in any weather
By rubbing boy and girl together.

We are the nation's nicest team,
Madison Avenue's magic scheme
To show how boy gets girl: my style
Succeeds by using Denta-Smile.

How merchandised that ceremony!
The minister was scrubbed and bony,
And all was sterile in that room
Except, one hoped, the eager groom.

Married, with advertising's blessing,
We can begin togethernessing.
Before I carry you, my bride,
Across the threshold and inside,
I'll take, to help my milk-fed bones,
Vitamins, minerals and hormones.

Now look how quickly I have fixed
A dry martini (ready-mixed).
So drink to our day, consecrated,
In chairs of leather, simulated.
While you are changing out of those
Nylon, dacron, rayon clothes,
I cook the dinner, without fail
Proving a real American male,
Humble, without too much endurance,
But lots of paid-up life insurance.

From the deep-freeze, to please your wish,
A TV dinner in its dish,
All ready-seasoned, heat it up.
Pour instant water in this cup
On instant coffee from a can.
Be proud, love, of your instant man.
Innocent food, mechanized manna
(Except the delicate banana),
Can you endure—forgive the question—
The messy horrors of digestion?

Even our love is pasteurized,
Our gentle hope homogenized.

And now our pure, hygienic night.
To our voluptuous delight
Your hair is up, restraints are down,
And cream is patted on your frown.
The brand-name mattress on the bed
Is wrapped in paper like fresh bread.
We can, to make our own campfire,
Turn the electric blanket higher.
We will cry, Darling, I do care,
In chastely air-conditioned air.

We've read the books, know what to do,
By science, wife, I offer you
This helpful, vacuum-packed, live nerve
(Just add devotion, dear, and serve).
Hurry! Out back I seem to hear
The landlord's Plymouth prowling near.

If this efficient plan produces
By chance (those awful natural juices!)
That product of a thousand uses,
A Junior, wrapped in elastic
Inexpensive bag of plastic
(Just break the seal and throw away)
From antiseptic throats we'll say:
It was an All-American day.

V-J DAY

John Ciardi

On the tallest day in time the dead came back
Clouds met us in the pastures past a world.
By short wave the releases of a rack
Exploded on the interphone's new word.

Halfway past Iwo we jettisoned to sea
Ten tons of arrows from the Eagle's claws.
They fell and followed. Half nostalgically
We watched them spout a fountain from the troughs.

Lightened, we banked like jays, antennae squawking.
The four wild metal halos of our props
Blurred into time. The interphone was talking
Abracadabra to the cumulus tops:

Dreamboat three-one to Yearsend—loud and clear,
Angels one-two, on course at one-six-nine.
Magellan to Balboa, Propwash to Century.
How do you read me? Bombay to Valentine.

Fading and out. And all the dead were homing.
(Wisecrack to Halfmast. Doom to Memory.)
On the tallest day in time we saw them coming,
Wheels jammed, and flaming, on a metal sea.

GREAT FARM

Philip Booth

In April, when raining is sunlight,
when dawn is a coarse young crow,
as willows bend to feather
the Great Farm springs to grow.

The orchard is loud: bees
and blossoms claim the bough;
a meadow of frogs, a sky
of swallows, flood the air now.

Two girls ride two white horses
(the world is green to plow!)
and sideways a big man with buckets
sets hugely to milk a big cow.

SUNDAY: NEW GUINEA

Karl Shapiro

The bugle sounds the measured call to prayers,
The band starts bravely with a clarion hymn,
From every side, singly, in groups, in pairs,
Each to his kind of service comes to worship Him.

Our faces washed, our hearts in the right place,
We kneel or stand or listen from our tents;
Half-naked natives with their kind of grace
Move down the road with balanced staffs like mendicants.

And over the hill the guns bang like a door
And planes repeat their mission in the heights.
The jungle outmaneuvers creeping war
And crawls within the circle of our sacred rites.

I long for our disheveled Sundays home,
Breakfast, the comics, news of latest crimes,
Talk without reference, and palindromes,
Sleep and the Philharmonic and the ponderous *Times*.

I long for lounging in the afternoons
Of clean intelligent warmth, my brother's mind,
Books and thin plates and flowers and shining spoons,
And your love's presence, snowy, beautiful, and kind.

from "IS 5"

E. E. Cummings

my sweet old etcetera
aunt lucy during the recent

war could and what
is more did tell you just
what everybody was fighting

for,
my sister

isabel created hundreds
(and
hundreds)of socks not to
mention shirts fleaproof earwarmers

etcetera wristers etcetera,my
mother hoped that

i would die etcetera
bravely of course my father used
to become hoarse talking about how it was
a privilege and if only he
could meanwhile my

self etcetera lay quietly
in the deep mud et

cetera
(dreaming,
et cetera,of
Your smile
eyes knees and of your Etcetera)

In the Great Tradition

POEMS WITH A HERITAGE

These are poems from the past. Many of the giants are here: Vergil, Dante, Shakespeare, Milton, Rilke. Verses from the Greek Anthology, haiku from Japan, ballads from ancient Spain and Ireland, lyrics from the middle ages, narratives from the nineteenth century—the history of poetry passes by in outline. There is only one poem from a contemporary writer. It is "Poem in October," written by the Byronic meteor Dylan Thomas. The reason it was chosen is because it represents the seemingly ageless stance of the poet at the height of his manhood confronting the world with his presence and inquiring, "What of my life?"

THE OLD FAMILIAR FACES

Charles Lamb

I have had playmates, I have had companions,
In my days of childhood, in my joyful school-days;
All, all are gone, the old familiar faces.

I have been laughing, I have been carousing,
Drinking late, sitting late, with my bosom cronies;
All, all are gone, the old familiar faces.

I loved a love once, fairest among women;
Closed are her doors on me, I must not see her—
All, all are gone, the old familiar faces.

I have a friend, a kinder friend has no man;
Like an ingrate, I left my friend abruptly;
Left him, to muse on the old familiar faces.

Ghost-like I paced round the haunts of my childhood.
Earth seemed a desert I was bound to traverse,
Seeking to find the old familiar faces.

Friend of my bosom, thou more than a brother,
Why wert not thou born in my father's dwelling?
So might we talk of the old familiar faces—

How some they have died, and some they have left me,
And some are taken from me; all are departed;
All, all are gone, the old familiar faces.

THE END OF THE YEAR

Su Tung P'o

Translated by Kenneth Rexroth

When a friend starts on a journey of a thousand miles,
As he is about to leave, he delays again and again.
When men part, they feel they may never meet again.
When a year has gone, how will you ever find it again?
I wonder where it has gone, this year that is ended?
Certainly someplace far beyond the horizon.
It is gone like a river which flows to the East,
And empties into the sea without hope of return.
My neighbors on the left are heating wine.
On the right they are roasting a fat pig.
They will have one day of joy
As recompense for a whole year of trouble.
We leave the bygone year without regret.
Will we leave so carelessly the years to come?
Everything passes, everything
Goes, and never looks back,
And we grow older and less strong.

CLEAR AFTER RAIN

Tu Fu

Translated by Kenneth Rexroth

Autumn, cloud blades on the horizon.
The west wind blows from ten thousand miles.
Dawn, in the clear morning air,
Farmers busy after long rain.
The desert trees shed their few green leaves.
The mountain pears are tiny but ripe.
A Tartar flute plays by the city gate.
A single wild goose climbs into the void.

VERSES WRITTEN DURING
A SLEEPLESS NIGHT

Alexander Pushkin
Translated by Babette Deutsch

Sleep evades me, there's no light:
Darkness wraps the earth with slumber,
Only weary tickings number
The slow hours of the night.
Parca, chattering woman-fashion,
Night, that offers no compassion,
Life, that stirs like rustling mice—
Why encage me in your vise?
Why the whispering insistence—
Are you but the pale persistence
Of a day departed twice?
What black failures do you reckon?
Do you prophesy or beckon?
I would know whence you are sprung,
I would study your dark tongue . . .

SONNET

Stéphane Mallarmé
Translated by Roger Fry

This virgin, beautiful and lively day
Will it tear with a stroke of its drunken wing
The hard, forgotten lake which haunts 'neath the frost
The transparent glacier of flights unflown!

A swan of past days recalls it is he
Magnificent but without hope who is freed
For not having sung the realm where to live
When sterile winter's ennui has shone forth.

All his neck will shake off this white agony
By space inflicted on the bird who denies it,
But not the horror of the soil where his plumage is
    caught.

Fantom that to this place his brightness assigns him,
He is stilled in the icy dream of contempt
Which clothes in his useless exile the Swan.

POEM IN OCTOBER

Dylan Thomas

It was my thirtieth year to heaven
Woke to my hearing from harbour and neighbour wood
And the mussel pooled and the heron
Priested shore
The morning beckon
With water praying and call of seagull and rook
And the knock of sailing boats on the net webbed wall
Myself to set foot
That second
In the still sleeping town and set forth.

My birthday began with the water-
Birds and the birds of the winged trees flying my name
Above the farms and the white horses
And I rose
In rainy autumn
And walked abroad in a shower of all my days.
High tide and the heron dived when I took the road
Over the border
And the gates
Of the town closed as the town awoke.

A springful of larks in a rolling
Cloud and the roadside bushes brimming with whistling
Blackbirds and the sun of October
Summery
On the hill's shoulder,
Here were fond climates and sweet singers suddenly
Come in the morning where I wandered and listened
To the rain wringing
Wind blow cold
In the wood faraway under me.

Pale rain over the dwindling harbour
And over the sea wet church the size of a snail
With its horns through mist and the castle
Brown as owls
But all the gardens
Of spring and summer were blooming in the tall tales
Beyond the border and under the lark full cloud.
There could I marvel
My birthday
Away but the weather turned around.

It turned away from the blithe country
And down the other air and the blue altered sky
Streamed again a wonder of summer
With apples
Pears and red currants
And I saw in the turning so clearly a child's
Forgotten mornings when he walked with his mother
Through the parables
Of sun light
And the legends of the green chapels

And the twice told fields of infancy
That his tears burned my cheeks and his heart moved in mine.
These were the woods the river and sea
Where a boy
In the listening
Summertime of the dead whispered the truth of his joy
To the trees and the stones and the fish in the tide.
And the mystery
Sang alive
Still in the water and singingbirds.

And there could I marvel my birthday
Away but the weather turned around. And the true
Joy of the long dead child sang burning
In the sun.
It was my thirtieth
Year to heaven stood there then in the summer noon
Though the town below lay leaved with October blood.
O may my heart's truth
Still be sung
On this high hill in a year's turning.

THE NIGHTINGALE

Francesco Petrarch
Translated by Thomas Lemesurier

That nightingale, whose strain so sweetly flows
   Mourning her ravish'd young or much-lov'd mate,
A soothing charm o'er all the valleys throws
   And skies, with notes well-tun'd to her and state:
And all the night she seems my kindred woes
   With me to weep and on my sorrow wait;
Sorrows that from my own fond fancy rose,
   Who deem'd a goddess could not yield to fate.
How easy to deceive who sleeps secure!
   Who could have thought that to dull earth would turn
Those eyes that as the sun shone bright and pure?
Ah! now what fortune wills I see full sure:
   That loathing life yet living I should see
   How few its joys, how little they endure!

MASS OF LOVE

Ancient Spanish Ballad
Translated by Anna Pursche

Dawn of a bright June morning,
   The birthday of Saint John,
When ladies and their lovers
   To hear High Mass are gone.

Yonder goes my lady,
   Among them all, the best;
In colored silk mantilla
   And many skirts she's dressed.

Embroidered is her bodice
   With gems of pearl and gold.
Her lips of beauty rare
   Beguiling sweetness hold.

Faint the touch of rouge
  On cheeks of fairest white,
Sparkling blue her eyes
  With subtle art made bright.

Proudly church she entered
  Radiant as sun above,
Ladies died of envy
  And courtiers, of love.

A singer in the choir
  His place lost in the creed;
The priest who read the lesson
  The pages did not heed,

And acolytes beside him
  No order could restore;
Instead of Amen, Amen,
  They sang Amor, Amor.

TOSSED ON A SEA OF TROUBLE

Archilochus
Translated by William Hay

Tossed on a sea of troubles, Soul, my Soul,
  Thyself do thou control;
And to the weapons of advancing foes
  A stubborn breast oppose:
Undaunted mid the hostile might
Of squadrons burning for the fight.

Thine be no boasting when the victor's crown
  Wins thee deserved renown;
Thine no dejected sorrow, when defeat
  Would urge a base retreat:
Rejoice in joyous things—nor overmuch
  Let grief thy bosom touch
Midst evil, and still bear in mind
How changeful are the ways of humankind.

PRAYER TO PEACE
From *Cresophontes*

Euripides
Translated by Moses Hadas

Peace, deep and rich,
of gods immortal the fairest,
I yearn for you: so long you tarry!
I fear old age and its bleakness
will overtake me ere again I see
your grace and your beauty
and lovely dances and songs
and garlanded merry-makers.
Come, lady Peace, come to our city;
ward hateful contention from our dwellings,
and bitter strife whose pleasure is the sharp sword.

SONNET XIX
On His Blindness

John Milton

When I consider how my light is spent
Ere half my days in this dark world and wide,
And that one talent, which is death to hide,
Lodged with me useless, though my soul more bent
To serve therewith my Maker, and present
My true account, lest He returning chide;
"Doth God exact day-labor, light denied?"
I fondly ask. But Patience, to prevent
That murmur, soon replies, "God doth not need
Either man's work or his own gifts; who best
Bear his mild yoke, they serve him best; his state
Is kingly; thousands at his bidding speed,
And post o'er land and ocean without rest;
They also serve who only stand and wait."

ANTONY'S ORATION
From *Julius Caesar*
William Shakespeare

Friends, Romans, countrymen, lend me your ears;
I come to bury Caesar, not to praise him.
The evil that men do lives after them;
The good is oft interred with their bones;
So let it be with Caesar. The noble Brutus
Hath told you Caesar was ambitious:
If it were so, it was a grievous fault,
And grievously hath Caesar answered it.
Here, under leave of Brutus and the rest—
For Brutus is an honorable man;
So are they all, all honorable men—
Come I to speak in Caesar's funeral.

He was my friend, faithful and just to me:
But Brutus says he was ambitious;
And Brutus is an honorable man.
He hath brought many captives home to Rome,
Whose ransoms did the general coffers fill:
Did this in Caesar seem ambitious?
When that the poor have cried, Caesar hath wept:
Ambition should be made of sterner stuff:
Yet Brutus says he was ambitious;
And Brutus is an honorable man.
You all did see that on the Lupercal
I thrice presented him a kingly crown,
Which he did thrice refuse: was this ambition?

Yet Brutus says he was ambitious;
And, sure, he is an honorable man.
I speak not to disprove what Brutus spoke,
But here I am to speak what I do know.
You all did love him once, not without cause:
What cause withholds you then to mourn for him?
O judgment! thou art fled to brutish beasts,
And men have lost their reason. Bear with me;
My heart is in the coffin there with Caesar,
And I must pause till it come back to me.

If you have tears, prepare to shed them now.
You all do know this mantle: I remember
The first time ever Caesar put it on;
'Twas on a summer's evening, in his tent,
That day he overcame the Nervii:
Look, in this place ran Cassius' dagger through:
See what a rent the envious Casca made:
Through this the well-beloved Brutus stabbed:
And as he plucked his cursed steel away,
Mark how the blood of Caesar followed it,
As rushing out of doors, to be resolved
If Brutus so unkindly knocked, or no:
For Brutus, as you know, was Caesar's angel:
Judge, O you gods, how dearly Caesar loved him!
This was the most unkindest cut of all;
For when the noble Caesar saw him stab,
Ingratitude, more strong than traitors' arms,
Quite vanquished him: then burst his mighty heart;
And, in his mantle muffling up his face,
Even at the base of Pompey's statue,
Which all the while ran blood, great Caesar fell.
O, what a fall was there, my countrymen!
Then I, and you, and all of us fell down,
Whilst bloody treason flourished over us.

SHE WAS A PHANTOM OF DELIGHT
William Wordsworth

She was a phantom of delight
When first she gleam'd upon my sight;
A lovely apparition, sent
To be a moment's ornament;
Her eyes as stars of Twilight fair;
Like Twilight's, too, her dusky hair;
But all things else about her drawn
From May-time and the cheerful dawn;
A dancing shape, an image gay,
To haunt, to startle, and waylay.

I saw her upon nearer view,
A spirit, yet a woman too!
Her household motions light and free,
And steps of virgin-liberty;
A countenance in which did meet
Sweet records, promises as sweet;
A creature not too bright or good
For human nature's daily food,
For transient sorrows, simple wiles,
Praise, blame, love, kisses, tears, and smiles.

And now I see with eye serene
The very pulse of the machine;
A being breathing thoughtful breath
A traveller between life and death:
The reason firm, the temperate will,
Endurance, foresight, strength, and skill;
A perfect woman, nobly plann'd
To warn, to comfort, and command;
And yet a Spirit still, and bright
With something of angelic light.

From THE BALLAD OF READING GAOL
Oscar Wilde

In Reading gaol by Reading town
    There is a pit of shame,
And in it lies a wretched man
    Eaten by teeth of flame,
In a burning winding-sheet he lies,
    And his grave has got no name.

And there, till Christ call forth the dead,
    In silence let him lie:
No need to waste the foolish tear,
    Or heave the windy sigh:
The man had killed the thing he loved,
    And so he had to die.

And all men kill the thing they love,
  By all let this be heard,
Some do it with a bitter look,
  Some with a flattering word,
The coward does it with a kiss,
  The brave man with a sword!

KUBLA KHAN

Samuel Taylor Coleridge

In Xanadu did Kubla Khan
  A stately pleasure-dome decree:
Where Alph, the sacred river, ran
Through caverns measureless to man
  Down to a sunless sea.
So twice five miles of fertile ground
With walls and towers were girdled round:
And there were gardens bright with sinuous rills,
Where blossomed many an incense-bearing tree;
And here were forests ancient as the hills,
Enfolding sunny spots of greenery.

But O! that deep romantic chasm which slanted
Down the green hill athwart a cedarn cover!
A savage place! as holy and enchanted
As e'er beneath a waning moon was haunted
By woman wailing for her demon-lover!
And from this chasm, with ceaseless turmoil seething,
As if this Earth in fast thick pants were breathing,
A mighty fountain momently was forced,
Amid whose swift half-intermitted burst
Huge fragments vaulted like rebounding hail,
Or chaffy grain beneath the thresher's flail:
And 'mid these dancing rocks at once and ever
It flung up momently the sacred river.

Five miles meandering with a mazy motion
Through wood and dale the sacred river ran,
Then reached the caverns measureless to man,
And sank in tumult to a lifeless ocean:
And 'mid this tumult Kubla heard from far
Ancestral voices prophesying war!

The shadow of the dome of pleasure
Floated midway on the waves;
Where was heard the mingled measure
From the fountain and the caves.
It was a miracle of rare device,
A sunny pleasure-dome with caves of ice!

A damsel with a dulcimer
In a vision once I saw:
It was an Abyssinian maid,
And on her dulcimer she played,
Singing of Mount Abora.
Could I revive within me
Her symphony and song,
To such a deep delight 'twould win me
That with music loud and long,
I would build that dome in air,
That sunny dome! those caves of ice!
And all who heard should see them there,
And all should cry, Beware! Beware!
His flashing eyes, his floating hair!
Weave a circle round him thrice,
And close your eyes with holy dread,
For he on honey-dew hath fed,
And drunk the milk of Paradise.

CHILDE HAROLD'S FAREWELL TO ENGLAND

George Gordon, Lord Byron

Adieu, adieu! my native shore
    Fades o'er the waters blue;
The night-winds sigh, the breakers roar,
    And shrieks the wild sea-mew.
Yon sun that sets upon the sea,
    We follow in his flight;
Farewell awhile to him and thee,
    My native land— Good-night.

A few short hours and he will rise
    To give the morrow birth;
And I shall hail the main and skies,
    But not my mother earth.
Deserted is my own good hall,
    Its hearth is desolate;
Wild weeds are gathering on the wall;
    My dog howls at the gate.

Come hither, hither, my little page!
    Why dost thou weep and wail?
Or dost thou dread the billow's rage,
    Or tremble at the gale?
But dash the tear-drop from thine eye;
    Our ship is swift and strong;
Our fleetest falcon scarce can fly
    More merrily along.

"Let winds be shrill, let waves roll high,
    I fear not wave nor wind:
Yet marvel not, Sir Childe, that I.
    Am sorrowful in mind;
For I have from my father gone,
    A mother whom I love,
And have no friends, save these alone,
    But thee—and One above.

"My father blessed me fervently,
   Yet did not much complain;
But sorely will my mother sigh
   Till I come back again."—
Enough, enough, my little lad!
   Such tears become thine eye;
If I thy guileless bosom had,
   Mine own would not be dry.

Songs from THE PRINCESS

Alfred, Lord Tennyson

Tears, idle tears, I know not what they mean,
Tears from the depth of some divine despair
Rise in the heart, and gather to the eyes,
In looking on the happy autumn-fields,
And thinking of the days that are no more.

Fresh as the first beam glittering on a sail,
That brings our friends up from the underworld,
Sad as the last which reddens over one
That sinks with all we love below the verge;
So sad, so fresh, the days that are no more.

Ah, sad and strange as in dark summer dawns
The earliest pipe of half-awakened birds
To dying ears, when unto dying eyes
The casement slowly grows a glimmering square;
So sad, so strange, the days that are no more.

Dear as remembered kisses after death,
And sweet as those by hopeless fancy feigned
On lips that are for others; deep as love,
Deep as first love, and wild with all regret;
O Death in Life, the days that are no more!

* * *

The splendor falls on castle walls
  And snowy summits old in story;
The long light shakes across the lakes,
  And the wild cataract leaps in glory.
Blow, bugle, blow, set the wild echoes flying,
Blow, bugle; answer, echoes, dying, dying, dying.

O, hark, O, hear! how thin and clear,
  And thinner, clearer, farther going!
O, sweet and far from cliff and scar
  The horns of Elfland faintly blowing!
Blow, let us hear the purple glens replying,
Blow, bugle; answer, echoes, dying, dying, dying.

O love, they die in yon rich sky,
  They faint on hill or field or river;
Our echoes roll from soul to soul,
  And grow for ever and for ever.
Blow, bugle, blow, set the wild echoes flying,
And answer, echoes, answer, dying, dying, dying.

SONG

John Donne

Goe, and catche a falling starre,
  Get with child a mandrake roote,
Tell me, where all past yeares are,
  Or who cleft the Divels foot,
Teach me to heare Mermaides singing,
  Or to keep off envies stinging,
        And finde
        What winde
Serves to advance an honest minde.

If thou beest borne to strange sights,
  Things invisible to see,
Ride ten thousand daies and nights,
  Till age snow white haires on thee,
Thou, when thou retorn'st, wilt tell mee
All strange wonders that befell thee,

And sweare
No where
Lives a woman true, and faire.

If thou findst one, let mee know,
  Such a Pilgrimage were sweet;
Yet doe not, I would not goe,
  Though at next doore wee might meet,
Though shee were true, when you met her,
And last, till you write your letter,
    Yet shee
    Will bee
False, ere I come, to two, or three.

TO THE VIRGINS, TO MAKE
MUCH OF TIME

Robert Herrick

Gather ye rose-buds while ye may:
Old Time is still a-flying;
And this same flower that smiles to-day,
To-morrow will be dying.

The glorious lamp of heaven, the sun,
The higher he's a-getting,
The sooner will his race be run,
And nearer he's to setting.

That age is best, which is the first,
When youth and blood are warmer;
But being spent, the worse and worst
Times will succeed the former.

Then be not coy, but use your time,
And while ye may, go marry;
For having lost but once your prime,
You may for ever tarry.

CASTILE

Miguel de Unamuno
Translated by Eleanor L. Turnbull

Oh, land of Castile, you do raise me up
to the sky in the rough palm of your hand;
to the sky that burns and refreshes you,
    the sky, your master.

Parched land, sinewy land and land of clear
horizons, mother of hearts and of arms,
the present takes in you the ancient coloring
    of long past glories.

At their outer edges, your bare brown fields
touch heaven with its concave meadow of sky,
the burning sun has its cradle in you,
    its tomb, its sanctuary.

The rounded dome of your space is all summit,
in you I feel myself raised up to heaven,
I breathe here on your desolate waste lands
    air from high mountains.

You are a vast altar, land of Castile,
into your air I shall set free my songs,
if worthy of you to the world they'll come
    down from the uplands.

TO LESBIA

Catullus
Translated by Abraham Cowley

LXXXV—Odi et amo. Quare id faciam, fortasse requiris

    I hate, and yet I love thee too;
    How can that be? I know not how;
    Only that so it is I know;
    And feel with torment that 'tis so.

SOLEMN HOUR

Rainer Maria Rilke
Translated by C. F. MacIntyre

Who weeps now anywhere in the world,
without cause weeps in the world,
weeps over me.

Who laughs now anywhere in the night,
without cause laughs in the night,
laughs at me.

Who goes now anywhere in the world,
without cause goes in the world,
goes to me.

Who dies now anywhere in the world,
without cause dies in the world,
looks at me.

THE PANTHER

Rainer Maria Rilke
Translated by Paul Engle

From going always over bars his glance
Holds nothing more, grown tired, as if there hurled
Against him but a thousand bars' expanse—
Beyond a thousand bars no other world.

The wary walking of the strong stride, dark
Around the littlest circle of his land
Is like a dance of power around an arc
Where, stupefied, a mighty Will may stand.

Only sometimes the live lid of the eye
Lifts, and an image enters quietly,
Travels the taut, tight limbs without a cry
And ceases, in the heart, to be.

ECCE PUER

James Joyce

Of the dark past
A child is born;
With joy and grief
My heart is torn.

Calm in his cradle
The living lies.
May love and mercy
Unclose his eyes!

Young life is breathed
On the glass;
The world that was not
Comes to pass.

A child is sleeping:
An old man gone.
O, father forsaken,
Forgive your son!

PIED BEAUTY

Gerard Manley Hopkins

Glory be to God for dappled things—
For skies of couple-colour as a brinded cow;
For rose-moles all in stipple upon trout that swim;
Fresh-firecoal chestnut-falls; finches' wings;
Landscape plotted and pieced—fold, fallow, and plough;
And all trades, their gear and tackle and trim.
All things counter, original, spare, strange;
Whatever is fickle, freckled (who knows how?)
With swift, slow; sweet, sour; adazzle, dim;
He fathers-forth whose beauty is past change:
     Praise him.

TO AN ATHLETE DYING YOUNG

A. E. *Housman*

The time you won your town the race
We chaired you through the market-place;
Man and boy stood cheering by,
And home we brought you shoulder-high.

To-day, the road all runners come,
Shoulder-high we bring you home,
And set you at your threshold down,
Townsman of a stiller town.

Smart lad, to slip betimes away
From fields where glory does not stay
And early though the laurel grows
It withers quicker than the rose.

Eyes the shady night has shut
Cannot see the record cut,
And silence sounds no worse than cheers
After earth has stopped the ears:

Now you will not swell the rout
Of lads that wore their honours out,
Runners whom renown outran
And the name died before the man.

So set, before its echoes fade,
The fleet foot on the sill of shade,
And hold to the low lintel up
The still-defended challenge-cup.

And round that early-laurelled head
Will flock to gaze the strengthless dead,
And find unwithered on its curls
The garland briefer than a girl's.

IV from CHILDHOOD
From *Illuminations*

Arthur Rimbaud
Translated by Louise Varèse

I am the saint at prayer on the terrace like the
peaceful beasts that graze down to the sea of Palestine.

I am the scholar of the dark armchair. Branches
and rain hurl themselves at the windows of my library.

I am the pedestrian of the highroad by way of
the dwarf woods; the roar of the sluices drowns my
steps. I can see for a long time the melancholy wash
of the setting sun.

I might well be the child abandoned on the jetty
on its way to the high seas, the little farm boy following
the lane, its forehead touching the sky.

The paths are rough. The hillocks are covered
with broom. The air is motionless. How far away
are the birds and the springs! It can only be the end
of the world ahead.

L'ENVOI
Rudyard Kipling

When Earth's last picture is painted, and the tubes are
    twisted and dried,
When the oldest colors have faded, and the youngest critic
    has died,
We shall rest, and, faith, we shall need it—lie down for an
    eon or two,
Till the Master of All Good Workmen shall set us to work
    anew!

And those that were good shall be happy: they shall sit in a
    golden chair;
They shall splash at a ten-league canvas with brushes of
    comets' hair;
They shall find real saints to draw from—Magdalene, Peter,
    and Paul;
They shall work for an age at a sitting and never be tired at
    all!

And only the Master shall praise us, and only the Master
    shall blame;
And no one shall work for money, and no one shall work
    for fame;
But each for the joy of the working, and each, in his separate
    star
Shall draw the Thing as he sees It for the God of Things as
    They Are!

THE CHARGE OF THE LIGHT BRIGADE

Alfred, Lord Tennyson

> Half a league, half a league,
>   Half a league onward,
> All in the valley of Death
>   Rode the six hundred.
> "Forward, the Light Brigade!
> Charge for the guns!" he said:
> Into the valley of Death
>   Rode the six hundred.
>
> "Forward, the Light Brigade!"
> Was there a man dismayed?
> Not though the soldier knew
>   Some one had blundered:
> Theirs not to make reply,
> Theirs not to reason why,
> Theirs but to do and die:
> Into the valley of Death
>   Rode the six hundred.

Cannon to right of them,
Cannon to left of them,
Cannon in front of them
  Volleyed and thundered;
Stormed at with shot and shell,
Boldly they rode and well,
Into the jaws of Death,
Into the mouth of Hell
  Rode the six hundred.

Flashed all their sabres bare,
Flashed as they turned in air
Sabring the gunners there,
Charging an army, while
  All the world wondered:
Plunged in the battery-smoke
Right through the line they broke
Cossack and Russian
Reeled from the sabre-stroke,
  Shattered and sundered.
Then they rode back, but not,
  Not the six hundred.

Cannon to right of them,
Cannon to left of them,
Cannon behind them
  Volleyed and thundered;
Stormed at with shot and shell,
While horse and hero fell,
They that had fought so well
Came through the jaws of Death,
Back from the mouth of Hell,
All that was left of them,
  Left of six hundred.

When can their glory fade?
O the wild charge they made!
  All the world wondered.
Honor the charge they made!
Honor the Light Brigade,
  Noble six hundred!

THE DAY IS DONE

Henry Wadsworth Longfellow

The day is done, and the darkness
    Falls from the wings of Night,
As a feather is wafted downward
    From an eagle in his flight.

I see the lights of the village
    Gleam through the rain and the mist,
And a feeling of sadness comes o'er me
    That my soul cannot resist:

A feeling of sadness and longing,
    That is not akin to pain,
And resembles sorrow only
    As the mist resembles the rain.

Come, read to me some poem,
    Some simple and heartfelt lay,
That shall soothe this restless feeling,
    And banish the thoughts of day.

Not from the grand old masters,
    Not from the bards sublime,
Whose distant footsteps echo
    Through the corridors of Time.

For, like strains of martial music,
    Their mighty thoughts suggest
Life's endless toil and endeavor;
    And to-night I long for rest.

Read from some humbler poet,
    Whose songs gushed from his heart,
As showers from the clouds of summer,
    Or tears from the eyelids start;

Who, through long days of labor,
    And nights devoid of ease,
Still heard in his soul the music
    Of wonderful melodies.

Such song have power to quiet
   The restless pulse of care,
And come like the benediction
   That follows after prayer.

Then read from the treasured volume
   The poem of thy choice,
And lend to the rhyme of the poet
   The beauty of thy voice.

And the night shall be filled with music,
   And the cares, that infest the day,
Shall fold their tents, like the Arabs,
   And as silently steal away.

IN SCHOOL DAYS

John Greenleaf Whittier

Still sits the school-house by the road,
   A ragged beggar sunning;
Around it still the sumachs grow,
   And blackberry-vines are running.

Within, the master's desk is seen,
   Deep-scarred by raps official;
The warping floor, the battered seats,
   The jack-knife's carved initial;

The charcoal frescos on its wall;
   Its door's worn sill, betraying
The feet that, creeping slow to school,
   Went storming out to playing;

Long years ago a winter sun
   Shone over it at setting;
Lit up its western window-panes,
   And low eaves' icy fretting.

It touched the tangled golden curls,
   And brown eyes full of grieving,
Of one who still her steps delayed
   When all the school were leaving.

For near her stood the little boy
    Her childish favor singled:
His cap pulled low upon a face
    Where pride and shame were mingled.

Pushing with restless feet the snow
    To right and left, he lingered;—
As restlessly her tiny hands
    The blue-checked apron fingered.

He saw her lift her eyes; he felt
    The soft hand's light caressing,
And heard the tremble of her voice,
    As if a fault confessing.

"I'm sorry that I spelt the word:
    I hate to go above you,
Because,"—the brown eyes lower fell,—
    "Because, you see, I love you!"

Still memory to a gray-haired man
    That sweet child-face is showing.
Dear girl! the grasses on her grave
    Have forty years been growing!

He lives to learn, in life's hard school,
    How few who pass above him
Lament their triumph and his loss,
    Like her,—because they love him.

ILL LUCK
From *The Flowers of Evil*

Charles Baudelaire
Translated by Roy Campbell

So huge a burden to support,
Your courage, Sisyphus, would ask;
Well though my heart attacks its task,
Yet Art is long and Time is short.

Far from the famed memorial arch
Towards a lonely grave I come.
My heart in its funereal march
Goes beating like a muffled drum.

—Yet many a gem lies hidden still
Of whom no pick-axe, spade, or drill
The lonely secrecy invades;
And many a flower, to heal regret,
Pours forth its fragrant secret yet
Amidst the solitary shades.

ODE ON SOLITUDE

Alexander Pope

Happy the man whose wish and care
    A few paternal acres bound,
Content to breathe his native air
    In his own ground.

Whose herds with milk, whose fields with bread,
    Whose flocks supply him with attire,
Whose trees in summer yield him shade,
    In winter fire.

Bless'd who can unconcern'dly find
    Hours, days, and years slide soft away,
In health of body, peace of mind,
    Quiet by day;

Sound sleep by night: study and ease
    Together mix'd; sweet recreation;
And innocence, which most does please,
    With Meditation.

Thus let me live, unseen, unknown,
    Thus unlamented let me die;
Steal from the world, and not a stone
    Tell where I lie.

DOVER BEACH

Matthew Arnold

The sea is calm to-night.
The tide is full, the moon lies fair
Upon the straits;—on the French coast the light
Gleams and is gone; the cliffs of England stand,
Glimmering and vast, out of the tranquil bay.
Come to the window, sweet is the night-air!
Only, from the long line of spray
Where the sea meets the moon-blanch'd sand,
Listen! you hear the grating roar
Of pebbles which the waves draw back, and fling,
At their return, up the high strand,
Begin, and cease, and then again begin,
With tremulous cadence slow, and bring
The eternal note of sadness in.

Sophocles long ago
Heard it on the Aegean, and brought
Into his mind the turbid ebb and flow
Of human misery; we
Find also in the sound a thought,
Hearing it by this distant northern sea.

The sea of faith
Was once, too, at the full, and round earth's shore
Lay like the folds of a bright girdle furl'd.
But now I only hear
Its melancholy, long, withdrawing roar,
Retreating, to the breath
Of the night-wind, down the vast edges drear
And naked shingles of the world.

Ah, love, let us be true
To one another! for the world, which seems
To lie before us like a land of dreams,
So various, so beautiful, so new,

Hath really neither joy, nor love, nor light,
Nor certitude, nor peace, nor help for pain;
And we are here as on a darkling plain
Swept with confused alarms of struggle and flight,
Where ignorant armies clash by night.

SPRING

Catullus
Translated by L. R. Lind

Now Spring brings back the tepid breeze,
Now Winter's raging gale is still
Beneath the West Wind's soothing breath.
And now, Catullus, you have left
The Phrygian fields, the fertile land
Of hot Nicaea disappears.
To Asia's famous cities we
Shall sail, and now our anxious hearts
Are eager for new wandering,
And now our steps are firm and joyful.

Dear band of comrades, fare you well,
Who long ago left home together
Return by many a different road.

ON MY SWEET MOTHER

Sappho
Translated by Thomas Moore

Oh, my sweet mother, 'tis in vain,
I cannot weave as once I wove,
So 'wildered is my heart and brain
With thinking of that youth I love.

From THE SATIRES

Juvenal
Translated by L. R. Lind

We are led on
By impulse of soul and by our blind desire
To ask for wives and children: but the gods
Know of what sort our wives and sons will be.
Yet, so that there may be something you can pray for,
As you devote the entrails and prophetic
Sausages made from white pigs on the altar,
Why, pray for a sound mind in a healthy body!
Ask for a brave heart not afraid of death
That will not place long life among the gifts
Of nature, that can bear whatever troubles,
That knows no anger, wishes nothing, thinks
The works and woe of Hercules are better
Than love and banquets and the downy cushions
Of Sardanapalus. I'm pointing out
The things that you can give yourself: the path
To peaceful life, the only one, leads on
Through virtue. Fortune, you would have no power.
If men had wisdom; it is we who make
A goddess of you and place you in the skies.

From ECLOGUE IV

Vergil
Translated by James Laughlin

For thee, little boy, will the earth pour forth gifts
All untilled, give thee gifts
First the wandering ivy and foxglove
Then colocasia and the laughing acanthus
Uncalled the goats will come home with their milk
No longer need the herds fear the lion
Thy cradle itself will bloom with sweet flowers

The serpent will die
The poison plant will wither
Assyrian herbs will spring up everywhere

And when thou art old enough to read of heroes
And of thy father's great deeds
Old enough to understand the meaning of courage
Then will the plain grow yellow with ripe grain
Grapes will grow on brambles
Hard old oaks drip honey.

TO HIS SOUL

Hadrian
Translated by Elinor Wylie

Little soul, like a cloud, like a feather,
My body's small guest and companion,
Where now do you rest, in what places—
Stripped naked, and rigid, and pallid,
Do you play as before, little jester?

ON THE NATURE OF THINGS *

I, 1–24

Lucretius
Translated by Basil Bunting

Darling of God and Men, beneath the gliding stars
you fill rich earth and buoyant sea with your presence
for every living thing achieves its life through you,
rises and sees the sun. For you the sky is clear,
the tempests still, Deft earth scatters her gentle flowers,
the level ocean laughs, the softened heavens glow
with generous light for you. In the first days of spring

when the untrammelled all-renewing southwind blows
the birds exult in you and herald your coming.
Then the shy cattle leap and swim the brooks for love.
Everywhere, through all seas, mountains and waterfalls,
love caresses all hearts and kindles all creatures
to overmastering lust and ordained renewals.
Therefore, since you alone control the sum of things
and nothing without you comes forth into the light
and nothing beautiful or glorious can be
without you, Alma Venus! trim my poetry
with your grace: and give peace to write and read and think.

MY WOMAN

Catullus
Translated by Gilbert Highet

My woman says she wants no other lover
    than me, not even Jupiter himself.
She says so. What a woman says to an eager sweetheart
    write on the wind, write on the rushing waves.

AUTUMN DAWN

Antonio Machado
Translated by Jean Rogers Longland

A highroad's barren scar
Among the grey rock-spires
And humble pastures far
Where strong black bulls are gazing. Brambles, thickets, briars.

The dew has drenched with cold
The landscape in the dark
And the poplars' frieze of gold,
Toward the river's arc.

A hint of dawn half seen
With purple crags for frame.
Beside his greyhounds keen,
His eager gun at rest, a hunter stalking game.

IF FREQUENTLY TO MASS

Christian de Pisan
Translated by J. G. Legge

If frequently to mass I go,
My beauty there I fain would see;
Fresh as a new-blown rose is she.

Men waste their time who gossip so;
Why should they talk maliciously,
If frequently to mass I go?

Nor road nor path my footsteps know,
Save one that leads where she may be.
How foolish he who fool calls me,
If frequently to mass I go.

ON THE DEATH OF HIS SON

Lewis Glyn Cothi
Translated by Gwyn Williams

One son was a jewel to me:
o Dwynwen, his father bewails his birth!
I have been left pain for love,
to ache for ever without a son.
My plaything is dead and my sides
are sick for Siôn y Glyn.
I moan continually
for a little story-book chieftain.

A sweet apple and a bird
the boy loved, and white pebbles,
a bow made of a thorn twig
and little brittle swords of wood.
He feared a pipe and a scarecrow
and begged his mother for a ball.
He'd sing for anyone,
singing io-o for a nut.
He'd make as though to flatter
and then fall out with me;
then make it up for a chip of wood
or a dice that he desired.
O, that Siôn, sweet innocent,
could live again like Lazarus.
Beuno brought seven heaven-dwellers
back again into this life.
Woe upon woe to my true heart
that Siôn's soul does not make eight.
O Mary, woe for his lying down
and woe to my side for his grave!
Siôn's death stands near me
like two barbs in my breast.
My son, child of my hearth,
my breast, my heart, my song,
my one delight before my death,
my knowing poet, my luxury,
my jewel, and my candle,
my sweet soul, my one betrayal,
my chick learning my song,
my chaplet of Iseult, my kiss,
my nest, (woe that he's gone!)
my lark, my little wizard.
My Siôn, my bow, my arrow,
my suppliant, my boyhood,
Siôn who sends to his father
a sharpness of longing and love.
No more smiles for my lips,
no more laughter from my mouth,
no more sweet entertainment,
no more begging for nuts,

no longer any playing ball
and no more singing aloud.
Farewell, whilst I live below,
my merry darling, my Siôn.

THE LINDEN TREE

Dietmar von Aist
Translated by Edgar Taylor

There sat upon the linden tree
    A bird and sang its strain;
So sweet it sang, that, as I heard,
    My heart went back again:
It went to one remembered spot,
    I saw the rose-trees grow,
And thought again the thoughts of love
    There cherished long ago.

A thousand years to me it seems
    Since by my fair I sat,
Yet thus to have been stranger long
    Was not my choice, but fate:
Since then I have not seen the flowers,
    Nor heard the birds' sweet song;
My joys have all too briefly passed,
    My griefs been all too long.

HARBINGERS

Bashō
Translated by Harold G. Henderson

Spring too, very soon!
    They are setting the scene for it—
        plum tree and moon.

From THE ILIAD

Homer
Translated by Edward, Earl of Derby

Meanwhile Achilles, plung'd
In bitter grief, from all the band apart,
Upon the margin of the hoary sea
Sat idly gazing on the dark-blue waves;
And to his Goddess-mother long he pray'd,
With outstretch'd hands, "Oh, mother! since thy son
To early death by destiny is doom'd,
I might have hoped the Thunderer on high,
Olympian Jove, with honour would have crown'd
My little space; but now disgrace is mine;
Since Agamemnon, the wide-ruling King,
Hath wrested from me, and still holds, my prize."
Weeping, he spoke; his Goddess-mother heard,
Beside her aged father where she sat
In the deep ocean-caves: ascending quick
Through the dark waves, like to a misty cloud,
Beside her son she stood; and as he wept,
She gently touched him with her hand.

SONNET

Dante Alighieri
Translated by D. G. Rossetti

Mine eyes beheld the blessed pity spring
   Into thy countenance immediately
    A while agone, when thou beheld'st in me
The sickness only hidden grief can bring;
And then I knew thou wast considering
   How abject and forlorn my life must be;
   And I became afraid that thou shouldst see
My weeping, and account it a base thing.

Therefore I went out from thee; feeling how
    The tears were straightway loosen'd at my heart
    Beneath thine eyes' compassionate control.
    And afterwards I said within my soul:
    "Lo! with this lady dwells the counterpart
Of the same Love who holds me weeping now."

ON THE ATHENIAN DEAD AT ECBATANA

Plato
Translated by Ralph Gladstone

Goodbye to the Aegean
that swelling strikes the coast,
Eretria and our neighbors
in Athens. Dead and lost
on Persian plains expanding
in endless length we lie,
and so we seize the moment
to tell the sea Goodbye.

CLEOBULUS' EPITAPH

Simonides
Translated by Richmond Lattimore

I am the maiden in bronze set over the tomb of Midas.
As long as water runs from well springs, and tall trees burgeon,
and the sun goes up the sky to shine, and the moon is brilliant,
as long as rivers shall flow and the wash of the sea's breakers,
so long remaining in my place on this tomb where the tears fall
I shall tell those who pass that Midas here lies buried.

SPRING SCENE

Taniguchi Buson
Translated by Harold G. Henderson

On the temple bell
    has settled, and is fast asleep,
        a butterfly.

LONELINESS

Hashin
Translated by Harold G. Henderson

No sky at all;
    no earth at all—and still
        the snowflakes fall. . . .

THE GARDEN OF PROSERPINE

Algernon Charles Swinburne

Here, where the world is quiet,
    Here, where all trouble seems
Dead winds' and spent waves' riot
    In doubtful dreams of dreams,
I watch the green field growing
For reaping folk and sowing,
For harvest-time and mowing,
    A sleepy world of streams.

I am tired of tears and laughter,
    And men that laugh and weep;
Of what may come hereafter
    For men that sow to reap:
I am weary of days and hours,
Blown buds of barren flowers,
Desires and dreams and powers,
    And everything but sleep.

Here life has death for neighbor,
  And far from eye or ear
Wan waves and wet winds labor,
  Weak ships and spirits steer;
They drive adrift, and whither
They wot not who make thither;
But no such winds blow hither,
  And no such things grow here.

No growth of moor or coppice,
  No heather-flower or vine,
But bloomless buds of poppies,
  Green grapes of Proserpine,
Pale beds of blowing rushes,
Where no leaf blooms or blushes
Save this whereout she crushes
  For dead men deadly wine.

Pale, without name or number,
  In fruitless fields of corn,
They bow themselves and slumber
  All night till light is born;
And like a soul belated,
In hell and heaven unmated,
By cloud and mist abated
  Comes out of darkness morn.

Though one were strong as seven,
  He too with death shall dwell,
Nor wake with wings in heaven,
  Nor weep for pains in hell;
Though one were fair as roses,
His beauty clouds and closes;
And well though love reposes,
  In the end it is not well.

Pale, beyond porch and portal,
  Crowned with calm leaves, she stands
Who gathers all things mortal
  With cold immortal hands;
Her languid lips are sweeter
Than Love's, who fears to greet her,
To men that mix and meet her
  From many times and lands.

She waits for each and other,
    She waits for all men born;
Forgets the earth her mother,
    The life of fruits and corn;
And spring and seed and swallow
Take wing for her and follow
Where summer song rings hollow
    And flowers are put to scorn.

There go the loves that wither,
    The old loves with wearier wings;
And all dead years draw thither,
    And all disastrous things;
Dead dreams of days forsaken,
Blind buds that snows have shaken,
Wild leaves that winds have taken,
    Red strays of ruined springs.

We are not sure of sorrow,
    And joy was never sure;
To-day will die to-morrow;
    Time stoops to no man's lure;
And Love, grown faint and fretful
With lips but half regretful
Sighs, and with eyes forgetful
    Weeps that no loves endure.

From too much love of living,
    From hope and fear set free,
We thank with brief thanksgiving
    Whatever gods may be,
That no life lives forever;
That dead men rise up never;
That even the weariest river
    Winds somewhere safe to sea.

Then star nor sun shall waken,
    Nor any change of light:
Nor sound of waters shaken,
    Nor any sound or sight:
Nor wintry leaves nor vernal,
Nor days nor things diurnal;
Only the sleep eternal
    In an eternal night.

SUMMER IS GONE·

Anonymous (9th century-Irish)
Translated by Sean O'Faolain

I have but one story—
The stags are moaning,
The sky is snowing,
Summer is gone.

Quickly the low sun
Goes drifting down
Behind the rollers,
Lifting and long.

The wild geese cry
Down the storm;
The ferns have fallen,
Russet and torn.

The wings of the birds
Are clotted with ice.
I have but one story—
Summer is gone.

A CHRISTMAS CRADLESONG

Lope de Vega
Translated by George Ticknor

Holy angels and blest,
    Through the palms as ye sweep
Hold their branches at rest
    For my babe is asleep.

And ye Bethlehem palm-trees,
    As stormy winds rush
In tempest and fury
    Your angry noise hush;—
Move gently, move gently,
    Restrain your wild sweep;
Hold your branches at rest
    My babe is asleep.

My babe all divine,
    With earth's sorrows oppressed,
Seeks in slumber an instant
    His grievings to rest;
He slumbers,—he slumbers,—
    O, hush then and keep
Your branches all still,—
    My babe is asleep.

Cold blasts wheel about him,—
    A rigorous storm,—
And ye see how, in vain,
    I would shelter his form;—
Holy angels and blest
    As above me ye sweep,
Hold these branches at rest,—
    My babe is asleep.

From THE BELLS

Edgar Allan Poe

Hear the mellow wedding bells—
    Golden bells!
What a world of happiness their harmony foretells!
    Through the balmy air of night
How they ring out their delight!—
From the molten-golden notes,
    And all in tune,
What a liquid ditty floats
To the turtle-dove that listens, while she gloats
    On the moon!
Oh, from out the sounding cells,
What a gush of euphony voluminously wells!
    How it swells!
    How it dwells
On the Future!—how it tells
Of the rapture that impels
To the swinging and the ringing

Of the bells, bells, bells—
Of the bells, bells, bells, bells,
  Bells, bells, bells—
To the rhyming and the chiming of the bells!

VII From ASIDES FROM THE CLOWNS

Jules LaForgue
Translated by William Jay Smith

My clear-cut heart, my tender soul,
You would be dipped one day in me
As one dips a macaroon in tea,
One's little finger held out.

So great is my love, so white, so green,
So very vigorous, and yet
Mere pas-de-deux, light silhouettes
Are all you find on that solid screen.

Adieu.—What now? You are weeping. Quite!
But tell me why you look down
When my star opens its dressing gown,
And sigh for noon at midnight.

The Inmost Leaf

POEMS WITH A PHILOSOPHY

Here is a sheaf of speculative, philosophical, and religious poems.
They were not selected to present a unified point of view. Several of
them are from the Bible and other books considered holy. Many of
them are inspirational poems written from a Christian persuasion.
Some of them place their faith primarily in man and his human capaci-
ties. Others search but cannot find. There is no single point of view
because there cannot be one. Time and condition change. But the
restless self-search, the urgent need to find a truth to cling to, these
appear to be a part of our human inheritance.

DEBATE WITH THE RABBI

Howard Nemerov

You've lost your religion, the Rabbi said.
   It wasn't much to keep, said I.
You should affirm the spirit, said he,
And the communal solidarity.
   I don't feel so solid, I said.

We are the people of the Book, the Rabbi said.
   Not of the phone book, said I.
Ours is a great tradition, said he,
And a wonderful history.
   But history's over, I said.

We Jews are creative people, the Rabbi said.
   Make something, then, said I.
In science and in art, said he,
Violinists and physicists have we.
   Fiddle and physic indeed, I said.

Stubborn and stiff-necked man! the Rabbi cried.
   The pain you give me, said I
Instead of bowing down, said he,
You go on in your obstinacy.
   We Jews are that way, I replied.

THE MORNING HOURS

In the Name of Allah, the Beneficent, the Merciful.
Translated by Mohammed Marmaduke Pickthall

By the morning hours
And by the night when it is stillest,
Thy Lord hath not forsaken thee nor doth He hate thee,
And verily the latter portion will be better for thee than the former,
And verily thy Lord will give unto thee so that thou wilt be content.
Did He not find thee an orphan and protect (thee)?
Did He not find thee wandering and direct (thee)?

Did He not find thee destitute and enrich (thee)?
Therefor the orphan oppress not,
Therefor the beggar drive not away,
Therefor of the bounty of thy Lord be thy discourse.

THE INNER MAN

Plato

Beauty depends on simplicity—I mean the true simplicity of
   a rightly and nobly ordered mind and character.
He is a fool who seriously inclines to weigh the
   beautiful by any other standard than that of the good.
The good is the beautiful.
Grant me to be beautiful in the inner man.

FIRE AND ICE

Robert Frost

Some say the world will end in fire,
Some say in ice.
From what I've tasted of desire
I hold with those who favor fire.
But if it had to perish twice,
I think I know enough of hate
To say that for destruction ice
Is also great
And would suffice.

From DEVOTIONS XVII

John Donne

No man is an island, entire of itself; every man is a piece of the
continent, a part of the main; . . . any man's death diminishes me,
because I am involved in mankind; and therefore never send to know
for whom the bell tolls; it tolls for thee.

A CREED

Edwin Markham

There is a destiny that makes us brothers;
  None goes his way alone:
All that we send into the lives of others
  Comes back into our own.

I care not what his temples or his creeds,
  One thing holds firm and fast—
That into his fateful heap of days and deeds
  The soul of man is cast.

A PSALM OF LIFE

Henry Wadsworth Longfellow

Tell me not, in mournful numbers,
  Life is but an empty dream!—
For the soul is dead that slumbers,
  And things are not what they seem.

Life is real! Life is earnest!
  And the grave is not its goal;
Dust thou art, to dust returnest,
  Was not spoken of the soul.

Not enjoyment, and not sorrow,
  Is our destined end or way;
But to act, that each to-morrow
  Finds us farther than to-day.

Art is long, and Time is fleeting,
  And our hearts, though stout and brave,
Still, like muffled drums, are beating
  Funeral marches to the grave.

In the world's broad field of battle,
  In the bivouac of Life,
Be not like dumb, driven cattle!
  Be a hero in the strife!

Trust no Future, howe'er pleasant!
    Let the dead Past bury its dead!
Act,—act in the living Present!
    Heart within, and God o'erhead!

Lives of great men all remind us
    We can make our lives sublime,
And, departing, leave behind us
    Footprints on the sands of time;

Footprints, that perhaps another,
    Sailing o'er life's solemn main,
A forlorn and shipwrecked brother,
    Seeing, shall take heart again.

Let us, then, be up and doing,
    With a heart for any fate;
Still achieving, still pursuing,
    Learn to labor and to wait.

ECCLESIASTES 3

To every thing there is a season, and a time
to every purpose under the heaven:

A time to be born, and a time to die; a
time to plant, and a time to pluck up that
which is planted;

A time to kill, and a time to heal; a time
to break down, and a time to build up;

A time to weep, and a time to laugh; a
time to mourn, and a time to dance;

A time to cast away stones, and a time
to gather stones together; a time to embrace,
and a time to refrain from embracing;

A time to get, and a time to lose; a time
to keep, and a time to cast away;

A time to rend, and a time to sew; a time
to keep silence, and a time to speak;

A time to love, and a time to hate; a
time of war, and a time of peace.

What profit hath he that worketh in
that wherein he laboureth?

I have seen the travail, which God hath
given to the sons of men to be exercised in it.

He hath made every thing beautiful in
his time: also he hath set the world in their
heart, so that no man can find out the work
that God maketh from the beginning to the end.

CALIBAN IN THE COAL MINES
Louis Untermeyer

God, we don't like to complain
   We know that the mine is no lark—
But—there's the pools from the rain;
But—there's the cold and the dark.

God, You don't know what it is—
   You, in Your well-lighted sky,
Watching the meteors whizz;
   Warm, with the sun always by.

God, if You had but the moon
   Stuck in Your cap for a lamp,
Even You'd tire of it soon,
   Down in the dark and the damp.

Nothing but blackness above,
   And nothing that moves but the cars—
God, if You wish for our love,
   Fling us a handful of stars!

A STONE, A LEAF, A DOOR

Thomas Wolfe

. . . A stone, a leaf, an unfound door;
Of a stone, a leaf, a door.
And of all the forgotten faces.

Naked and alone we came into exile.
In her dark womb
We did not know our mother's face;
From the prison of her flesh have we come
Into the unspeakable and incommunicable prison
Of this earth.

Which of us has known his brother?
Which of us has looked into his father's heart?
Which of us has not remained forever prison-pent?
Which of us is not forever a stranger and alone?

O waste of loss, in the hot mazes, lost,
Among bright stars
On this most weary unbright cinder, lost!
Remembering speechlessly
We seek the great forgotten language,
The lost lane-end into heaven,
A stone, a leaf, an unfound door.

THE TIGER

William Blake

Tiger! Tiger! burning bright,
In the forests of the night,
What immortal hand or eye
Could frame thy fearful symmetry?

In what distant deeps or skies
Burnt the fire of thine eyes?
On what wings dare he aspire?
What the hand dare seize the fire?

And what shoulder, and what art,
Could twist the sinews of thy heart?
And when thy heart began to beat,
What dread hand and what dread feet?

What the hammer? what the chain?
In what furnace was thy brain?
What the anvil? what dread grasp
Dare its deadly terrors clasp?

When the stars threw down their spears,
And watered heaven with their tears,
Did He smile His work to see?
Did He who made the Lamb, make thee?

Tiger! Tiger! burning bright,
In the forests of the night,
What immortal hand or eye
Dare frame thy fearful symmetry?

MY HEART'S IN THE HIGHLANDS

Robert Burns

My heart's in the Highlands, my heart is not here;
My heart's in the Highlands a-chasing the deer;
A-chasing the wild deer, and following the roe,—
My heart's in the Highlands wherever I go.

Farewell to the Highlands, farewell to the North,
The birthplace of valor, the country of worth;
Wherever I wander, wherever I rove,
The hills of the Highlands for ever I love.

Farewell to the mountains high covered with snow;
Farewell to the straths and green valleys below;
Farewell to the forests and wild-hanging woods;
Farewell to the torrents and loud-pouring floods.

My heart's in the Highlands, my heart is not here;
My heart's in the Highlands a-chasing the deer,
A-chasing the wild deer, and following the roe,—
My heart's in the Highlands wherever I go.

THE TRAPPIST ABBEY: MATINS

Thomas Merton

When the full fields begin to smell of sunrise
And the valleys sing in their sleep,
The pilgrim moon pours over the solemn darkness
Her waterfalls of silence,
And then departs, up the long avenue of trees.

The stars hide, in the glade, their light, like tears,
And tremble where some train runs, lost,
Baying in eastward mysteries of distance,
Where fire flares, somewhere, over a sink of cities.

Now kindle in the windows of this ladyhouse, my soul,
Your childish, clear awakeness:
Burn in the country night
Your wise and sleepless lamp.
For, from the frowning tower, the windy belfry,
Sudden the bells come, bridegrooms,
And fill the echoing dark with love and fear.

Wake in the windows of Gethsemani, my soul, my sister,
For the past years, with smokey torches, come,
Bringing betrayal from the burning world
And bloodying the glade with pitch flame.

Wake in the cloisters of the lonely night, my soul, my sister,
Where the apostles gather, who were, one time, scattered,
And mourn God's blood in the place of His betrayal,
And weep with Peter at the triple cock-crow.

TEMPT ME NO MORE; FOR I

C. Day Lewis

Tempt me no more; for I
Have known the lightning's hour,
The poet's inward pride,
The certainty of power.

Bayonets are closing round.
I shrink; yet I must wring
A living from despair
And out of steel a song.

Though song, though breath be short,
I'll share not the disgrace
Of those that ran away
Or never left the base.

Comrades, my tongue can speak
No comfortable words,
Calls to a forlorn hope,
Gives work and not rewards.

Oh keep the sickle sharp
And follow still the plough:
Others may reap, though some
See not the winter through.

Father, who endest all,
Pity our broken sleep;
For we lie down with tears
And waken but to weep.

And if our blood alone
Will melt this iron earth,
Take it. It is well spent
Easing a saviour's birth.

ON GIVING
From *The Prophet*

Kahlil Gibran

You give but little when you give of your possessions.
It is when you give of yourself that you truly give.
For what are your possessions but things you keep and guard for fear
    you may need them tomorrow?
And tomorrow, what shall tomorrow bring to the overprudent dog
    burying bones in the trackless sand as he follows the pilgrims to
    the holy city?

And what is fear of need but need itself?

Is not dread of thirst when your well is full, the thirst that is un-
quenchable?

There are those who give little of the much which they have—and
they give it for recognition and their hidden desire makes their
gifts unwholesome.

And there are those who have little and give it all.

These are the believers in life and the bounty of life, and their coffer
is never empty.

There are those who give with joy, and that joy is their reward.

And there are those who give with pain and that pain is their baptism.

And there are those who give and know not pain in giving, nor do
they seek joy, nor give with mindfulness of virtue;

They give as in yonder valley the myrtle breathes its fragrance into
space.

Through the hands of such as these God speaks, and from behind
their eyes He smiles upon the earth.

It is well to give when asked, but it is better to give unasked, through
understanding;

And to the open-handed the search for one who shall receive is joy
greater than giving.

And is there aught you would withhold?

All you have shall some day be given;

Therefore give now, that the season of giving may be yours and not
your inheritors'.

A PRAYER

Alfred Noyes

Angels, where you soar
Up to God's own light,
Take my own lost bird
On your hearts to-night;
And, as grief once more
Mounts to heaven and sings,
Let my love be heard
Whispering in your wings.

A BREATH OF AIR

James Wright

I walked, when love was gone,
Out of the human town,
For an easy breath of air.
Beyond a break in the trees,
Beyond the hangdog lives
Of old men, beyond girls:
The tall stars held their peace.
Looking in vain for lies
I turned, like earth, to go.
An owl's wings hovered, bare
On the moon's hills of snow.

And things were as they were.

CHRISTMAS SONGS

Gerta Kennedy

Bring every child
bring each branch and stem
bent, beautiful, or wild;

bring each thirsty face
and every beast and bird
beyond the holy word
that our lady
of the snows,
lady of blue and of the rose
may affirm
earth's whole grace.
Her embroidered hem
as she passes
will bless the worm,
bless the smallest grasses.

Bring every child
bring each branch and stem
bent, beautiful, or wild.

Turn all clocks to the wall.
Let omens appear on the skies
as our god is born again
at the turn of the year,
born into men.

Let night fall
and day rise
outside history;
outside of time
again the mystery
rises prime,
bearing its prize,
bearing its deep surprise.
Come again joy!
joy, pity and mirth
come again to the earth
in deep December.

The splendors unfold,
velvet and gold,
odors of roses,
of wine.
Pity is holy
laughter's divine.

Joy and pity
pity and mirth
come again to the earth
for all men to remember.

From THE RUBAIYAT OF OMAR KHAYYAM

Edward FitzGerald

XIII

Some for the Glories of this World; and some
Sigh for the Prophet's Paradise to come;
  Ah, take the Cash, and let the Credit go,
Nor heed the rumble of a distant Drum!

XVI

The Worldly Hope men set their Hearts upon
Turns Ashes—or it prospers; and anon,
  Like Snow upon the Desert's dusty Face,
Lighting a little hour or two—was gone.

XXIV

Ah, make the most of what we yet may spend,
Before we too into the Dust descend;
  Dust into Dust, and under Dust to lie,
Sans Wine, sans Song, sans Singer, and—sans End!

LXIII

Oh threats of Hell and Hopes of Paradise!
One thing at least is certain—This Life flies:
  One thing is certain and the rest is Lies;
The Flower that once has blown for ever dies.

LXIV

Strange, is it not? that of the myriads who
Before us passed the door of Darkness through,
  Not one returns to tell us of the Road,
Which to discover we must travel too.

LXVI

I sent my Soul through the Invisible
Some letter of that After-life to spell:
  And by and by my Soul returned to me,
And answered, "I Myself am Heaven and Hell."

The Moving Finger writes; and, having writ,
Moves on: nor all your Piety nor Wit
   Shall lure it back to cancel half a Line
Nor all your Tears wash out a Word of it

ON CHILDREN
From *The Prophet*

Kahlil Gibran

. . . Your children are not your children.
They are the sons and daughters of Life's longing for itself.
They come through you but not from you,
And though they are with you yet they belong not to you.
You may give them your love but not your thoughts.
For they have their own thoughts.
You may house their bodies but not their souls,
For their souls dwell in the house of tomorrow, which you cannot visit,
not even in your dreams.
You may strive to be like them, but seek not to make them like you.
For life goes not backward nor tarries with yesterday . . .

BREAK, BREAK, BREAK

Alfred, Lord Tennyson

Break, break, break,
   On thy cold gray stones, O Sea!
And I would that my tongue could utter
   The thoughts that arise in me.

O well for the fisherman's boy,
   That he shouts with his sister at play!
O well for the sailor lad,
   That he sings in his boat on the bay!

And the stately ships go on
  To their haven under the hill;
But O for the touch of a vanished hand,
  And the sound of a voice that is still!

Break, break, break,
  At the foot of thy crags, O Sea!
But the tender grace of a day that is dead
  Will never come back to me.

COMPOSED UPON WESTMINSTER BRIDGE

William Wordsworth

Earth has not anything to show more fair:
Dull would he be of soul who could pass by
A sight so touching in its majesty:
This city now doth like a garment wear
The beauty of the morning; silent, bare,
Ships, towers, domes, theaters, and temples lie
Open unto the fields, and to the sky;
All bright and glittering in the smokeless air.
Never did sun more beautifully steep
In his first splendor, valley, rock, or hill;
Ne'er saw I, never felt, a calm so deep!
The river glideth at his own sweet will:
Dear God! the very houses seem asleep;
And all that mighty heart is lying still!

IN COMMON

Gene Derwood

Here am I, this carrot eating,
Orange but hard common,
Out the window sun is treating,
Laying still its gold on,
The color still is yellow,
Red now, but a late hello.

Does this living feel and starting,
Cry when out of earth it's sucked?
Is there tear in every parting,
Even from loose earth when plucked?
The last day shall we be very
Terrorized or merry?

Health itself is bled from this
Wandering dynamic in my veins,
What can be the vegetable bliss
Compensatory for the pains?
Here's sweet carrot, here am I,
Souls immortal we descry.

THE KILLING

Edwin Muir

That was the day they killed the Son of God
On a squat hill-top by Jerusalem.
Zion was bare, her children from their maze
Sucked by the demon curiosity
Clean through the gates. The very halt and blind
Had somehow got themselves up to the hill.

After the ceremonial preparation,
The scourging, nailing, nailing against the wood,
Erection of the main-trees with their burden,
While from the hill rose an orchestral wailing,
They were there at last, high up in the soft spring day.
We watched the writhings, heard the moanings, saw
The three heads turning on their separate axles
Like broken wheels left spinning. Round his head
Was loosely bound a crown of plaited thorn
That hurt at random, stinging temple and brow
As the pain swung into its envious circle.
In front the wreath was gathered in a knot
That as he gazed looked like the last stump left
Of a death-wounded deer's great antlers. Some

Who came to stare grew silent as they looked,
Indignant or sorry. But the hardened old
And the hard-hearted young, although at odds
From the first morning, cursed him with one curse,
Having prayed for a Rabbi or an armed Messiah
And found the Son of God. What use to them
Was a God or a Son of God? Of what avail
For purposes such as theirs? Beside the cross-foot,
Alone, four women stood and did not move
All day. The sun revolved, the shadow wheeled,
The evening fell. His head lay on his breast,
But in his breast they watched his heart move on
By itself alone, accomplishing its journey,
Their taunts grew louder, sharpened by the knowledge
That he was walking in the part of death,
Far from their rage. Yet all grew stale at last,
Spite, curiosity, envy, hate itself,
They waited only for death and death was slow
And came so quietly they scarce could mark it.
They were angry then with death and death's deceit.

I was a stranger, could not read these people
Or this outlandish deity. Did a God
Indeed in dying cross my life that day
By chance, he on his road and I on mine?

GOD'S WORLD

Edna St. Vincent Millay

O world, I cannot hold thee close enough!
Thy winds, thy wide gray skies!
Thy mists, that roll and rise!
Thy woods, this autumn day, that ache and sag
And all but cry with color! That gaunt crag
To crush! To lift the lean of that black bluff!
World, world, I cannot get thee close enough!

Long have I known a glory in it all
But never knew I this.
Here such a passion is
As stretcheth me apart. Lord, I do fear
Thou'st made the world too beautiful this year.
My soul is all but out of me—let fall
No burning leaf; prithee, let no bird call.

MEN SAY THEY KNOW MANY THINGS

Henry David Thoreau

Men say they know many things;
But lo! they have taken wings—
The arts and sciences,
And a thousand appliances;
The wind that blows
Is all that any body knows.

MATTHEW 5:1–10

And seeing the multitudes, he went up
into a mountain: and when he was set,
his disciples came unto him:

And he opened his mouth, and taught
them, saying,

Blessed are the poor in spirit: for
theirs is the kingdom of heaven.

Blessed are they that mourn: for they
shall be comforted.

Blessed are the meek: for they shall
inherit the earth.

Blessed are they which do hunger and
thirst after righteousness: for they shall
be filled.

Blessed are the merciful: for they
shall obtain mercy.

Blessed are the pure in heart: for they
shall see God.

Blessed are the peacemakers: for they
shall be called the children of God.

Blessed are they which are persecuted
for righteousness' sake: for theirs is
the kingdom of heaven.

COME GREEN AGAIN

Winfield Townley Scott

If what heals can bless
Can what blesses heal?
And all come green again
That was bodied forth
Years and years ago?
Years before my time.

Yet things I deepest learned
Turn into memory
As though no man's creation
But enlarges mine;
As though no man's existence
But was also mine
In its lonesomeness.

Henry Thoreau bent
In his boat on Walden Pond
Whistling his wooden flute
Under midnight stars
Across the stars in the water.

Hawthorne and Melville parting
At night in Liverpool,
Parting on a rainy corner
For the final time,
Something unsaid between them.

Mark Twain in moonlight
Standing in his Hartford house,
That wounded, beautiful man,
His hands at his white hair
While he sang "Nobody knows
The troubles I see but Jesus."

Then in broad daylight
The ladies of Camden drawing
Their skirts and kids aside
To avoid the dirty man
As Whitman hobbled past,
His basket on his arm
Filled with his book for sale.

Can such existences
Help but heal our hearts
Or such lonesomeness
Help but bless in us
That everlasting change
Which is our changelessness
And our humbleness?
And all come green again.

What I have learned enough
To have as air to breathe
Returns as memory
Of undiminished love:
That no man's creation
But enlarges me.
O all come green again.

MY PRAYER

Henry David Thoreau

Great God, I ask thee for no meaner pelf
Than that I may not disappoint myself;
That in my action I may soar as high
As I can now discern with this clear eye.

And next in value, which thy kindness lends,
That I may greatly disappoint my friends,
Howe'er they think or hope that it may be,
They may not dream how thou'st distinguished me.

That my weak hand may equal my firm faith,
And my life practise more than my tongue saith;
   That my low conduct may not show,
     Nor my relenting lines,
   That I thy purpose did not know,
     Or overrated thy designs.

From THE TEMPEST

William Shakespeare

The cloud-capp'd towers, the gorgeous palaces,
The solemn temples, the great globe itself,
Yea, all which it inherit, shall dissolve;
And, like this insubstantial pageant faded,
Leave not a wrack behind.

I AM!

Written in Northampton County Asylum

John Clare

I am! yet what I am none cares or knows,
My friends forsake me like a memory lost;
I am the self-consumer of my woes,
They rise and vanish in oblivious host,
Like shades in love and death's oblivion lost;
And yet I am! and live with shadows tost

Into the nothingness of scorn and noise,
Into the living sea of waking dreams,
Where there is neither sense of life nor joys,
But the vast shipwreck of my life's esteems;
And e'en the dearest—that I loved the best—
Are strange—nay, rather stranger than the rest.

I long for scenes where man has never trod;
A place where woman never smil'd or wept;
There to abide with my creator, GOD,
And sleep as I in childhood sweetly slept:
Untroubling and untroubled where I lie;
The grass below—above the vaulted sky.

DAWN

Frederick George Scott

The immortal spirit hath no bars
    To circumscribe its dwelling place;
My soul hath pastured with the stars
    Upon the meadow-lands of space.

My mind and ear at times have caught,
    From realms beyond our mortal reach,
The utterance of Eternal Thought
    Of which all nature is the speech.

And high above the seas and lands,
    On peaks just tipped with morning light
My dauntless spirit mutely stands
    With eagle wings outspread for flight.

CHARTLESS

Emily Dickinson

I never saw a moor,
I never saw the sea;
Yet know I how the heather looks,
And what a wave must be.

I never spoke with God,
Nor visited in heaven;
Yet certain am I of the spot
As if the chart were given.

From MACBETH

William Shakespeare

Tomorrow, and tomorrow, and tomorrow,
Creeps in this petty pace from day to day
To the last syllable of recorded time,
And all our yesterdays have lighted fools
The way to dusty death. Out, out, brief candle!
Life's but a walking shadow, a poor player
That struts and frets his hour upon the stage
And then is heard no more; it is a tale
Told by an idiot, full of sound and fury,
Signifying nothing.

INVICTUS

William Ernest Henley

Out of the night that covers me,
  Black as the pit from pole to pole,
I thank whatever gods may be
  For my unconquerable soul.

In the fell clutch of circumstance
  I have not winced nor cried aloud.
Under the bludgeonings of chance
  My head is bloody, but unbowed.

Beyond this place of wrath and tears
  Looms but the Horror of the shade,
And yet the menace of the years
  Finds and shall find me unafraid.

It matters not how strait the gate,
  How charged with punishments the scroll,
I am the master of my fate:
  I am the captain of my soul.

AT SET OF SUN

George Eliot

If you sit down at set of sun
And count the acts that you have done,
   And, counting, find
One self-denying deed, one word
That eased the heart of him who heard—
   One glance most kind,
That fell like sunshine where it went—
Then you may count that day well spent.

But, if, through all the livelong day,
You've cheered no heart, by yea or nay—
   If, through it all
You've nothing done that you can trace
That brought the sunshine to one face—
   No act most small
That helped some soul and nothing cost—
Then count that day as worse than lost.

THE ARROW AND THE SONG

Henry Wadsworth Longfellow

I shot an arrow into the air,
It fell to earth, I knew not where;
For so swiftly it flew, the sight
Could not follow it in its flight.

I breathed a song into the air,
It fell to earth, I knew not where;
For, who has sight so keen and strong
That it can follow the flight of song?

Long, long afterward, in an oak
I found the arrow, still unbroke;
And the song, from beginning to end,
I found again in the heart of a friend.

I THINK CONTINUALLY OF THOSE
WHO WERE TRULY GREAT

Stephen Spender

I think continually of those who were truly great.
Who, from the womb, remembered the soul's history
Through corridors of light where the hours are suns
Endless and singing. Whose lovely ambition
Was that their lips, still touched with fire,
Should tell of the Spirit clothed from head to foot in song.
And who hoarded from the Spring branches
The desires falling across their bodies like blossoms.

What is precious is never to forget
The essential delight of the blood drawn from ageless springs
Breaking through rocks in worlds before our earth.
Never to deny its pleasure in the simple morning light
Nor its grave evening demand for love.
Never to allow gradually the traffic to smother
With noise and fog the flowering of the spirit.

Near the snow, near the sun, in the highest fields
See how these names are fêted by the waving grass
And by the streamers of white cloud
And whispers of wind in the listening sky.
The names of those who in their lives fought for life
Who wore at their hearts the fir'es centre.
Born of the sun they travelled a short while towards the sun,
And left the vivid air signed with their honour.

EVERYONE SANG

Siegfried Sassoon

Everyone suddenly burst out singing;
And I was filled with such delight
As prisoned birds must find in freedom
Winging wildly across the white
Orchards and dark green fields; on; on; and out of sight.

Everyone's voice was suddenly lifted,
And beauty came like the setting sun.
My heart was shaken with tears, and horror
Drifted away. . . . O, but everyone
Was a bird; and the song was wordless; the singing will never be done.

THERE IS A TIDE

From *Julius Caesar*

William Shakespeare

There is a tide in the affairs of men,
Which, taken at the flood, leads on to fortune;
Omitted, all the voyage of their life
Is bound in shallows and in miseries:
And we must take the current when it serves,
Or lose our ventures.

THE WHALE

Herman Melville

The ribs and terrors in the whale
   Arched over me a dismal gloom,
While all God's sun-lit waves rolled by,
   And left me deepening down to doom.

I saw the opening maw of hell,
   With endless pains and sorrows there;
Which none but they that feel can tell—
   Oh, I was plunging to despair.

In black distress, I called my God,
   When I could scarce believe Him mine,
He bowed His ear to my complaints—
   No more the whale did me confine.

With speed He flew to my relief
   As on a radiant dolphin borne;
Awful, yet bright, as lightning shone
   The face of my Deliverer God.

My song for ever shall record
　　That terrible, that joyful hour;
I give the glory to my God,
　　His all the mercy and the power.

WANDERER'S NIGHT SONG

Johann Wolfgang von Goethe
Translated by Henry Wadsworth Longfellow

O'er all the hill-tops
Is quiet now,
In all the tree-tops
Hearest thou
Hardly a breath;
The birds are asleep in the trees:
Wait; soon like these
Thou too shalt rest.

IF I COULD ONLY LIVE AT THE PITCH
THAT IS NEAR MADNESS

Richard Eberhart

If I could only live at the pitch that is near madness,
When everything is as it was in my childhood
Violent, vivid, and of infinite possibility:
That the sun and the moon broke over my head.

Then I cast time out of the trees and fields,
Then I stood immaculate in the Ego;
Then I eyed the world with all delight,
Reality was the perfection of my sight.

And time has big handles on the hands,
Fields and trees a way of being themselves.
I saw battalions of the race of mankind
Still stolid, demanding a moral answer.

I gave the moral answer and I died
And into a realm of complexity came
Where nothing is possible but necessity
And the truth wailing there like a red babe.

REQUIEM

Robert Louis Stevenson

Under the wide and starry sky
Dig the grave and let me lie.
Glad did I live and gladly die,
    And I laid me down with a will.

This be the verse you grave for me:
Here he lies where he longed to be;
Home is the sailor, home from sea,
    And the hunter home from the hill.

CLOSE TO ME

Gabriela Mistral
Translated by Langston Hughes

Tiny fleece of my own flesh
woven deep within me,
tiny fleece so hating cold,
sleep close to me!

The partridge sleeps in the clover
alert to the barking dogs:
but my breathing does not disturb you.
Sleep close to me!

Trembling little blade of grass
frightened at life,
do not turn loose my breasts:
sleep close to me!

I who have lost everything
shiver at the thought of sleep.
Do not slip from my arms:
sleep close to me!

THE GIFT

William Carlos Williams

As the wise men of old brought gifts
    guided by a star
        to the humble birthplace
of the god of love,
    the devils
        as an old print shows
retreated in confusion.
    What could a baby know
        of gold ornaments
or frankincense and myrrh,
    of priestly robes
        and devout genuflections?
But the imagination
    knows all stories
        before they are told
and knows the truth of this one
    past all defection
The rich gifts
    so unsuitable for a child
        though devoutly proffered,
stood for all that love can bring.
    The men were old
        how could they know
of a mother's needs
    or a child's
        appetite?
But as they kneeled
    the child was fed.

                They saw it
and
        gave praise!
        A miracle
had taken place,
    hard gold to love,
a mother's milk!
        before
            their wondering eyes.
The ass brayed
        the cattle lowed.
                It was their nature.
All men by their nature give praise.
    It is all
        they can do.
The very devils
        by their flight give praise.
            What is death,
beside this?
        Nothing. The wise men
            came with gifts
and bowed down
        to worship
            this perfection.

STAR OF THE NATIVITY

Boris Pasternak
Translated by Eugene M. Kayden

It was wintertime.
The wind blew hard from the plain.
And the infant was cold in the cave
On the slope of a hill.
He was warmed by the breath of an ox.
The cattle huddled
Within the cave.
A warm mist drifted over the manger.

On a cliff afar the shepherds, awake,
Shook off the wisps of straw
And hayseed of their beds,
And sleepily gazed in the vastness of night.

They beheld the fields in drifted snows,
Gravestones and fences,
The shafts of a cart,
And a sky of stars above the graveyard;

And near them, unseen until then,
Like a watchman's candle
One star alone and shy
That shone on the road to Bethlehem.

At times it looked like a hayrick aflame,
Apart from God and the sky;
Like a barn on fire,
Like a farmstead ablaze in the night.

It reared in the sky like a flaming stack
Of straw and hay,
In the midst of a Creation
Amazed by this new star in the world.

And the flame grew steadily wider,
Large as a portent.
Then three stargazers
Hastened to follow the marvelous light.

Behind them, their camels with gifts.
Their caparisoned asses, each one smaller
In size, came daintily down the hillside.

And all new matters that were to come after
Arose as a vision of wonder in space.
All thoughts of ages, all dreams, new worlds,
All the future of galleries and of museums,
All the games of fairies, works of inventors,
And the yule trees, and the dreams all children dream:
The tremulous glow of candles in rows,
The gold and silver of angels and globes
(A wind blew, raging, long from the plain),
And the splendor of tinsel and toys under trees.

A part of the pond lay hidden by alders;
A part could be seen afar from the cliff
Where rooks were nesting among the treetops.
The shepherds could see each ass and camel
Trudging its way by the water mill.
"Let us go and worship the miracle,"
They said, and belted their sheepskin coats.

Their bodies grew warm, walking through snows.
There were footprints that glinted like mica
Across bright fields, on the way to the inn.
But the dogs on seeing the tracks in starshine
Growled loud in anger as if at a flame.

The frosty night was like a fairy tale.
And phantoms from mountain ridges in snows
Invisibly came to walk in the crowd.
The dogs grew fearful of ghosts around
And huddled beside the shepherd lads.

Across these valleys and mountain roads,
Unbodied, unseen by mortal eyes,
A heavenly host appeared in the throng,
And each footprint gleamed as an angel's foot.

At dawn the cedars lifted their heads.
A multitude gathered around the cave.
"Who are ye?" said Mary. They spoke: "We come
As shepherds of flocks, as envoys of heaven;
In praise of the Child and thy glory we come."
"The cave is too crowded. Abide ye a while."

Before dawnlight, in gloom, in ashen dark,
The drivers and shepherds stamped in the cold.
The footmen quarreled with mounted men;
Beside the well and the water trough
The asses brayed and the camels bellowed.

The dawn! It swept the last of the stars
Like grains of dust from the vaulted sky.
Then Mary allowed the Magi alone
To enter the cleft of the mountainside.

He slept in His manger in radiant light
As a moonbeam sleeps in a hollow tree.
The breath of the ox and the ass kept warm
His hands and feet in the cold of night.

The Magi remained in the twilight cave;
They whispered softly, groping for words.
Then someone in darkness touched the arm
Of one near the manger, to move him aside;
Behold, like a guest above the threshold,
The Star of the Nativity gazed on the Maid.

LAMENT

Rainer Maria Rilke
Translated by C. F. MacIntyre

Oh, everything is far
and long ago.
I believe that star
these thousand years is dead,
though I still see its light.
I believe, in that boat
passing though the night
something fearful was said.
In the house a clock
struck . . .
Where did it strike? . . .
I would like to walk
out of my heart
under the wide sky.
I would like to pray.
One of all these stars
must still exist.
I believe I know
which one
still lasts
and stands like a city, white
in the sky at the end of the beam of light . . .

JOHANNES MILTON, SENEX

Robert Bridges

Since I believe in God the Father Almighty
Man's Maker and Judge, Overruler of Fortune,
'Twere strange should I praise anything and refuse Him praise,
Should love the creature forgetting the Creator,
Nor unto Him in suff'ring and sorrow turn me:
Nay how cou'd I withdraw me from His embracing?

But since that I have seen not, and cannot know Him,
Nor in my earthly temple apprehend rightly
His wisdom and the heav'nly purpose eternal;
Therefore will I be bound to no studied system
Nor argument, nor with delusion enslave me,
Nor seek to please Him in any foolish invention
Which my spirit within me, that loveth beauty
And hateth evil, hath reprov'd as unworthy:

But I cherish my freedom in loving service,
Gratefully adoring for delight beyond asking
Or thinking, and in hours of anguish and darkness
Confiding always on His excellent greatness.

PRAYER OF ST. FRANCIS OF ASSISI

Lord, make me an instrument of your peace.
Where there is hatred, let me sow love;
Where there is injury, pardon;
Where there is doubt, faith;
Where there is despair, hope;
Where there is darkness, light;
And where there is sadness, joy.
O, Divine Master, grant that I may not so much seek to be consoled,
    as to console;
To be understood as to understand;
To be loved as to love;
For it is in giving that we receive;
It is in pardoning that we are pardoned;
It is in dying that we are born to eternal life.

SILENTIUM

Fyodor Tyutchev
Translated by Avrahm Yarmolinsky

Be silent, secret, and conceal
Whate'er you think, whate'er you feel.
Within your soul your dreams should rise
And set like stars that fill the skies
With splendor on their nightly route:
Admire them, scan them, and be mute.

How can a heart at will unfold
Its tale? Can any soul be told
By what it is you live and die?
A thought when spoken is a lie.
The springs men dig for they pollute:
Drink secret waters and be mute.

Within yourself learn how to live.
Magic that is not fugitive
Lies, a rich treasure, in the mind,
Thoughts that the glare of day will blind
And the wild din without confute:
Heed that low music, and be mute.

TWENTY-THIRD PSALM

The Lord is my shepherd; I shall not want.
He maketh me to lie down in green pastures:
    he leadeth me beside the still waters.
He restoreth my soul: he leadeth me in the
paths of righteousness for his name's sake.
    Yea, though I walk through the valley
        of the shadow of death,
I will fear no evil: for thou art with me;
    thy rod and thy staff they comfort me.
    in the presence of mine enemies:
    thou anointest my head with oil;
        my cup runneth over.
    Surely goodness and mercy
shall follow me all the days of my life:
       and I will dwell
in the house of the Lord for ever.

HEAVENLY GRASS

Tennessee Williams

My feet took a walk in heavenly grass.
All day while the sky shone clear as glass.
My feet took a walk in heavenly grass,
All night while the lonesome stars rolled past.
Then my feet come down to walk on earth,
And my mother cried when she give me birth.
Now my feet walk far and my feet walk fast,
But they still got an itch for heavenly grass.
But they still got an itch for heavenly grass.

LAMENT

Edna St. Vincent Millay

Listen, children:
Your father is dead.
From his old coats
I'll make you little jackets;
I'll make you little trousers
From his old pants.
There'll be in his pockets
Things he used to put there,
Keys and pennies
Covered with tobacco;
Dan shall have the pennies
To save in his bank;
Anne shall have the keys
To make a pretty noise with.
Life must go on,
And the dead be forgotten;
Life must go on,
Though good men die;
Anne, eat your breakfast;
Dan, take your medicine;
Life must go on;
I forget just why.

The Children's Hour

POEMS FOR AND ABOUT CHILDREN

A poet is closer to childhood than most of us because he has not lost his sense of wonder. He still sees a thing as fresh, new, and unique. When he feels or tastes or smells something, it is as though this particular touch or taste or smell is the first of its kind since the dawn of the world, and he the first to experience it. Whatever the reason, poets are often at their best when writing for or about children. The poems offered here range from nonsense to heartbreak. Some are classics, and some others deserve to be.

SIMPLES

James Joyce

Of cool sweet dew and radiance mild
The moon a web of silence weaves
In the still garden where a child
Gathers the simple salad leaves.

A moondew stars her hanging hair
And moonlight kisses her young brow
And, gathering, she sings an air:
Fair as the wave is, fair, art thou!

Be mine, I pray, a waxen ear
To shield me from her childish croon
And mine a shielded heart for her
Who gathers simples of the moon.

SPRING AND FALL:

To a Young Child

Gerard Manley Hopkins

Márgarét, are you gríeving
Over Goldengrove unleaving?
Leáves, líke the things of man, you
With your fresh thoughts care for, can you?
Áh! ás the heart grows older
It will come to such sights colder
By and by, nor spare a sigh
Though worlds of wanwood leafmeal lie;
And yet you wíll weep and know why.
Now no matter, child, the name:
Sórrow's spríngs áre the same.
Nor mouth had, no nor mind, expressed
What heart heard of, ghost guessed:
It ís the blight man was born for
It is Margaret you mourn for.

MUTTERINGS OVER THE CRIB
OF A DEAF CHILD

James Wright

"How will he hear the bell at school
Arrange the broken afternoon,
And know to run across the cool
Grasses where the starlings cry,
Or understand the day is gone?"

Well, someone lifting curious brows
Will take the measure of the clock.
And he will see the birchen boughs
Outside sagging dark from the sky,
And the shade crawling upon the rock.

"And how will he know to rise at morning?
His mother has other sons to waken,
She has the stove she must build to burning
Before the coals of the nighttime die;
And he never stirs when he is shaken."

I take it the air affects the skin,
And you remember, when you were young,
Sometimes you could feel the dawn begin,
And the fire would call you, by and by,
Out of bed and bring you along.

"Well, good enough. To serve his needs
All kinds of arrangements can be made.
But what will you do if his finger bleeds?
Or a bobwhite whistles invisibly
And flutes like an angel off in the shade?"

He will learn pain. And, as for the bird,
It is always darkening when that comes out.
I will putter as though I had not heard,
And lift him into my arms and sing
Whether he hears my song or not.

CHILD ON TOP OF A GREENHOUSE
Theodore Roethke

The wind billowing out the seat of my britches,
My feet crackling splinters of glass and dried putty,
The half-grown chrysanthemums staring up like accusers,
Up through the streaked glass, flashing with sunlight,
A few white clouds all rushing eastward,
A line of elms plunging and tossing like horses,
And everyone, everyone pointing up and shouting!

A DUTCH LULLABY
Eugene Field

WYNKEN, Blynken, and Nod one night
    Sailed off in a wooden shoe—
Sailed on a river of misty light
    Into a sea of dew.
"Where are you going, and what do you wish?"
    The old moon asked the three.
"We have come to fish for the herring-fish
    That live in this beautiful sea;
    Nets of silver and gold have we,"
        Said Wynken,
        Blynken,
        And Nod.

The old moon laughed and sung a song
    As they rocked in the wooden shoe,
And the wind that sped them all night long
    Ruffled the waves of dew;
The little stars were the herring-fish
    That lived in the beautiful sea;
"Now cast your nets wherever you wish,
    But never afeard are we"—
So cried the stars to the fishermen three,
        Wynken,
        Blynken,
        And Nod.

All night long their nets they threw
    For the fish in the twinkling foam,
Then down from the sky came the wooden shoe,
    Bringing the fishermen home.
'T was all so pretty a sail, it seemed
    As if it could not be;
And some folks thought 't was a dream they'd dreamed
    Of sailing that beautiful sea.
    But I shall name you the fishermen three:
        Wynken,
        Blynken,
        And Nod.

Wynken and Blynken are two little eyes,
    And Nod is a little head,
And the wooden shoe that sailed the skies
    Is a wee one's trundle-bed;
So shut your eyes while mother sings
    Of the wonderful sights that be,
And you shall see the beautiful things
    As you rock in the misty sea
    Where the old shoe rocked the fishermen three—
        Wynken,
        Blynken,
        And Nod.

THE DUEL

Eugene Field

The gingham dog and the calico cat
Side by side on the table sat;
'Twas half past twelve, and (what do you think!)
Nor one nor t'other had slept a wink!
    The old Dutch clock and the Chinese plate
    Appeared to know as sure as fate
There was going to be a terrible spat.
    (I wasn't there: I simply state
    What was told to me by the Chinese plate!)

The gingham dog went, "Bow-wow-wow!"
And the calico cat replied, "Mee-ow!"
The air was littered, an hour or so,
With bits of gingham and calico,
   While the old Dutch clock in the chimney-place
   Up with its hands before its face,
   For it always dreaded a family row!
      (Now mind; I'm only telling you
      What the old Dutch clock declares is true!)

The Chinese plate looked very blue,
And wailed, "Oh, dear! what shall we do!"
But the gingham dog and the calico cat
Wallowed this way and tumbled that,
   Employing every tooth and claw
   In the awfullest way you ever saw—
And, oh! how the gingham and calico flew!
      (Don't fancy I exaggerate—
      I got my news from the Chinese plate!)

Next morning, where the two had sat
They found no trace of dog or cat:
And some folks think unto this day
That burglars stole that pair away!
   But the truth about the cat and pup
   Is this: they ate each other up!
Now what do you really think of that!
      (The old Dutch clock it told me so,
      And that is how I came to know.)

From THE BAREFOOT BOY

John Greenleaf Whittier

Blessings on thee, little man,
Barefoot boy, with cheek of tan!
With thy turned-up pantaloons,
And thy merry whistled tunes;
With thy red lip, redder still
Kissed by strawberries on the hill;

With the sunshine on thy face,
Through thy torn brim's jaunty grace,
From my heart I give thee joy,—
I was once a barefoot boy!
Prince thou art,—the grown-up man
Only is republican.

POLITENESS

A. A. *Milne*

If people ask me,
I always tell them:
"Quite well, thank you, I'm very glad to say."
If people ask me,
I always answer,
"Quite well, thank you, how are you today?"
I always answer,
I always tell them,
If they ask me
Politely. . . .

BUT SOMETIMES

    I wish

      That they wouldn't.

A VISIT FROM ST. NICHOLAS

Clement Clarke Moore

'Twas the night before Christmas, when all through the house
Not a creature was stirring, not even a mouse;
The stockings were hung by the chimney with care,
In hopes that St. Nicholas soon would be there;
The children were nestled all snug in their beds,
While visions of sugar-plums danced in their heads;
And mamma in her 'kerchief, and I in my cap,

Had just settled our brains for a long winter's nap,
When out on the lawn there arose such a clatter,
I sprang from the bed to see what was the matter.
Away to the window I flew like a flash,
Tore open the shutters and threw up the sash.
The moon on the breast of the new-fallen snow
Gave the lustre of mid-day to objects below,
When, what to my wondering eyes should appear,
But a miniature sleigh, and eight tiny reindeer,
With a little old driver, so lively and quick,
I knew in a moment it must be St. Nick.
More rapid than eagles his coursers they came,
And he whistled, and shouted, and called them by name;
"Now, Dasher! now, Dancer! now, Prancer and Vixen!
On, Comet! on Cupid! on, Donder and Blitzen!
To the top of the porch! to the top of the wall!
Now dash away! dash away! dash away all!"
As dry leaves that before the wild hurricane fly,
When they meet with an obstacle, mount to the sky,
So up to the house-top the coursers they flew,
With the sleigh full of toys, and St. Nicholas too.
And then, in a twinkling, I heard on the roof
The prancing and pawing of each little hoof.
As I drew in my head, and was turning around,
Down the chimney St. Nicholas came with a bound.
He was dressed all in fur, from his head to his foot,
And his clothes were all tarnished with ashes and soot;
A bundle of toys he had flung on his back,
And he looked like a peddler just opening his pack.
His eyes—how they twinkled—his dimples how merry!
His cheeks were like roses, his nose like a cherry!
His droll little mouth was drawn up like a bow,
And the beard of his chin was as white as the snow;
The stump of a pipe he held tight in his teeth,
And the smoke it encircled his head like a wreath;
He had a broad face and a little round belly,
That shook, when he laughed, like a bowlful of jelly.
He was chubby and plump, a right jolly old elf,
And I laughed when I saw him, in spite of myself;
A wink of his eye and a twist of his head,

Soon gave me to know I had nothing to dread;
He spoke not a word, but went straight to his work,
And filled all the stockings; then turned with a jerk,
And laying his finger aside of his nose,
And giving a nod, up the chimney he rose;
He sprang to his sleigh, to his team gave a whistle,
And away they all flew like the down of a thistle.
But I heard him exclaim, ere he drove out of sight,
"Happy Christmas to all, and to all a good-night."

THE OWL AND THE PUSSY-CAT

Edward Lear

The Owl and the Pussy-cat went to sea
   In a beautiful pea-green boat:
They took some honey, and plenty of money
   Wrapped up in a five-pound note.
The Owl looked up to the stars above,
   And sang to a small guitar,
"O lovely Pussy, O Pussy, my love,
   What a beautiful Pussy you are,
     You are,
     You are!
   What a beautiful Pussy you are!"

Pussy said to the Owl, "You elegant fowl,
   How charmingly sweet you sing!
Oh! let us be married; too long we have tarried:
   But what shall we do for a ring?"
They sailed away, for a year and a day,
   To the land where the bong-tree grows;
And there in a wood a Piggy-wig stood,
   With a ring at the end of his nose,
     His nose,
     His nose,
   With a ring at the end of his nose.

"Dear Pig, are you willing to sell for one shilling
   Your ring?" Said the Piggy, "I will."
So they took it away, and were married next day
   By the Turkey who lives on the hill.
They dined on mince and slices of quince,
   Which they ate with a runcible spoon;
And hand in hand, on the edge of the sand,
   They danced by the light of the moon,
      The moon,
      The moon,
   They danced by the light of the moon.

THE TALE OF CUSTARD THE DRAGON
Ogden Nash

Belinda lived in a little white house,
With a little black kitten and a little gray mouse,
And a little yellow dog and a little red wagon,
And a realio, trulio, little pet dragon.

Now the name of the little black kitten was Ink,
And the little gray mouse, she called her Blink,
And the little yellow dog was sharp as Mustard,
But the dragon was a coward, and she called him Custard.

Custard the dragon had big sharp teeth,
And spikes on top of him and scales underneath,
Mouth like a fireplace, chimney for a nose,
And realio, trulio daggers on his toes.

Belinda was as brave as a barrel full of bears,
And Ink and Blink chased lions down the stairs,
Mustard was as brave as a tiger in a rage,
But Custard cried for a nice safe cage.

Belinda tickled him, she tickled him unmerciful,
Ink, Blink and Mustard, they rudely called him Percival,
They all sat laughing in the little red wagon
At the realio, trulio, cowardly dragon.

Belinda giggled till she shook the house,
And Blink said Weeck! which is giggling for a mouse,
Ink and Mustard rudely asked his age,
When Custard cried for a nice safe cage.

Suddenly, suddenly they heard a nasty sound,
And Mustard growled, and they all looked around.
Meowch! cried Ink, and Ooh! cried Belinda,
For there was a pirate, climbing in the winda.

Pistol in his left hand, pistol in his right,
And he held in his teeth a cutlass bright,
His beard was black, one leg was wood;
It was clear that the pirate meant no good.

Belinda paled, and she cried Help! Help!
But Mustard fled with a terrified yelp,
Ink trickled down to the bottom of the household,
And little mouse Blink strategically mouseholed.

But up jumped Custard, snorting like an engine,
Clashed his tail like irons in a dungeon,
With a clatter and a clank and a jangling squirm
He went at the pirate like a robin at a worm.

The pirate gaped at Belinda's dragon,
And gulped some grog from his pocket flagon,
He fired two bullets, but they didn't hit,
And Custard gobbled him, every bit.

Belinda embraced him, Mustard licked him,
No one mourned for his pirate victim.
Ink and Blink in glee did gyrate
Around the dragon that ate the pyrate.

Belinda still lives in her little white house,
With her little black kitten and her little gray mouse,
And her little yellow dog and her little red wagon,
And her realio, trulio little pet dragon.

Belinda is as brave as a barrel full of bears,
And Ink and Blink chase lions down the stairs.
Mustard is as brave as a tiger in a rage,
But Custard keeps crying for a nice safe cage.

CRADLE SONG

William Blake

Sleep, sleep, beauty bright,
Dreaming in the joys of night;
Sleep, sleep; in thy sleep
Little sorrows sit and weep.

Sweet babe, in thy face
Soft desires I can trace,
Secret joys and secret smiles,
Little pretty infant wiles.

As thy softest limbs I feel
Smiles as of the morning steal
O'er thy cheek, and o'er thy breast
Where thy little heart doth rest.

O the cunning wiles that creep
In thy little heart asleep!
When thy little heart doth wake,
Then the dreadful night shall break.

THE CHILDREN'S HOUR

Henry Wadsworth Longfellow

Between the dark and the daylight,
   When the night is beginning to lower,
Comes a pause in the day's occupations,
   That is known as the Children's Hour.

I hear in the chamber above me
   The patter of little feet,
The sound of a door that is opened
   And voices soft and sweet.

From my study I see in the lamplight,
   Descending the broad hall stair,
Grave Alice and laughing Allegra,
   And Edith with golden hair.

A whisper, and then a silence:
　　Yet I know by their merry eyes
They are plotting and planning together
　　To take me by surprise.

A sudden rush from the stairway,
　　A sudden raid from the hall!
By three doors left unguarded
　　They enter my castle wall!

They climb up into my turret
　　O'er the arms and back of my chair;
If I try to escape, they surround me;
　　They seem to be everywhere.

They almost devour me with kisses,
　　Their arms about me entwine
Till I think of the Bishop of Bingen
　　In his Mouse-Tower on the Rhine!

Do you think, O blue-eyed banditti,
　　Because you have scaled the wall,
Such an old mustache as I am
　　Is not a match for you all?

I have you fast in my fortress,
　　And will not let you depart,
But put you down into the dungeon
　　In the round-tower of my heart.

And there will I keep you forever,
　　Yes, forever and a day,
Till the walls shall crumble to ruin,
　　And moulder in dust away!

A CRADLE SONG

William Butler Yeats

The angels are stooping
Above your bed;
They weary of trooping
With the whimpering dead.

God's laughing in heaven
To see you so good;
The Shining Seven
Are gay with His mood.

I kiss you and kiss you,
My pigeon, my own;
Ah, how I shall miss you
When you have grown.

THERE WAS AN OLD PERSON OF WARE

Edward Lear

There was an old person of Ware,
Who rode on the back of a bear:
When they asked, "Does it trot?" he said,
    "Certainly not
He's a Moppsikon Floppsikon bear!"

THE RIVER IS A PIECE OF SKY

John Ciardi

From the top of a bridge
The river below
Is a piece of sky—
    Until you throw
    A penny in
    Or a cockleshell
    Or a pebble or two
    Or a bicycle bell
    Or a cobblestone
    Or a fat man's cane—
And then you can see
It's a river again.

The difference you'll see
When you drop your penny:
The river has splashes,
The sky hasn't any.

PUSSY-CAT, PUSSY-CAT

Pussy-Cat, Pussy-Cat,
　　Where have you been?
I've been to London
　　To visit the Queen.
Pussy-Cat, Pussy-Cat,
　　What did you there?
I frightened a little mouse
　　Under a chair.

SWEET AND LOW

Alfred, Lord Tennyson

Sweet and low, sweet and low,
　Wind of the western sea,
Low, low, breathe and blow,
　Wind of the western sea!
Over the rolling waters go,
Come from the dying moon, and blow,
　Blow him again to me;
While my little one, while my pretty one sleeps.

Sleep and rest, sleep and rest,
　Father will come to thee soon;
Rest, rest, on mother's breast,
　Father will come to thee soon;
Father will come to his babe in the nest,
Silver sails all out of the west
　Under the silver moon;
Sleep, my little one, sleep, my pretty one, sleep.

THE REASON FOR THE PELICAN
John Ciardi

The reason for the pelican
Is difficult to see:
His beak is clearly larger
Than there's any need to be.

It's not to bail a boat with—
He doesn't own a boat,
Yet everywhere he takes himself
He has that beak to tote.

It's not to keep his wife in—
His wife has got one, too.
It's not a scoop for eating soup.
It's not an extra shoe.

It isn't quite for anything.
And yet you realize
It's really quite a splendid beak
In quite a splendid size.

THE LAND OF COUNTERPANE
Robert Louis Stevenson

When I was sick and lay a-bed,
I had two pillows at my head,
And all my toys beside me lay
To keep me happy all the day.

And sometimes for an hour or so
I watched my leaden soldiers go,
With different uniforms and drills,
Among the bed-clothes, through the hills;

And sometimes sent my ships in fleets
All up and down among the sheets;
Or brought my trees and houses out,
And planted cities all about.

I was the giant great and still
That sits upon the pillow-hill,
And sees before him, dale and plain,
The pleasant land of counterpane.

THE FAIRY SHIP

Gabriel Setoun

I saw a ship a-sailing,
    A-sailing on the sea;
And oh! it was all laden
    With pretty things for thee!

There were comfits in the cabin,
    And apples in the hold;
The sails were made of silk,
    And the masts were made of gold.

The four and twenty sailors
    That stood between the decks,
Were four-and-twenty white mice,
    With chains about their necks.

The captain was a duck,
    With a jacket on his back;
And when the ship began to move
    The captain said, "Quack! Quack!"

BUBBLES

George H. Shorey

Bubble, Bubble, light and airy
Are you the palace of a fairy?
Perhaps you're only a Brownie moon;
Or maybe an elfin's toy balloon.

A goblin lives in there, I know
Who bursts the bubble when I blow;
And in my eye the naughty sprite
Kicks and scratches with all his might.

In streaks and splashes of yellow and blue,
The fairy painters are painting you.
I know, O bubble, light and airy,
You are the palace of a fairy.

THE FAIRY ARTIST

Nellie M. Garabrant

O there is a little artist,
    Who paints in the cold night hours;
Pictures for wee, wee children
    Of wondrous trees and flowers.
Pictures of snow-white mountains,
    Touching the snow-white sky;
Pictures of distant oceans,
    Where pigmy ships sail by,
The moon is the lamp he paints by,
    His canvas, the window pane;
His brush is the frozen snow-flake,
    Jack Frost, the artist's name.

SIMPLE SIMON AND THE PIEMAN

Simple Simon met a pieman,
    Going to the fair;
Says Simple Simon to the pieman,
    Let me taste your ware.

Says the pieman to Simple Simon,
    Show me first your penny;
Says Simple Simon to the pieman,
    Indeed I have not any.

Simple Simon went a-fishing,
    For to catch a whale;
All the water he had got
    Was in his mother's pail.

Simple Simon went to look
    If plums grew on a thistle;
He pricked his fingers very much,
    Which made poor Simon whistle.

He went for water in a sieve
    But soon it all fell through;
And now poor Simple Simon
    Bids you all adieu.

SING A SONG OF SIXPENCE

Sing a song of sixpence,
    A pocket full of rye;
Four and twenty blackbirds,
    Baked in a pie.

When the pie was opened,
    The birds began to sing;
Was not that a dainty dish,
    To set before the king?

The king was in his counting-house,
    Counting out his money;
The queen was in the parlour,
    Eating bread and honey.

The maid was in the garden,
　　Hanging out the clothes,
When down came a blackbird
　　And pecked off her nose.

They sent for the king's doctor,
　　Who sewed it on again,
And he sewed it on so neatly,
　　The seam was never seen.

HER FAVORITES

Mattie Lee Hausgen

My favorite dress
I must confess
Is not my red or blue or pink
(They're fine, I think),
But I like climbing trees and walls—
My favorite dress is overalls!
My favorite hat has nothing on it;
It's just my everyday sunbonnet.
My favorite summer shoes, you say?
Ha! I go barefoot all the day!

BINKER

A. A. Milne

Binker—what I call him—is a secret of my own,
And Binker is the reason why I never feel alone.
Playing in the nursery, sitting on the stair,
Whatever I am busy at, Binker will be there.

Oh, Daddy is clever, he's a clever sort of man,
And Mummy is the best since the world began,
And Nanny is Nanny, and I call her Nan—
　　But they can't
　　See
　　Binker.

Binker's always talking, 'cos I'm teaching him to speak:
He sometimes likes to do it in a funny sort of squeak,
And he sometimes likes to do it in a hoodling sort of
    roar . . .
And I have to do it for him 'cos his throat is rather sore.

Oh, Daddy is clever, he's a clever sort of man,
And Mummy knows all that anybody can,
And Nanny is Nanny, and I call her Nan—
    But they don't
    Know
    Binker

Binker's brave as lions when we're running in the park;
Binker's brave as tigers when we're lying in the dark;
Binker's brave as elephants. He never, never cries . . .
Except (like other people) when the soap gets in his
    eyes.

Oh, Daddy is Daddy, he's a Daddy sort of man,
And Mummy is as Mummy as anybody can,
And Nanny is Nanny, and I call her Nan . . .
    But they're not
    Like
    Binker.

Binker isn't greedy, but he does like things to eat,
So I have to say to people when they're giving me a
    sweet,
"Oh, Binker wants a chocolate, so could you give me
    two?"
And then I eat it for him, 'cos his teeth are rather new.

Well, I'm very fond of Daddy, but he hasn't time to
    play,
And I'm very fond of Mummy, but she sometimes goes
    away,
And I'm often cross with Nanny when she wants to brush
    my hair . . .

But Binker's always Binker, and is certain to be there.

LOST
Carl Sandburg

Desolate and lone,
All night long on the lake
Where fog trails and mist creeps,
The whistle of a boat
Calls and cries unendingly,
Like some lost child
In tears and trouble,
Hunting the harbor's breast
And the harbor's eyes.

A FAIRY'S LIFE
From *The Tempest*
William Shakespeare

Where the bee sucks there suck I:
In a cowslip's bell I lie:
There I couch when owls do cry.
On the bat's back I do fly
After summer merrily.
Merrily, merrily shall I live now,
Under the blossom that hangs on the bough.

HICKORY, DICKORY, DOCK

Hickory, dickory, dock,
The mouse ran up the clock;
The clock struck one,
The mouse ran down,
Hickory, dickory, dock.

BED IN SUMMER

Robert Louis Stevenson

In winter I get up at night
And dress by yellow candle-light.
In summer, quite the other way,
I have to go to bed by day.

I have to go to bed and see
The birds still hopping on the tree,
Or hear the grown-up people's feet
Still going past me on the street.

And does it not seem hard to you,
When all the sky is clear and blue,
And I should like so much to play,
To have to go to bed by day?

THE HOUSE OF CARDS

Christina Rossetti

A house of cards
    Is neat and small:
Shake the table,
    It must fall.

Find the Court cards
    One by one;
Raise it, roof it,—
    Now it's done:—
Shake the table!
    That's the fun.

The Humor Sampler

POETS AT PLAY

A collection of humorous verse is like a spread of canapes. If you try one, you can't stop at a dozen. We hope you will find here many a morsel to please your taste and to make you ask for more. A good appetizer should sharpen the appetite rather than satisfy it. Perhaps this is what we have done. Try one and see.

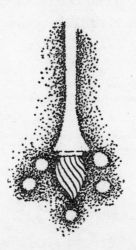

EDGAR A. GUEST CONSIDERS "THE GOOD OLD WOMAN WHO LIVED IN A SHOE" AND THE GOOD OLD TRUTHS SIMULTANEOUSLY

Louis Untermeyer

It takes a heap o' children to make a home that's true,
And home can be a palace grand or just a plain, old
    shoe;
But if it has a mother dear and a good old dad or two,
Why, that's the sort of good old home for good old me
    and you.

Of all the institutions this side the Vale of Rest
Howe'er it be it seems to me a good old mother's best;
And fathers are a blessing, too, they give the place a
    tone;
In fact each child should try and have some parents
    of his own.

The food can be quite simple; just a sop of milk and
    bread
Are plenty when the kiddies know it's time to go to
    bed.
And every little sleepy-head will dream about the day
When he can go to work because a Man's Work is his
    Play.

And, oh, how sweet his life will seem, with nought to
    make him cross,
And he will never watch the clock and always mind
    the boss.
And when he thinks (as may occur), this thought will
    please him best:
That ninety million think the same—including
                         Eddie Guest.

TOURIST TIME

F. R. Scott

This fat woman in canvas knickers
Gapes seriously at everything.
We might be a city of the dead
Or cave men
Instead of simple town folk.

We have nothing to show
That can't be seen better somewhere else,
Yet for this woman the wonder ceases not.

Madam, the most extraordinary thing in this town
Is the shape of your legs.

O communication!
O rapid transit!

MONEY

Richard Armour

Workers earn it,
Spendthrifts burn it,
Bankers lend it,
Women spend it,
Forgers fake it,
Taxes take it,
Dying leave it,
Heirs receive it,
Thrifty save it,
Misers crave it,
Robbers seize it,
Rich increase it,
Gamblers lose it . . .
I could use it.

PROHIBITION

Don Marquis

prohibition makes you
 want to cry
into your beer and
denies you the beer
to cry into

THE TREE

Alfred Kreymborg

I am four monkeys.
One hangs from a limb,
tail-wise,
chattering at the earth;
another is cramming his belly with coconut;
the third is up in the top branches,
quizzing the sky;
and the fourth—
he's chasing another monkey.

How many monkeys are you?

A MEMORY

L. A. G. Strong

When I was as high as that
I saw a poet in his hat.
I think the poet must have smiled
At such a solemn gazing child.

Now wasn't it a funny thing
To get a sight of J. M. Synge,
And notice nothing but his hat?
Yet life is often queer like that.

I LIKE TO QUOTE

Mitchell D. Follansbee

I like to quote the fragrant lines of Keats,
  And often I am caught by Shelley's tone,
And yet for clever thoughts and quaint conceits
  Give me some little lyric of my own.

ON THE VANITY OF EARTHLY GREATNESS

Arthur Guiterman

The tusks that clashed in mighty brawls
Of mastodons are billiard balls.

The sword of Charlemagne the Just
Is ferric oxide, known as rust.

The grizzly bear whose potent hug
Was feared by all is now a rug.

Great Caesar's bust is on the shelf,
And I don't feel so well myself!

DOUBLE DUTY

W. E. Farbstein

Mothers who raise
  A child by the book
    Can, if sufficiently vexed,
Hasten results
  By applying the book
    As well as applying the text.

US POTES

Franklin P. Adams

Swift was sweet on Stella;
    Poe had his Lenore;
Burns's fancy turned to Nancy
    And a dozen more.

Pope was quite a trifler;
    Goldsmith was a case;
Byron'd flirt with any skirt
    From Liverpool to Thrace.

Sheridan philandered;
    Shelly, Keats, and Moore
All were there with some affair
    Far from lit'rachoor.

Fickle is the heart of
    Each immortal bard.
Mine alone is made of stone—
    Gotta work too hard.

GETTIN' BORN

Anthony Euwer

When once a chic busts through a egg
    He gives three little squeals,
Then works out backwards through a hole
    By kickin' with his heels.

Or maybe he'll keep peckin' 'round,
    With now and then some cursin',
Until his head pokes through and then
    Comes all his little person.

Or like as not he'll puff his chest,
    A grunt and then some kickin'—
He's standin' there out in the air,
    A promissory chicken.

HORSES

Richard Armour

They head the list
   Of bad to bet on,
But I insist
   They're worse to get on.

SAID ARISTOTLE UNTO PLATO

Owen Wister

Said Aristotle unto Plato,
   "Have another sweet potato?"
Said Plato unto Aristotle,
   "Thank you, I prefer the bottle."

ON SOME SOUTH AFRICAN NOVELISTS

Roy Campbell

You praise the firm restraint with which they write—
I'm with you there, of course:
They use the snaffle and the curb all right,
But where's the bloody horse?

THE GREAT AUK'S GHOST

Ralph Hodgson

The Great Auk's ghost rose on one leg,
   Sighed thrice and three times winkt,
And turned and poached a phantom egg,
   And muttered, "I'm extinct."

A DRINK WITH SOMETHING IN IT
Ogden Nash

There is something about a Martini,
A tingle remarkably pleasant;
A yellow, a mellow Martini;
I wish that I had one at present.
There is something about a Martini,
Ere the dining and dancing begin,
And to tell you the truth,
It is not the vermouth—
I think that perhaps it's the gin.

There is something about an old-fashioned
That kindles a cardiac glow;
It is soothing and soft and impassioned
As lyric by Swinburne or Poe.
There is something about an old-fashioned
When dusk has enveloped the sky,
And it may be the ice,
Or the pineapple slice,
But I strongly suspect it's the rye.

There is something about a mint julep.
It is nectar imbibed in a dream,
As fresh as the bud of the tulip,
As cool as the bed of the stream.
There is something about a mint julep,
A fragrance beloved by the lucky.
And perhaps it's the tint
Of the frost and the mint,
But I think it was born in Kentucky.

There is something they put in a highball
That awakens the torpidest brain,
That kindles a spark in the eyeball,
Gliding singing through vein after vein.
There is something they put in a highball
Which you'll notice one day, if you watch;
And it may be the soda,
But judged by the odor,
I rather believe it's the Scotch.

Then here's to the heartening wassail,
Wherever good fellows are found;
Be its master instead of its vassal,
And order the glasses around.
For there's something they put in the wassail
That prevents it from tasting like wicker;
Since it's not tapioca,
Or mustard, or mocha,
I'm forced to conclude it's the liquor.

THE HEIGHT OF THE RIDICULOUS

Oliver Wendell Holmes

I wrote some lines once on a time
    In wondrous merry mood,
And thought, as usual, men would say
    They were exceeding good.

They were so queer, so very queer,
    I laughed as I would die;
Albeit, in the general way,
    A sober man am I.

I called my servant, and he came;
    How kind it was of him,
To mind a slender man like me,
    He of the mighty limb!

"These to the printer," I exclaimed,
    And, in my humorous way,
I added (as a trifling jest),
    "There'll be the devil to pay."

He took the paper, and I watched,
    And saw him peep within;
At the first line he read, his face
    Was all upon the grin.

He read the next; the grin grew broad,
    And shot from ear to ear;
He read the third; a chuckling noise
    I now began to hear.

The fourth; he broke into a roar;
    The fifth; his waistband split;
The sixth; he burst five buttons off,
    And tumbled in a fit.

Ten days and nights, with sleepless eye,
    I watched that wretched man,
And since, I never dare to write
    As funny as I can.

JABBERWOCKY

Lewis Carroll

'Twas brillig, and the slithy toves
    Did gyre and gimble in the wabe;
All mimsy were the borogoves,
    And the mome raths outgrabe.
"Beware the Jabberwock, my son!
    The jaws that bite, the claws that catch!
Beware the Jubjub bird, and shun
    The frumious Bandersnatch!"

He took his vorpal sword in hand;
    Long time the manxome foe he sought.—
So rested he by the Tumtum tree,
    And stood awhile in thought.

And as in uffish thought he stood,
    The Jabberwock, with eyes of flame,
Came whiffling through the tulgey wood,
    And burbled as it came!

One, two! One, two! And through and through
    The vorpal blade went snicker-snack!
He left it dead, and with its head
    He went galumphing back.

"And hast thou slain the Jabberwock?
　　Come to my arms, my beamish boy!
O frabjous day! Callooh! Callay!"
　　He chorted in his joy.

'Twas brillig, and the slithy toves
　　Did gyre and gimble in the wabe;
All mimsy were the borogoves,
　　And the mome raths outgrabe.

RESUMÉ

Dorothy Parker

Razors pain you;
Rivers are damp;
Acids stain you;
And drugs cause cramp.
Guns aren't lawful;
Nooses give;
Gas smells awful;
You might as well live.

TO A THESAURUS

Franklin P. Adams

O precious codex, volume, tome,
Book, writing, compilation, work
Attend the while I pen a pome,
A jest, a jape, a quip, a quirk.

For I would pen, engross, indite,
Transcribe, set forth, compose, address,
Record, submit—yea, even write
An ode, an elegy to bless—

To bless, set store by, celebrate,
Approve, esteem, endow with soul,
Commend, acclaim, appreciate,
Immortalize, laud, praise, extol.

Thy merit, goodness, value, worth,
Expedience, utility—
O manna, honey, salt of earth,
I sing, I chant, I worship thee!

How could I manage, live, exist,
Obtain, produce, be real, prevail,
Be present in the flesh, subsist,
Have place, become, breathe or inhale.

Without thy help, recruit, support,
Opitulation, furtherance,
Assistance, rescue, aid, resort,
Favor, sustention, and advance?

Alas! alack! and well-a-day!
My case would then be dour and sad,
Likewise distressing, dismal, gray,
Pathetic, mournful, dreary, bad.

* * * * *

Though I could keep this up all day,
This lyric, elegiac song,
Meseems hath come the time to say
Farewell! adieu! good-by! so long!

THE PURPLE COW

Gelette Burgess

I never saw a Purple Cow;
    I never Hope to See One;
But I can Tell you, Anyhow,
    I'd rather See than Be One.

AH, YES, I WROTE THE "PURPLE COW"

Gelette Burgess

Ah, yes, I wrote the "Purple Cow"—
I'm sorry, now, I Wrote it!
But I can Tell you, Anyhow,
I'll Kill you if you Quote it!

A LADY THINKS SHE IS THIRTY

Ogden Nash

Unwillingly Miranda wakes,
Feels the sun with terror,
One unwilling step she takes,
Shuddering to the mirror.

Miranda in Miranda's sight
Is old and gray and dirty;
Twenty-nine she was last night;
This morning she is thirty.

Shining like the morning star,
Like the twilight shining,
Haunted by a calendar,
Miranda sits a-pining.

Silly girl, silver girl,
Draw the mirror toward you;
Time who makes the years to whirl
Adorned as he adored you.

Time is timelessness for you;
Calendars for the human;
What's a year, or thirty, to
Loveliness made woman?

Oh, Night will not see thirty again,
Yet soft her wing, Miranda;
Pick up your glass and tell me, then—
How old is Spring, Miranda?

THE TWINS

Henry Sambrooke Leigh

In form and feature, face and limb,
    I grew so like my brother,
That folks got taking me for him,
    And each for one another.
It puzzled all our kith and kin,
    It reached a fearful pitch;
For one of us was born a twin,
    Yet not a soul knew which.

One day, to make the matter worse,
    Before our names were fixed,
As we were being washed by nurse,
    We got completely mixed;
And thus, you see, by fate's decree,
    Or rather nurse's whim,
My brother John got christened me,
    And I got christened him.

This fatal likeness even dogged
    My footsteps when at school,
And I was always getting flogged,
    For John turned out a fool.
I put this question, fruitlessly,
    To every one I knew,
"What would you do, if you were me,
    To prove that you were you?"

Our close resemblance turned the tide
    Of my domestic life,
For somehow, my intended bride
    Became my brother's wife.
In fact, year after year the same
    Absurd mistakes went on,
And when I died, the neighbors came
    And buried brother John.

WHAT'S THE USE
Ogden Nash

Sure, deck your lower limbs in pants;
Yours are the limbs, my sweeting.
You look divine as you advance—
Have you seen yourself retreating?

I TAKE 'EM AND LIKE 'EM
Margaret Fishback

I'm fonder of carats than carrots,
And orchids are nicer than beans,
But life in a series of garrets
Has made me receptive to greens.

ON HIS BOOKS
Hilaire Belloc

When I am dead, I hope it may be said:
'His sins were scarlet, but his books were read.'

GRANDMAMMA'S BIRTHDAY
Hilaire Belloc

Dear Grandmamma, with what we give,
We humbly pray that you may live
For many, many happy years:
Although you bore us all to tears.

ENIGMA FOR CHRISTMAS SHOPPERS

Phyllis McGinley

It is a strange, miraculous thing
About department stores,
How elevators upward wing
By twos and threes and fours,

How pale lights gleam, how cables run
All day without an end,
Yet how reluctant, one by one,
The homing cars descend.

They soar to Furniture, or higher,
They speed to Gowns and Gifts,
But when the bought weighs down the buyer,
Late, late, return the lifts.

Newton, himself, beneath his tree,
Would ponder this and frown:
How what goes up so frequently
So seldom cometh down.

THE READER WRITES

Carl Crane

What poets mean by what they mean
Is tougher than It's ever been.

Some swear that Ezra Pound's the ticket;
I get lost in Ezra's thicket.

I'm stumped by what the lilacs bring
To T. S. Eliot in the spring.

I sit up late at night deciding
What goes on in Laura Riding.

Ah, never will the masses know
What Auden means, who loves them so.

Rare is the nugget I can fish out
From subtleties the poets dish out;

In fact, I think it's time we had some
Poets who are plain and gladsome,

Who shun the effort it must cost
To seem more deep than Robert Frost.

THE HIPPOPOTAMUS

Hilaire Belloc

I shoot the Hippopotamus
With bullets made of platinum,
Because if I use leaden ones
His hide is sure to flatten 'em.

EXPERIENCE

Dorothy Parker

Some men break your heart in two,
Some men fawn and flatter,
Some men never look at you;
And that cleans up the matter.

JUST AND UNJUST

Lord Bowen

The rain it raineth on the just
And also on the unjust fella;
But chiefly on the just, because
The unjust steals the just's umbrella.

I STAND CORRECTED

Margaret Fishback

When I was happy in my youth
I laid my state of mind to love,
But now, to tell the dismal truth,
I see I didn't know whereof
I spoke. For I have lately found—
With great dissatisfaction—that
Though love can make the world go round,
It often makes the world go flat.

UNFORTUNATE COINCIDENCE

Dorothy Parker

By the time you swear you're his,
Shivering and sighing,
And he vows his passion is
Infinite, undying—
Lady, make a note of this:
One of you is lying.

WHEN ADAM DAY BY DAY

A. E. Housman

When Adam day by day
Woke up in Paradise,
He always used to say
"Oh, this is very nice."

But Eve from scenes of bliss
Transported him for life.
The more I think of this
The more I beat my wife.

THE RIDDLE
Ralph Hodgson

He told himself and he told his wife,
His boy and his dog the Facts of Life.
Guess who'd known them all along;
Guess who'd found them in a song;
Guess who knew he'd got them wrong.

BREATHES THERE A MAN
Samuel Hoffenstein

Breathes there a man with hide so tough
Who says two sexes aren't enough?

THE TIDES OF LOVE
T. A. Daly

Flo was fond of Ebenezer—
"Eb," for short, she called her beau.
Talk of Tides of Love, great Caesar!
You should see them—Eb and Flo.

AN AWFUL RESPONSIBILITY
Keith Preston

I am the captain of my soul;
I rule it with stern joy;
And yet I think I had more fun,
When I was cabin boy.

TO THE TERRESTRIAL GLOBE

Sir W. S. Gilbert

Roll on, thou ball, roll on!
Through pathless realms of Space
   Roll on!
What though I'm in a sorry case?
What though I cannot meet my bills?
What though I suffer toothache's ills?
What though I swallow countless pills?
Never you mind!
   Roll on!

Roll on, thou ball, roll on!
Through seas of inky air
   Roll on!
It's true I have no shirts to wear;
It's true my butcher's bill is due;
It's true my prospects all look blue—
But don't let that unsettle you:
Never you mind!
   Roll on!
            [It rolls on.]

THE FLEA

Roland Young

And here's the happy, bounding flea—
You cannot tell the he from she.
The sexes look alike, you see;
But she can tell and so can he.

THE DIGNITY OF LABOR

Robert Bersohn

Labor raises honest sweat;
Leisure puts you into debt.

Labor gives you rye and wheat;
Leisure gives you naught to eat.

Labor makes your riches last;
Leisure gets you nowhere fast.

Labor makes you bed at eight;
Leisure lets you stay up late.

Labor makes you swell with pride;
Leisure makes you shrink inside.

Labor keeps you fit and prime,
But give me leisure every time.

THE HONEY BEE

Don Marquis

the honey bee is sad and cross
and wicked as a weasel
and when she perches on you boss
she leaves a little measle

THE APE

Roland Young

The sacred ape, now, children, see.
He's searching for the modest flea.
If he should turn around we'd find
He has no hair on his behind.

THE ASS
Edwin Allan

The ass
    is decidedly middlecrass:
    conventional, obtuse,
    Reason, abuse,
    are equally no use.
    It is a platitude
    that only a halter
    can alter
    the middlecrass assitude.

COLD FACT
Dick Emmons

By the time he's suited
And scarved and booted
And mittened and capped
And zipped and snapped
And tucked and belted,
The snow has melted.

LINES FOR CUSCUSCARAWAY
AND MIRZA MURAD ALI BEG

T. S. Eliot

How unpleasant to meet Mr. Eliot!
With his features of clerical cut,
And his brow so grim
And his mouth so prim
And his conversation, so nicely
Restricted to What Precisely

And If and Perhaps and But.
How unpleasant to meet Mr. Eliot!
With a bobtail cur
In a coat of fur
And a porpentine cat
And a wopsical hat:
How unpleasant to meet Mr. Eliot!
      (Whether his mouth be open or shut).

JUST DROPPED IN

William Cole

Secretary of State John Foster Dulles conferred today
with Burnese Premier U Nu. He said later he had come
here neither to woo neutral Burma nor to be wooed . . .
His reception was studiously polite.—The New York
Times.

He did not come to woo U Nu,
And there wasn't much of a state to-do,
And they sat around and talked, those two,
And there isn't a doubt that they mentioned Chou.

When reporters asked "A political coup?"
He waved them aside with a light "Pooh-pooh."
But he didn't just come to admire the view,
Which he certainly knew you knew, U Nu.

THE TERMITE

Ogden Nash

Some primal termite knocked on wood
And tasted it, and found it good,
And that is why your Cousin May
Fell through the parlor floor today.

HOW TO TREAT ELVES

Morris Bishop

I met an elf-man in the woods,
    The wee-est little elf!
Sitting under a mushroom tall—
    'Twas taller than himself!

"How do you do, little elf," I said,
    "And what do you do all day?"
"I dance'n fwolic about," said he,
    "'N scuttle about and play;

"I s'prise the butterflies, 'n when
    A katydid I see,
'Katy didn't!' I say, and he,
    Says 'Katy did!' to me!

"I hide behind my mushroom stalk
    When Mister Mole comes froo,
'N only jus' to fwighten him
    I jump out 'n say 'Boo!'

"'N then I swing on a cobweb swing
    Up in the air so high,
'N the cwickets chirp to hear me sing
    'Upsy-daisy-die!'

"'N then I play with the baby chicks,
    I call them, chick chick chick!
'N what do you think of that?" said he.
    I said, "It makes me sick.

"It gives me sharp and shooting pains
    To listen to such drool."
I lifted up my foot, and squashed
    The God damn little fool.

NOTE ON INTELLECTUALS

W. H. Auden

To the man-in-the-street, who, I'm sorry to say
    Is a keen observer of life,
The word Intellectual suggests straight away
    A man who's untrue to his wife.

CASEY AT THE BAT

Ernest Lawrence Thayer

The outlook wasn't brilliant for the Mudville nine that day;
The score stood four to two, with but one inning more to
    play;
And so, when Cooney died at first, and Barrows did the same,
A sickly silence fell upon the patrons of the game.

A straggling few got up to go in deep despair. The rest
Clung to the hope which springs eternal in the human breast;
They thought, if only Casey could but get a whack, at that,
They'd put up even money now, with Casey at the bat.

But Flynn preceded Casey, as did also Jimmy Blake,
And the former was a pudding and the latter was a fake;
So upon that stricken multitude grim melancholy sat,
For there seemed but little chance of Casey's getting to the
    bat.

But Flynn let drive a single, to the wonderment of all,
And Blake, the much despised, tore the cover off the ball;
And when the dust had lifted, and they saw what had
    occurred,
There was Jimmy safe on second, and Flynn a-hugging third.

Then from the gladdened multitude went up a joyous yell,
It bounded from the mountain-top, and rattled in the dell;
It struck upon the hillside, and recoiled upon the flat;
For Casey, mighty Casey, was advancing to the bat.

There was ease in Casey's manner as he stepped into his
 place,
There was pride in Casey's bearing, and a smile on Casey's
 face;
And when, responding to the cheers, he lightly doffed his hat,
No stranger in the crowd could doubt 'twas Casey at the bat.

Ten thousand eyes were on him as he rubbed his hands with
 dirt,
Five thousand tongues applauded when he wiped them on
 his shirt;
Then while the writhing pitcher ground the ball into his hip,
Defiance gleamed in Casey's eye, a sneer curled Casey's lip.

And now the leather-covered sphere came hurtling through
 the air,
And Casey stood a-watching it in haughty grandeur there;
Close by the sturdy batsman the ball unheeded sped.
"That ain't my style," said Casey. "Strike one," the
 umpire said.

From the benches, black with people, there went a muffled
 roar,
Like the beating of the storm-waves on a stern and distant
 shore;
"Kill him! kill the umpire!" shouted someone on the stand.
And it's likely they'd have killed him had not Casey raised
 his hand.

With a smile of Christian charity great Casey's visage shone;
He stilled the rising tumult; he bade the game go on;
He signalled to the pitcher, and once more the spheroid flew,
But Casey still ignored it, and the umpire said, "Strike two."

"Fraud!" cried the maddened thousands, and the echo
 answered, "Fraud!"
But a scornful look from Casey, and the audience was awed;
They saw his face grow stern and cold, they saw his muscles
 strain,
And they knew that Casey wouldn't let that ball go by again.

441

The sneer is gone from Casey's lips, his teeth are clenched in
    hate,
He pounds with cruel violence his bat upon the plate;
And now the pitcher holds the ball, and now he lets it go,
And now the air is shattered by the force of Casey's blow.

Oh! somewhere in this favored land the sun is shining bright,
The band is playing somewhere, and somewhere hearts are
    light;
And somewhere men are laughing, and somewhere children
    shout,
But there is no joy in Mudville—mighty Casey has struck
    out.

Index of Authors

A

Adams, Franklin P., 421, 426
Adams, Léonie, 112
Agee, James, 203, 276
Aiken, Conrad, 107, 218
Aist, Dietmar von, 342
Aldington, Richard, 225
Alighieri, Dante, 343
Allan, Edwin, 437
Amis, Kingsley, 65
Archilochus, 313
Armour, Richard, 418, 422
Arnold, Matthew, 335
Auden, W. H., 121, 165, 440

B

Baird, Martha, 295
Baudelaire, Charles, 203, 333
Bashō, 342
Belloc, Hilaire, 430, 432
Belvin, William, 57
Benét, Rosemary, 190, 274
Benét, Stephen Vincent, 235, 274
Benn, Gottfried, 81, 263
Berryman, John, 239
Bersohn, Robert, 436
Betjeman, John, 115, 176, 181
Bishop, Elizabeth, 92, 168
Bishop, John Peale, 284
Bishop, Morris, 439
Björnson, Björnstjerne, 150, 154
Blake, Marie, 261
Blake, William, 180, 257, 358, 404
Blok, Alexander, 227

Bodenheim, Maxwell, 210
Bogan, Louise, 80
Booth, Philip, 53, 302
Bowen, Lord, 432
Bowie, Beverly, 198
Brecht, Bertolt, 118, 294
Bridges, Robert, 187, 252, 386
Brontë, Emily, 192
Brooke, Rupert, 175
Browning, Elizabeth Barrett, 213, 228
Browning, Robert, 184, 213, 237
Bryant, William Cullen, 290
Burgess, Gelette, 427, 428
Burns, Robert, 359
Buson, Taniguchi, 345
Byron, George Gordon, 171, 320

C

Campbell, Roy, 95, 422
Campbell, Wilfred, 250
Cane, Melville, 95, 165
Carducci, Giousé, 133
Carroll, Lewis, 425
Catullus, 324, 336, 339
Char, René, 75
Ciardi, John, 82, 104, 301, 405, 407
Clare, John, 373
Cleghorn, Sarah N., 193
Cocteau, Jean, 110
Cole, William, 438
Coleridge, Samuel Taylor, 246, 318
Cothi, Lewis Glyn, 340
Coulette, Henri, 67

444

447

Index of Titles

450

I

J

K

L

Index of First Lines

I have seen, O desolate one, the voice has its tower, 112
I have sung, to deceive the evil-sounding clock of time 110
I hear America singing, the varied carols I hear, 293
I heard a bird at dawn 259
I know that I shall meet my fate 138
I like to quote the fragrant lines of Keats, 420
I make a pact with you, Walt Whitman— 108
I met an elf-man in the woods, 439
I must go down to the seas again, to the lonely sea and the sky, 245
I must have passed the crest a while ago 181
I never saw a moor, 374
I never saw a Purple Cow; 427
I saw a ship a-sailing, 408
I saw a young snake glide 99
I shall go away. And the birds will still be there, 136
I shoot the Hippopotamus 432
I shot an arrow into the air, 376
I should have seen the sign: "Fresh paint," 138
I speak of that great house 45
I think continually of those who were truly great. 377
I think I could turn and live with animals, they are so placid and self-contained; 253
I thought I heard a knock on the door, 137
I used to see her in the door, 214
I wake to sleep, and take my waking slow. 74
I wakened to a calling, 87
I walked, when love was gone, 363
I wandered lonely as a cloud 243
I wanted the gold, and I sought it; 297
I was the patriarch of the shining land, 277
I went to the city 283
I will arise and go now, and go to Innisfree, 142
I will exchange a city for a sunset, 261
I wrote some lines once on a time 424
I'm fonder of carats than carrots, 430
I'm going out to clean the pasture spring; 291
I'm longing for the forest; 129
I'm nobody! Who are you? 173
If frequently to mass I go, 340
If I could only live at the pitch that is near madness 379

461

Peace, deep and rich, 314
Peace, the one-time radiant goddess, 157
Pile the bodies high at Austerlitz and Waterloo. 264
prohibition makes you 419
Pussy-Cat, Pussy-Cat, 406
Quietness clings to the air. 263
Razors pain you; 426
Restrained, 81
Riches I hold in light esteem, 192
Roll on, thou ball, roll on! 435
Said Aristotle unto Plato, 422
September six o'clock: 92
Samuel Sewall, in a world of wigs, 58
Shall I compare thee to a Summer's day? 222
Shall I love him, 137
She came out of the frost, 227
She died in the upstairs bedroom 176
She is all so slight 225
She was a phantom of delight 316
She was all that you loved and cherished, 152
Simple Simon met a pieman, 409
Since I believe in God the Father Almighty 386
Since I must love your north 113
Sing a song of sixpence, 410
Sing we for love and idleness, 223
Sink the world! Can that dismay us? 155
Sleep evades me, there's no light: 309
Sleep, my darling, sleep; 94
Sleep, sleep, beauty bright, 404
Slowly flutters the snow from ash-coloured heavens in silence; 133
Slowly, silently, now the moon 236
Snow falls on the cars in Doctors' Row and hoods and headlights; 107
So huge a burden to support, 333
Some for the Glories of this World; and some 365
Some men break your heart in two, 432
Some primal termite knocked on wood 438
Some say the world will end in fire, 354
Sound the flute! 257
Speech after long silence; it is right, 212
Spring morning! 135

468

B-40